Smaller Manufacturing Enterprises in an International Context

A Longitudinal Exploration

Smaller Manufacturing Enterprises in an International Context

A Longitudinal Exploration

George Tesar
University of Wisconsin-Whitewater, USA & Umeå University, Sweden

Hamid Moini
University of Wisconsin-Whitewater, USA

John Kuada
Aalborg University, Denmark

Olav Jull Sørensen
Aalborg University, Denmark

Imperial College Press

ICP

Published by

Imperial College Press
57 Shelton Street
Covent Garden
London WC2H 9HE

Distributed by

World Scientific Publishing Co. Pte. Ltd.
5 Toh Tuck Link, Singapore 596224
USA office: 27 Warren Street, Suite 401-402, Hackensack, NJ 07601
UK office: 57 Shelton Street, Covent Garden, London WC2H 9HE

British Library Cataloguing-in-Publication Data
A catalogue record for this book is available from the British Library.

SMALLER MANUFACTURING ENTERPRISES IN AN INTERNATIONAL CONTEXT
A Longitudinal Exploration

ISBN-13 978-1-84816-495-6
ISBN-10 1-84816-495-5

Typeset by Stallion Press
Email: enquiries@stallionpress.com

Printed in Singapore.

This book is dedicated to

my Sluníčko,

my wife Mitra and daughter Sheila,

Gitte, Esi, and Senyo for their love and understanding,

*my five grandchildren — Kristian, Anna, Bastian, Jacob,
and the little one, Oskar.*

Preface

This book examines how smaller manufacturing enterprises have internationalized their operations from 1974 to 2009, a period of 35 years. During these years, academic researchers and management consultants have discussed internationalization across many levels of management with little definition of what internationalization is and how it impacts managerial decision making. Few of these discussions concerning internationalization have involved a long-term look at the phenomenon. In addition, most of these discussions have generally focused on larger enterprises that led the internationalization efforts. Only a few researchers and consultants have considered smaller manufacturing enterprises and the fact that many of these enterprises were forced to internationalize their operations.

Many of the smaller enterprises that, over time, were required to enter the competitive world of international markets are manufacturing their own unique products, contributing to the development of new technologies, and introducing major innovations that help their large customers compete more effectively and efficiently in the global marketplace. Smaller manufacturing enterprises are unique; they tend to operate in a single local environment subject to economic, political, and social conditions that give them a unique character. This is particularly true in the U.S. state of Wisconsin.

This book reports on the authors' special opportunity to follow a large number of smaller manufacturing enterprises in Wisconsin for over 35 years — an opportunity to study them from a distance and close up — by interviewing their managers and getting their responses to a series of surveys. With willing managers of Wisconsin smaller manufacturing enterprises, we discussed how they make decisions, how they plan, what strengths and weaknesses they have, and how they look at the outside world of international markets. They willingly cooperated by contributing their time and we thank them. They want to remain anonymous in order to protect the identities of their enterprises.

For many of these managers, their primary focus was on manufacturing a quality product at a competitive price. They are engineers, scientists, or entrepreneurs who started their enterprises because they believed that they could contribute something to society. They also believed that they had something new to offer and that they could stimulate industrial progress. Many of them have done just that. Sometimes, they complained that academics and consultants do not understand them. They are not just any small- or medium-sized enterprise; they are different because they manufacture real and significant products.

Internationalization of their operations is frequently not considered as a mainstream management issue. Smaller manufacturing enterprises are concerned with engineering and scientific issues that require rational and objective decision making. For many of them, internationalization is a secondary concern that surfaces only when environmental conditions around them change — when competition forces them to sell their products in foreign markets or to source for supplies wherever they can purchase them economically.

The authors of this study had the opportunity to interact not only with Wisconsin smaller manufacturing enterprises, but also with similar enterprises in other countries — the Czech Republic, Denmark, and Sweden. It became clear early on that there are many similarities among smaller manufacturing enterprises in other countries.

However, one fundamental difference became clear in our information gathering: European managers tended to be much more open about their operations and strategies at the time of the interviews. The Danish and Swedish managers were much more willing to discuss complicated and sometimes challenging issues concerning their management styles, and we very much appreciate their openness. Both the Danish and Swedish research cases represent real companies and the managers' names. The Czech managers were more cautious, perhaps because they are relatively new to the ways of scientific research. We thank them all.

This research is not intended to be definitive on how smaller manufacturing enterprises internationalize their operations. Rather, we hope that it will provide an interesting look at how smaller manufacturing enterprises approach the world of international commerce, how they prepare themselves for it, and what really draws them into it. We hope that not only students of international management will benefit from our research, but that engineers and scientists will also gain a more comprehensive perspective on what it takes to internationalize their smaller manufacturing enterprises.

Contents

Preface   vii

Introduction   Historical Perspective on Internationalization   1
                   of Smaller Manufacturing Enterprises

Part I   **Decision-Making Process among Smaller**   11
             Manufacturing Enterprises

Chapter 1   Managers of Smaller Manufacturing Enterprises   13

Chapter 2   The Types of Goals Set by Managers of Smaller   25
                Manufacturing Enterprises

Chapter 3   Strengths and Weaknesses of Smaller   33
                Manufacturing Enterprises

Chapter 4   Future Operations and Planning Processes   47
                among Smaller Manufacturing Enterprises

Part II   **Decision to Internationalize among Managers**   55
              of Smaller Manufacturing Enterprises

Chapter 5   The Internationalization Process   57

Chapter 6   The Decision to Consider Internationalization   67

Chapter 7   Perceived Obstacles to Internationalization   79

Part III   **Operations**   87

Chapter 8   Start of International Operations   89

Chapter 9   The Motivations for Internationalization   101

Part IV   Decision to Internationalize and Integrate   **111**

Chapter 10   Summary and Overview of Research Cases: 113
                 A Wisconsin Perspective

10.1   Alpha Technology Corporation   118
10.2   Bio-technology and Horticulture Unlimited   126
10.3   Outdoor Advertising Company   137
10.4   Packaging Container Services   145
10.5   PJ Manufacturing Inc.   153
10.6   Process Controls International   165

Chapter 11   Summary and Overview of Research Cases: 175
                 A European Perspective

11.1   Czech Cases   180
       11.1.1   ABC Plastic Limited   180
       11.1.2   KMF Limited   194
11.2   Danish Cases   207
       11.2.1   Cembrit Holding   207
       11.2.2   Migatronic   218
       11.2.3   Scan Tracking Systems   236
11.3   Swedish Cases   247
       11.3.1   Martinsons Trä AB   247
       11.3.2   Norrmejerier   258
       11.3.3   Seaflex AB   269

Chapter 12   Comparison of the Wisconsin and European   279
                 Perspectives

Part V   Conclusions and Suggestions for Future   **283**
          Research

Chapter 13   Conclusions   285

Chapter 14   Recommendations for Future Research   289

Selected Bibliography on Internationalization   291

Index   297

Introduction

Historical Perspective on Internationalization of Smaller Manufacturing Enterprises

This book provides a historical perspective on how smaller manufacturing enterprises operate, grow, and internationalize in a single environment, i.e. in the U.S. state of Wisconsin. The study on which this work is based focuses on individual managers — frequently owners of smaller manufacturing enterprises — who managed these enterprises in both their growing and sometimes declining years. These owner-managers might be easily classified into several managerial types with different managerial abilities, skills, and approaches to decision making. These decision-making propensities and capabilities are clearly reflected in their market positioning efforts, competitive posturing, and efforts to internationalize. For a majority of these enterprises, over the years, the internationalization efforts (among other challenges) were most critical.

The Objective

Our objective is not to contribute to the diversity of studies that over the years have broadened the understanding of internationalization among small- and medium-sized enterprises. Our objective instead is to focus exclusively on the subset of smaller manufacturing enterprises and provide a longitudinal perspective on their internationalization experiences. At the same time, in a small way, we would like to compare the internationalization experiences of smaller manufacturing

1

firms in Wisconsin with those in other parts of the world. Based on our professional experiences, and by convenience, we selected smaller manufacturing enterprises from the Czech Republic, Denmark, and Sweden. These comparisons are useful in attempting to understand internationalization as a managerial phenomenon in different countries. The smaller manufacturing enterprises in Denmark and Sweden have experienced internationalization for a much longer time than have their Wisconsin counterparts. The Czech Republic is a relatively new country, and their smaller manufacturing firms represent a fairly new development in their economy and offer different perspectives on the internationalization experience.

Internationalization

This book focuses primarily on the international context in which smaller manufacturing enterprises grow and operate today. An important component of the internationalization context is the concept of *internationalization* itself combined with the notion of international competition. At the beginning of this study, the issue of internationalization had not yet emerged. The emphasis instead was on exporting — increased export activities promoted by local and state governments. Many smaller manufacturing enterprises received unsolicited orders that they frequently did not fill because they did not know how. In the international climate of the mid-1970s and early 1980s, sales revenue derived from exports was only marginally important. Today, the situation is different: international sales are essential to the survival of these enterprises.

The internationalization of smaller manufacturing enterprises is essential because the traditional domestic market boundaries no longer exist. International competition has taken over and is forcing enterprises, regardless of size, to grow and operate on a broader and more international level. Competition at this level also demands that enterprises systematically re-examine their competitive posture, assess their market position, and evaluate their technological competence in the international context. Traditional relationships in consumer and business-to-business markets have given way to memberships in international supply chains, participation in complex value chains, and the reliance on international outsourcing. As a result, smaller manufacturing enterprises have become more integrated into these predominantly internationally based relationships.

Information Technology and Internationalization

The internationalization phenomenon is partly driven by the global marketplace which is, to a greater extent, a byproduct of the information technology revolution. Information technology has changed how smaller manufacturing enterprises communicate and exchange information. When these enterprises placed their webpages on the Internet, they instantly opened themselves to the broad international world. The Internet conveyed to the world that these companies do exist. Another easily accessible link is electronic mail, or email; which makes it possible for smaller manufacturing firms to communicate with their existing or potential customers anywhere in the world. From this perspective, Wisconsin enterprises have, in a way, become global enterprises.

Almost immediately after the smaller manufacturing enterprises posted their webpages on the Internet, they started receiving unsolicited inquiries and orders, occasionally accompanied by a confirmed letter of credit. As a result, many of them were overwhelmed by the volume of foreign attention they received. Even today, some enterprises choose to respond to these requests and some do not. Those who have decided to respond have had to internationalize their current business model. Unfortunately, very few managers understand how to successfully internationalize their growth strategies and operations to meet the needs of their international customers.

Internationalization as a Reality

The majority of managers realize that, in the present global economy, they need to internationalize their enterprises if they are to survive. This reality is particularly significant for the older and more traditional enterprises that, over many years, approached internationalization as an evolutionary process. However, for some of the recently formed smaller manufacturing enterprises, the internationalization process is more dramatic. New business start-ups that internalized information technology in the form of Internet communication as part of their business models had no choice but to include internationalization as an essential component of their fundamental business model. Consequently, over the years, internationalization has become an inevitable challenge for both established traditional smaller manufacturing enterprises and new start-ups.

Complexity of Internationalization

Internationalizing smaller manufacturing enterprises is not a simple process. The impact of internationalization varies depending on the nature of the industry and the type of product or market, as well as on the management style of each decision maker within each smaller manufacturing enterprise. For some smaller manufacturing enterprises, internationalization is externally driven by a number of outside forces, while for others it is internally driven by employees who have some vested interest in the global marketplace.

Individuals who influence the internationalization process among smaller manufacturing enterprises, either internally or externally, tend to be accountants, attorneys, consultants, government specialists in international commerce, and the managers themselves. These individuals, or groups of individuals, have their own motivations and objectives for helping smaller manufacturing enterprises internationalize. However, their inputs into the internationalization process are important. Some of these inputs relate to the managerial issues of internationalization, while others relate to public policy considerations. While managerial issues concerned with internationalization have implications for the market and competitive effectiveness and efficiency of the enterprise, public policy considerations are more complex. All levels of governments are interested in the internationalization of smaller manufacturing enterprises for several reasons. Smaller manufacturing enterprises that become successful international competitors create jobs, increase tax revenue, promote economic growth, and stabilize the economy. But more than that, they also provide the necessary foundations for new industries, create strong competitive advantages within geographic regions, create industrial clusters, and consolidate knowledge areas and industries. Consequently, smaller manufacturing enterprises provide internationally competitive foundations for regions, states, and countries.

The major deficiency of internationalization is the realization that the field of international management lacks a comprehensive and uniform theory of internationalization, especially among the smaller manufacturing enterprises. Existing theories are eclectic, normative, and frequently prescriptive. Many current theories are founded in substantially diverse cultural and historical settings. Others are based on sets of broad generalizations gathered from incomplete data from relatively diverse groups of small- and medium-sized enterprises that do not fully represent the traditional smaller manufacturing enterprises.

Discussions concerning the growth and operations of small- and medium-sized enterprises have gone on for more than 40 years. By now, economists, sociologists, technologists, and even enterprise managers accept the notion that small- and medium-sized enterprises provide a necessary economic, social, and technological foundation upon which larger enterprises grow and mature. Such enterprises serve as sources for novel ideas, new technologies, innovative products, and pioneering management styles. As a result of these inventive activities, numerous industries have emerged. The growth of new industries extends opportunities for existing markets to offer new products and services, enables banks and other financial institutions to provide a variety of financial services, and allows for the injection of new technology into stagnant industries. Even governments encourage start-ups of small- and medium-sized enterprises because they represent potential sources of tax revenue, employment opportunities, and economic stability.

Small- and Medium-Sized Enterprises vs. Smaller Manufacturing Enterprises

Even though not all small- and medium-sized enterprises are the same, the literature tends to combine different types of small- and medium-sized enterprises into one category. The present study is specifically about smaller manufacturing enterprises. Smaller manufacturing enterprises differ significantly from service enterprises, which only offer services and have different economic, social, or technological objectives. Smaller manufacturing enterprises constitute a homogeneous subgroup of small- and medium-sized enterprises. Their common dimension is manufacturing. Manufacturing represents the entire process of creating the physical form of a product, component, accessory, major piece of equipment, or even a large production facility. Smaller manufacturing enterprises create value. The contents of this book refer entirely to smaller manufacturing enterprises.

The Longitudinal Study

The survey presented here was a long-term study. For more than 35 years, this study examined both the domestic and international growth and operations of almost 500 smaller manufacturing enterprises that existed in a single environment and that were subject to the same economic, social, legal, technological, and lifestyle surroundings. As each state in the United States is unique, so it is with the state of Wisconsin. Wisconsin has its own economic climate that directly impacts the operational stability of its enterprises. It has its own homogeneous social climate that, because of its early immigrants, very much reflects Northern and Central European social values. Its legal environment addresses, in a very specific and traditionally progressive manner, the relationship between the Government of the State of Wisconsin and its commerce. Wisconsin is known as being technologically innovative. Mostly through its public universities, it maintains innovative educational programs in sciences, engineering, and medicine, among others. A significant number of graduates from such programs remain in Wisconsin and start their own businesses. In addition, Wisconsin's physical environment and consequential lifestyles mirror its geographic location and abundance of outdoor activities. The behavior of businesses over the past 35 years or more while this study was underway clearly demonstrated that Wisconsin-based smaller manufacturing enterprises tend to operate in a similar fashion.

The study that provided the basis for this appraisal of growth and operations of smaller manufacturing enterprises consisted of several stages. It started in the early 1970s with a series of 23 interviews with managers of Wisconsin smaller manufacturing enterprises. The selected enterprises were listed in the Classified Directory of Wisconsin Manufacturers, published by the Wisconsin Manufacturers Association. Thirty enterprises were originally selected for these interviews. The researchers used a consensus-building interview methodology for this part of the study. The objective was to find common factors among the enterprises that could provide a foundation for a much broader study. Sufficient consensus was reached during the 23rd interview, after which the interviewing process was stopped.

Responses from the managers were generally the same, with some exceptions. The series of interviews focused on three major areas: the managerial profile and orientation of each enterprise; the general formulation of their marketing and growth strategies; and issues directly related to components of growth, i.e. product and market development, market penetration, diversification, and development of exports. Exports, as a concept, was a proxy for the concept of internationalization, which was introduced in about 1995. Except for information about export operations, much overlap occurred in the findings from these interviews. Approximately one third of the enterprises interviewed exported their products. The important factors identified during the interviews were used in the second stage of the study.

A questionnaire, based on the input from the series of interviews, was designed and mailed to a sample of Wisconsin smaller manufacturing enterprises. A total of 474 enterprises responded to the survey. The first mailing produced interesting perspectives on how the smaller manufacturing enterprises were growing and operating at that time. Key findings included a strong focus on the product and process as well as a lack of marketing, but the export factor (which was also included) became important.

Ten years later, using the same research instrument and methodology, 288 of the original enterprises were still operational and responded to a second survey. Very little had changed among the smaller manufacturing enterprises in Wisconsin. The internationalization issue remained significant, the product and process focus was constant, and the enterprises lacked marketing abilities. Another 10 years later, again using the same research instrument and methodology, 101 of the original enterprises responded to a third survey. The third mail survey did not produce any major surprises either. Twenty years after the original survey, the enterprises had changed very little in terms of their growth and operations; however, a shift in operations towards internationalization had occurred. Approximately 10 years after the third mail survey, only 82 enterprises from the original sample of 474 could be identified.

The attrition rate is interesting and important. During the past 30 years or more, some of the original enterprises simply ceased operations; others were sold or had merged with other entities, within or outside of Wisconsin; some changed their names; and in some cases they moved out of state or abroad. The 82 enterprises that remained had not changed considerably over the years. Nevertheless, there were some changes. To determine the nature of these changes, a series of interviews using the consensus methodology approach was used again and six abridged research cases were collected — they are a part of this research. A series of six interviews was conducted with randomly selected enterprises from the surviving list of 82. Ownership changes, issues of top management succession, and internationalization were important topics of discussion during the interviews.

In addition to changes in ownership and issues of top management succession, the issue of changes in management style also became an important consideration. In some cases, the original founder and owner-manager had been replaced by a professional manager with a vested interest in the enterprise. Some of the remaining enterprises introduced a variety of new products; some entered new domestic and foreign markets, i.e. internationalized their operations; and some diversified into other businesses. Also, over the duration of this study, a number of the enterprises had taken on a completely new character. Some progressed from being fabricators of equipment tailored to customers' specifications to highly efficient manufacturers of upscale branded product lines, while others advanced from lines of low-technology products to high-technology engineered and manufactured installations.

For six of these transformed enterprises, the authors examined how current management perceives growth and operations in the contemporary international environment. This was an interesting and challenging exercise. In some instances, we had a more comprehensive perspective on the enterprise and its history than the present manager in charge. The six interviews provided invaluable information. Six short research cases were prepared and are included in this book.

Our Approach

Our perspectives on internationalization are based on three approaches. The first approach consists of a systematic and formally structured survey study of a sample of smaller manufacturing enterprises in a homogeneous business environment that was conducted three times during the period of the study. The second approach is based on a collection of research cases obtained from smaller manufacturing enterprises that were a part of the study in Wisconsin and research cases developed from interviews with enterprises in the three other countries of the Czech Republic, Denmark, and Sweden. Finally, there were opportunities to personally interact directly with the managers of some of the enterprises. During these interactions, we asked questions and observed how decisions concerning their own internationalization were made and implemented. Over the years, these opportunities offered an important insight into the internationalization process of smaller manufacturing enterprises in Wisconsin. How much our observations and conclusions can be extended to other states or countries is subject to conjecture.

It is important to point out, however, that this study is only an attempt to understand how, over many years, the smaller manufacturing enterprises have dealt with their internationalization issues and concerns. This is not a complete picture of internationalization among the entire population of smaller manufacturing enterprises found globally. Our research is a composite of experiences of a specific group of smaller manufacturing enterprises supplemented with limited experience of similar enterprises in other countries.

We hope that this book will provide opportunities for other researchers, doctoral students, and even practitioners to find concepts, ideas, or generalizations suitable for further research in the area of the internationalization of smaller manufacturing enterprises. We need to know more about internationalization as a concept. We need to know even more about how the concept is implemented among smaller manufacturing enterprises trying to become a part of the large global marketplace. As academics, researchers, public policy specialists, and even as managers, we need to know more about how internationalization as a managerial concept is used to confront international competition and assist managers of smaller (existing and emerging) manufacturing enterprises to survive.

Part I

Decision-Making Process among Smaller Manufacturing Enterprises

The objective in Part I is to explore how managers of smaller manufacturing enterprises approach the internationalization decision. More specifically, who are these managers? How do they view internationalization in the context of future operations? What strengths or weaknesses do they perceive as a basis for internationalization? What goals do they set that are consistent with their internationalization efforts? Answers to these questions provide additional insights into the internationalization process among smaller manufacturing enterprises.

Chapter 1

Managers of Smaller Manufacturing Enterprises

It is an accepted notion that smaller manufacturing enterprises provide the necessary foundation for economic growth and technological innovation. Smaller manufacturing enterprises play an important role in local, regional, and national development. At the same time, they fuel the growth of larger enterprises and, occasionally, are responsible for the introduction and growth of new industries. Biotechnology, computer, software, and nanotechnology are some of the industries introduced as a result of innovations carried out by small manufacturing start-ups. The initial ideas that helped form these industries came from research and development undertaken by smaller manufacturing enterprises, frequently managed and operated by owner-managers responsible for the initial innovation.

The Role of Smaller Manufacturing Enterprises in the Economy

Developmental economists consider smaller manufacturing enterprises to be necessary factors in building a sound industrial foundation for local, regional, and national economies. Smaller manufacturing enterprises help introduce the entrepreneurial skills needed to build and grow large stable enterprises, which create employment, increase the tax base, and stabilize and grow the economy. Thriving larger manufacturing enterprises can successfully compete in international markets, thus further strengthening the economy.

Sociologists view smaller manufacturing enterprises as social institutions which are capable of building important networks that tend to stabilize social environments and population clusters, leading to a better quality of life. Sociologists also point out that smaller manufacturing enterprises are managed by individuals who have innovative ideas for delivering new and alternative solutions for societal problems. Smaller manufacturing enterprises tend to be more independent, creative, and technologically focused. Depending on the management style of the key decision maker, many smaller manufacturing enterprises ignore geographical borders and socio-cultural differences.

Technologists, on the other hand, consider smaller manufacturing enterprises as essential outlets for technological creativity and market innovations. A majority of smaller high-technology manufacturing start-ups are founded by individuals with advanced degrees in engineering, sciences, or medicine. Many high-technology start-ups are seedlings for new high-technology industries, or building blocks for more robust technological infrastructures. According to some technologists, smaller manufacturing start-ups with lower levels of technology are typically founded by other types of professionals who have innovative product ideas or product improvements that can be marketed in existing markets, and provide only incremental technological improvements. These start-ups frequently contribute to innovation within supply and value chains. They may be as important as their high-technology counterparts.

Smaller manufacturing enterprises contribute to greater economic stability, strengthen social bonds, and create technologically based competitive advantages for a region. They also provide the necessary regional stimulus for the growth and support of infrastructural components such as financial institutions, venture capitalists, patent attorneys, and consulting services, among others. All of these activities contribute to economic growth in a region. Some economic development specialists argue that it does not matter if smaller manufacturing enterprises are high- or low-technology generators; it is their mere presence that is important.

Managers

Smaller manufacturing enterprises reflect their managers, especially owner-managers, since the managers are frequently also the owners. Enterprises managed by owner-managers tend to exhibit special characteristics. At the beginning, there tends to be an absence of specialized staff for individual business functions. The owner-manager usually performs all necessary functions, with the exception of routine accounting procedures. The typical smaller manufacturing enterprise, at its inception, finds it difficult to obtain sufficient capital. The owner-manager also lacks a fundamental understanding of marketing and competition principles. The owner-manager typically has a new idea, conceptualizes a new product or formulates a manufacturing process, and attempts to commercialize it. Starting a new enterprise facilitates the process.

As an enterprise grows, the management style often changes. By trial and error, the owner-manager learns how to bring innovations to the market and how to manage the enterprise from day to day. The organizational structure begins to change and specializations within the enterprise begin to form. These changes contribute to growth, and the owner-manager explores additional internal and external opportunities. However, in some situations, the growth challenges the owner-manager's abilities. When an owner-manager can no longer manage the enterprise, new management must be introduced. Many of these transitions lead to major organizational and ownership changes. Some smaller manufacturing enterprises are sold; others merge with competing enterprises or are completely liquidated.

A number of participants in this study illustrate this phenomenon. Most owner-managers of smaller manufacturing enterprises who started with a single product and a relatively low level of technology tended to stay with the product for a long time. At some point, they expanded and entered new regional, national, or even foreign markets. Others found it more convenient to diversify into a new business instead of introducing new products or entering new markets. It is apparent that a number of the single-product enterprises realized that a new product was needed to grow the enterprise further. Some were able to find a new product and they continued to grow.

Smaller manufacturing enterprises that offered high-technology products followed a different path. Initially, they behaved like their lower-technology counterparts. However, when their enterprises started to grow, these owner-managers realized that, as engineers, scientists, or medical professionals, they were not qualified to manage the growth. They recognized their professional shortcomings and proceeded to introduce professional managers to their enterprises. The recognition of their managerial shortcomings often initiated actions leading to the introduction of a new organizational model. For most owner-managers, this was the time to step back and let professional managers direct the entire enterprise. For others, it was time to sell stock, offer equity, or sell the enterprise. A few managers stayed with the new organization to serve as functional managers or consultants and watch the enterprise grow. It is interesting to note that many high-technology owner-managers who left their original enterprises started another venture shortly after they left.

Consequently, smaller manufacturing enterprises, regardless of their level of technology, are typically started by a variety of owner-managers. Earlier in this study, they were engineers working for large corporations; scientists working in university, research, or corporate laboratories; managers or executives interested in managing their own enterprises; academics; and medical professionals interested in less stressful jobs. Most of these early start-ups dealt with products of relatively low technology. Later in the study, high-technology start-ups were founded by highly educated professionals working in similar settings but interested in much more complex scientific issues. For example, a doctoral student started a biotechnology venture or a medical doctor founded a small enterprise to manufacture medical equipment.

Although these owner-managers all perceived their ideas, products, or processes as unique and as having inherent competitive advantages, they lacked the necessary marketing and financial skills to bring the perceived competitive advantage to the market. Furthermore, most of the owner-managers focused on the product and its manufacturing process rather than on customers or markets. Some owner-managers believed in their ideas, products, or processes to the point that they went into a lengthy procedure to promote them. Very few owner-managers had the professional managerial abilities to direct the venture professionally.

Growth was important to the managers of smaller manufacturing enterprises, but growth is also an ambiguous managerial construct. Growth is often defined as an absolute increase in the physical size of the enterprise as measured by employment, sales volume, or capital investment. This classification approach does not produce any significant insight into the actual operations of the enterprise. Other growth models are needed because expansion among smaller manufacturing enterprises may be due to two fundamentally different forces. On the one hand, external changes in the economic climate may force an enterprise to change; consequently, the enterprise would respond and grow accordingly. On the other hand, major managerial and organizational changes are often driven from within and are not related to the physical size of the enterprise. Managers with varying managerial decision-making styles stimulate growth in different ways. This study suggests that a manager's ability to make decisions is closely related to the degree of internal growth.

In order to understand the concept of growth among smaller manufacturing enterprises, it is necessary to examine some of the patterns of growth faced by these enterprises. Smaller manufacturing enterprises play an important role in the entire manufacturing sector. Some smaller manufacturing enterprises begin as custom fabricators — they build equipment and machinery to customers' specifications. Their expertise is inherent in the efficiency and effectiveness of their manufacturing process. They may remain so and even grow successfully. Other custom fabricators, at some point, begin to improve their manufacturing expertise further and make manufacturing improvements to build a better product. They may make suggestions on how to improve product performance, improve maintenance, and simplify technical support. When custom manufacturers acquire a certain level of fabrication knowledge and technical understanding of the products they create, they may decide to build their own proprietary products. In such instances, their customers may prefer to purchase the improved proprietary product rather than re-engineer their internally designed products, and thus save development and engineering costs.

Some smaller manufacturing enterprises tend to be very innovative and make additional improvements to their products. They learn how to introduce new technology into the products and integrate it into product lines, production processes, or the technological settings of their clients. For example, some may upgrade pneumatically operated production equipment by introducing electronic computer-based controls that are faster and more reliable, and thereby gain a competitive advantage. Occasionally, smaller manufacturing enterprises will also introduce a service to accompany their equipment and thus fully integrate the equipment, programming it to become a part of the customer's manufacturing process.

Upgrading from relatively low-technology fabrication processes to providing and integrating high-technology equipment presents enormous opportunities for growth. Enterprises using this technological expansion path have experienced not only rapid growth, but also major shifts in management. Changing from a fabrication shop to a product manufacturer and eventually a technology integrator requires different management styles, different decision-making approaches, and a proper understanding of growth itself.

Additional growth opportunities and the decision-making process needed to support eventual growth opportunities can be examined from two perspectives — technological and marketing. The technological perspective suggests that the transition from a fabrication shop to a product manufacturer to a technology integrator may be a relatively natural process for a manager with an engineering or scientific background. However, from a marketing perspective, when product development, pricing strategies, and sales need to be introduced to maintain existing markets and enter new markets, the same managers may not be able to introduce marketing as the necessary framework for decision making. In fact, they may be very good technologists but not very capable marketing specialists. These developments are clearly apparent within this study. Successful growth among smaller manufacturing enterprises requires carefully balanced decisions between marketing expertise and technical knowledge.

Based on the results of this study, managers of smaller manufacturing enterprises can be classified into three categories: those who wish to develop a comfortable standard of living for themselves; those who promote their enterprises and their products; and those who manage to grow in response to the needs of their enterprises.

Craftsman Managers

The first category includes managers who establish an enterprise with the objective of developing a comfortable standard of living as a result of managing a successful surviving enterprise. This manager is primarily a *craftsman* who is directly involved with the operations of the enterprise. This manager determines policies and procedures, and is very much involved with the product and its manufacturing process. The craftsman manager is typically an uninspiring leader who maintains employee bonds through their assigned roles.

The findings in this study suggest that such managers are not interested in innovation because current operational business models are based on their previous work experience and little uncertainty or risk is involved. One interesting managerial construct that has been constant over time is that small manufacturing enterprises maintain a share of the market because they are capable of supplying products that are totally uneconomical for larger enterprises to produce. It is interesting to note that craftsman managers determine how successful they are and how much they need to grow to maintain the standard of living they want to enjoy. Other craftsman managers change with experience; they adjust their managerial styles, and eventually reorganize and restructure their enterprises by introducing new business models.

Very few enterprises in this category are interested in internationalization or, more specifically, in marketing their products in foreign markets. If they are, they will most likely use an export agent, distributor, or manufacturer's sales agent to do so. Craftsman managers perceive uncertainty and risk in exporting their products directly, and want to charge higher prices for their products because they believe that profits are lower in foreign markets.

Promoter Managers

The second category of managers studied were promoters of their enterprises and their products. The *promoter* managers tend to have very strong entrepreneurial skills and charismatic leadership qualities that motivate employees to strive for a better future. Some promoter managers are also environmentally aware and socially responsible. However, the promoter manager tends to be somewhat impulsive. Although the manager attempts to formulate policies, the policies are frequently improved or changed, sometimes on a day-to-day basis. It can be suggested that, because of the established policies, promoter managers also begin to introduce managerial functions. With a promoter manager in place, functional orientation develops early and typically begins with manufacturing and sales functions, followed closely by other functions such as engineering.

Internal innovation becomes important when the manager, as a promoter, begins to realize that the product or the manufacturing process is less competitive. At the same time, the promoter manager realizes that rapid growth and the expansion of organizational complexity bring uncertainty; however, growth makes it possible for the enterprise to expand its market operations and improve its competitive position. The promoter manager at some point begins to feel the burden of management, as decision making becomes burdensome and difficult; the promoter manager will then hire additional staff to help oversee these procedures. These changes make it even more difficult to successfully manage the enterprise.

Knowledge about the enterprise, its market success, and the self-promotional tendencies of the promoter manager tend to attract outside attention. Competitors, potential merger partners, and other interested investors approach the various participants about potentially acquiring the enterprise. This situation presents a difficult challenge to promoter managers. Some decide to pursue unsolicited offers, while others realize that they have to change their management style in order to accommodate the growth and market success of the enterprise.

The present study suggests that promoter-managed enterprises became attractive acquisition targets in the mid-1980s and early 1990s. During this period, such enterprises faced major internationalization efforts for the first time, both internally and externally. Internally, they were pressured by their occasional foreign customers, governments offered assistance and other incentives for their international expansion, and their domestic competitive positions were eroding. Externally, they were asked to merge with foreign partners or join emerging supply chains; and an increasing number of smaller manufacturing enterprises were asked to source abroad for supplies, parts, and components to reduce costs. These issues were difficult to resolve.

Rational Managers

The final category of managers examined in this study was *rational* managers. Rational managers include those managers who were classified as promoter managers, but who managed to grow in response to the needs of their enterprises. These managers have strong entrepreneurial skills, but their main objective is to rationally and objectively allocate the resources available to their enterprises. Their primary objective is to secure a stable market share. Their management style demands that policies be carefully defined and well established within the organizational hierarchy consisting of professional managers and technical experts.

Rational managers tend to reorganize and restructure smaller manufacturing enterprises into entities that are able to compete in both domestic and international markets. They plan systematically for technical development and automatically introduce innovation. Their employees are highly skilled and perform homogeneous functions within set standards that are determined by the overall philosophy and core competence of the enterprise. Job descriptions encompass all areas of the enterprise. Each enterprise managed by a rational manager tends to have its own unique business model.

The rational managers overseeing smaller manufacturing enterprises in this study tend not to differentiate between domestic and international markets. The growth of the enterprise is driven by a successful internal business model and by the manager's broad opportunistic perspective of the global marketplace. Rational managers typically understand their markets and offer highly competitive technologies. In addition, because of their success, they are frequently approached by international customers, suppliers, investors, and even potential competitors to forge relationships and alliances.

Managerial Perspectives

The three categories of managers described above can be viewed from varying perspectives. In some cases, the craftsman managers — the original founders of their enterprises — can grow with the needs of their enterprises by making the right decisions. These managers improve their skills and anticipate what their enterprises will need in the next growth stage. The same tendencies apply to the next category of managers, the promoter managers. If they made the transition from craftsman managers to promoter managers, it is likely that they can also make the change to rational managers. These transitions can be achieved through education, experience, or competitive forces.

It is important to realize that some managers are simply not capable of changing their management style and their ability to make decisions. Some craftsman managers cannot move on to become promoter managers or, eventually, rational managers. They do not possess the necessary foresight and ability to anticipate what is needed to achieve higher growth. When managers managing smaller manufacturing enterprises cannot cope with the needs of their enterprises, they typically resign and are replaced. The replacement process can be complicated. Some craftsman managers are directly replaced by rational managers, but not always. Depending on who owns the enterprise, the next-level manager, a promoter manager, may be hired. There appears to be a natural expectation of growth and continuity in smaller manufacturing enterprises that suggests a traditional development and evolution process for the enterprise. Introducing a rational manager would not only interrupt the traditional process, but would dramatically change the organizational structure of the enterprise. Few smaller manufacturing enterprises would survive such a drastic management change from craftsman manager directly to a rational manager, due to the differences in how each would structure the enterprise and make decisions.

The differences in decision-making styles among the three categories of managers of smaller manufacturing enterprises are important to this study for several reasons. First, individual managers need to understand how and when to make appropriate decisions to grow an enterprise and, if they do not have this understanding, they need to know when to step back and let a more qualified manager take over. Second, the manager needs to anticipate the decisions that are needed to reinforce the growth of the enterprise and, at the same time, identify its market and technological needs. If the manager is not able to make these decisions, the enterprise will not grow. At this point, a more suitable manager needs to take over. Third, the enterprise must survive within the framework of the external environment. The new, highly competitive global marketplace demands greater attention from managers of smaller manufacturing enterprises. The managers must constantly be aware of their competition and their position in the global marketplace. Not all managers of smaller manufacturing enterprises are able to do so. The decision on how to compete and when to internationalize can be overwhelming for inexperienced managers and, again, they may have to be replaced by more experienced managers.

Conclusion

The main objective of this study was to examine how managers of smaller manufacturing enterprises make decisions in an international context over a longer time period. The decision-making process that underscores the tentative choice to internationalize is complex and often difficult for an individual manager. It is important to examine various aspects of enterprise management in order to determine which factors individual managers consider essential and which elements lead to a decision to internationalize one's company. The results of this study provide valuable insight into the understanding of how managers make decisions about when and how to internationalize their businesses. In particular, the findings suggest ways in which managers of smaller manufacturing enterprises plan, how these managers perceive their competitive advantage, and which performance goals are important to them.

Chapter 2

The Types of Goals Set by Managers of Smaller Manufacturing Enterprises

Whether or not to internationalize depends on which goals managers choose. A typical expectation is that individual enterprises will strive for profitability; however, there appears to be exceptions. Some smaller manufacturing enterprises set alternative goals, depending on their stage of growth and market position; other enterprises set broader goals relevant to their operations and, in some instances, to the economy. The horizons for achieving these goals differ considerably from one enterprise to another. Some start-up enterprises set short-term goals, perhaps six to twelve months; while larger and more mature small manufacturing enterprises may set long-term goals, perhaps two to four years.

Goal Setting

The goals set by managers of smaller manufacturing enterprises tell us a great deal about their short- and long-term focus and operations. A relatively small number of enterprises, from their founding, tend to be aware of their external environment; they consider themselves a part of the economy, the society, or even the international community. Other enterprises tend to be internally oriented, which means they take into account only the key managerial and operational aspects of the enterprise, usually market and financial performance. In smaller owner-manager enterprises, the owner-manager may be interested only in generating sufficient profit to support the anticipated activities necessary to establish a satisfactory position in the marketplace.

Promoter manager-based enterprises might be interested only in sales and market performance. Finally, rational manager-based enterprises may set their goals in a more strategic manner to reinforce and secure their competitive position in the marketplace.

Identifying Goals

Since managers of smaller manufacturing enterprises may have a port-folio of potential goals, at the beginning of this study we asked them to identify the goals they considered most important to their enterprises. The managers were able to identify five goals (listed in alphabetical order): (1) contribution to the development of the U.S. economy; (2) development and/or security of their markets; (3) high growth rate; (4) high profit rate; and (5) security of their investments. Initially, the managers perceived all five goals to be internal to the enterprise and, therefore, under their control. However, the goals can also be viewed as external factors because some managers who helped to identify them also pointed out that their own success in managing their enterprises was dependent on how well the economy was per-forming. If the economy was expanding, their enterprises could do well; if the economy was contracting, the success of their enterprises could be limited.

In the process of identifying these goals, none of the managers suggested that export (now international) operations were perceived as viable goals. At the beginning of the study, the main focus was on profits, growth, and markets. Since markets at that time tended to be identified in geographical terms, it is unlikely that goals concerning markets actually included foreign markets.

Contribution to the Development of the U.S. Economy

At the time managers identified the meaning and importance of these five goals, those factors were found to be related to management style. *Contribution to the development of the U.S. economy* was alpha-betically the first goal identified at the start of the study. Most managers had a simple explanation for what it meant to contribute to the development of the U.S. economy: to create jobs. This response was particularly relevant in the context of their geographical orientation. Managers served their narrow geographical region by employing individuals who then spent their income and paid taxes in the local economy. The notion that their enterprise had a significant impact on the overall national economy was not relevant for many of the managers. Some of the more mature enterprises managed by rational managers perceived the contribution factor more broadly. They believed that they indirectly contributed to the national economy by supplying larger national enterprises with technologically up-to-date quality products so that final products could be marketed competitively at the national level. Although this is a rather simplistic view, some managers did believe that they had an indirect impact on the national economy through their national customers with manufacturing bases in their geographical areas.

Development and/or Security of Markets

One managerial goal was to *develop and secure their markets* once an enterprise established itself in the market and was able to hold on to that market for a reasonable length of time, perhaps over a two-year period. Most managers indicated that it normally takes about a year for a new enterprise to establish itself in the market and another year to formalize its position. According to managers, it takes even longer to survive. Managers tend to describe the development of their markets as a reactive process in which customers request information about a product and its applications, information to strengthen sales relationships, and information on the terms of delivery, among other requests. Many start-up enterprises are not able to fully satisfy these requests. As enterprises grow and become more functionally focused, the information requested by customers becomes more readily available and the notion of market development acquires a new meaning. For some enterprises, the development of their markets included monitoring the information needed to maintain a balance between customer demands and competitive pressures. Rational managers of more mature enterprises viewed market development as an expansion of existing markets, and defined entry into new markets based mainly on how their products were used rather than on the basis of geography.

The related part of this goal, securing markets as a part of market development, was also perceived differently depending on the life cycle stage of each enterprise. For craftsman and promoter managers, securing the market suggested that the enterprises tried to build personal rapport with their customers, gain customer loyalty, and give customer satisfaction. Many managers who operated mainly in nearby markets were not always aware of their competition and assumed that, because they saw their products as unique, there was only minimal competition or no competition at all. Rational managers were aware of their competition, and consequently defined their competitive position differently. They viewed competition as a market force that had to be challenged by maintaining product quality at competitive prices. Some managers suggested that appropriate technology was necessary to secure their markets.

High Growth Rate

Managers also initially identified a *high growth rate* as an important factor in smaller enterprises. The interpretation of this goal was consistent among responding managers: they wanted their enterprises to grow rapidly. They pointed out that, in order to accomplish their other goals, they needed to make certain that their enterprises were growing. Managers typically looked for above-average growth rates for their industry. Some managers suggested that, because they had something unique to offer in the marketplace or perhaps were instrumental in founding a new industry, they were entitled to higher growth rates.

High Profit Rate on Investment

At the beginning of the study, managers indicated that a *high profit rate* on their investment was a major goal. For most managers, the goal was to have operations that were more profitable than the average profit rate in their respective industries.

Security of Investments

The final goal specified by the managers was *security of their investments*. Defining this goal was complicated by what different managers perceived and defined as their investments. The concept of investment for smaller manufacturing enterprises operated by craftsman managers differs considerably from that of promoter managers or even rational managers. Craftsman managers typically considered the investment to be financial investment: the amount of capital needed to start an enterprise, perform the most rudimentary tasks to manufacture the product, and get it to the customer. Promoter managers tended to think of investment as more than just a financial concern. The financial investment provided the foundation, but security of investment from the perspective of promoter managers included the technology represented in the product as well as the manufacturing technology. It also included the promotional efforts of the managerial team. The central notion of this goal was the security of the entire enterprise. Finally, rational managers tended to define this goal as the security of the total assets owned by the enterprise — more specifically, the combination of financial, physical, and human resources owned by each enterprise, which translated into its ability to competitively market technologically advanced products. Ownership of marketing know-how and technology was a major portion of the rational manager's investment.

Importance of Goals

These goals were tested three times over the span of the study. The results from the three surveys produced no significant differences among the goals, with the exception of *development and/or security of markets*. This goal had the highest level of response in all three surveys. Approximately 73% of the respondents considered *development and/or security of markets* important. Using the same measures, the three surveys showed that this goal was important in 1974, became significantly more important during the mid-1980s when competition intensified both domestically and internationally, and was somewhat less important in the mid-1990s.

These findings suggest that smaller manufacturing enterprises felt relatively secure in the mid-1970s, when they perceived that their markets were secure against domestic competition. In the mid-1980s, the situation changed dramatically. Foreign competition began to confront regionally oriented smaller manufacturing enterprises, and they had to take action against their competitors. They were also challenged by various government agencies to enter foreign markets and face competitors directly. Those enterprises that survived to the mid-1990s learned how to address their domestic and foreign competition and, in some cases, also learned how to take advantage of outsourcing and offshore manufacturing; some also opted to join global supply and value chains by the mid-1990s. By this time, they felt that their markets were again relatively secure.

No substantial differences existed among responses to the other goals, although response levels differed considerably. Approximately 64% of the respondents, averaged over the three surveys, perceived that a *high profit rate* on their investment, measured on a scale from 0 to 100, was important to them. About 63% of respondents indicated that *security of investments* was more important to them. Although the managers of the smaller manufacturing enterprises considered *high growth rate* important at the beginning of the study, the response rates were considerably lower in importance. The average response rate over the three surveys, measured on the same scale, was just over 40%.

The first goal identified at the beginning of the study, *contribution to the development of the U.S. economy*, produced dramatically lower response rates. Only about 20% of the respondents to the three surveys, on average, ranked the importance of this goal as being 50% or greater. More specifically, for the 1974 and 1985 surveys, the rate of responses was approximately 23%; in the 1995 survey, the response rate dropped to about 16%. It appears from these findings that in the 1970s, and even in the 1980s, approximately one quarter of managers were inclined to contribute to the development of the U.S. economy. In the 1990s, the economy changed: markets became more unstable, both domestic and international competition became more intensive, and smaller manufacturing enterprises fell behind technologically.

In general, they had a difficult time competing and, therefore, became more reluctant to contribute to the development of the U.S. economy.

It is interesting to note that the rate of responses to those goals that were 50% or higher in importance, measured on a scale from 0 to 100, was approximately 50%, and that this was consistent for all respondents when the three surveys were compared. This finding supports the importance of all five goals initially identified by the managers responsible for smaller manufacturing enterprises. In fact, all five goals were of some or major importance to these enterprises. In summary, it appears that managers of smaller manufacturing enterprises were primarily concerned about developing and securing their markets. They were equally concerned about securing their investments by generating profit. They wanted to grow, but they were not necessarily interested in contributing to the development of the U.S. economy.

Not all smaller manufacturing enterprises survived throughout the span of the study. As suggested before, some could not compete and closed their operations, some were sold, others merged with domestic or foreign competitors, and some even changed their identity. But some enterprises survived. In 2008, we were still able to find 82 original and consistent respondents to the three surveys. Based on a randomly selected sample of six surviving smaller manufacturing enterprises, we prepared six research cases in which we covered the issues and topics listed in the original questionnaire and used for the three consecutive surveys.

Significant differences were found in the importance and ranking of goals identified by the managers of the smaller manufacturing enterprises when the responses to the three surveys of the six enterprises still in existence in 2008 were compared to the rest of the respondents to the three surveys. In terms of *high growth rate*, the six surviving enterprises responded at approximately 68%. In other words, the six surviving enterprises considered *high growth rate* to be much more important — they wanted to grow. The goal of *high profit rate* was equally important for the two categories of respondents; but for the six survivors, it was not as important as *high growth rate*.

The two respondent categories also differed in their response to the *security of investments* goal. The response rate for the six surviving enterprises was somewhat lower than for the other category of respondents, which suggests that each of the six survivors was more willing to face risk than were the other enterprises. This finding also suggests that the six surviving enterprises were technologically more advanced and may have had stronger management, especially in the mid-1990s.

Conclusion

In conclusion, the managers of smaller manufacturing enterprises were setting somewhat inappropriate goals for themselves due to their relative ambivalence towards their external environment, especially the U.S. economy. Because of their mainly regional orientation, they were concerned about isolated markets and did not closely monitor their competition and market development, particularly from the mid-1980s and beyond. These findings also suggest that the owners did not plan or set goals for entering foreign or global markets. In fact, it appears that the smaller manufacturing enterprises felt relatively comfortable in their narrow markets and did not perceive the need to internationalize their marketing strategies.

Setting relevant goals and striving to achieve them may have an important bearing on a company's decision to internationalize. At the same time, one might argue that the notion of internationalization as a strategic growth and marketing philosophy for smaller manufacturing enterprises was not introduced until the mid-1980s. Before that time, the idea of internationalization was known as "exporting". Other forms of foreign market involvement, such as licensing, joint ventures, and direct investment in foreign markets, were relatively complex for smaller manufacturing enterprises in the mid-1970s.

Chapter 3
Strengths and Weaknesses of Smaller Manufacturing Enterprises

The strengths of smaller manufacturing enterprises are closely related to their future operations and planning. Smaller manufacturing enterprises are initially established because their owner-managers perceive that the enterprise has a competitive advantage in the marketplace. Typically, these perceived advantages, as expressed by individual managers, make it possible for the enterprises to operate from a credulous competitive position. This apparent advantage may last for a relatively long time for some smaller manufacturing enterprises operating in a small geographic marketplace. Thus, this perceived advantage also falsely enables the enterprise to be more concerned about day-to-day operational challenges than about the need to plan for the future.

Owner-managers in this study considered perceived advantages among smaller manufacturing enterprises to be a strength. Depending on how these executives perceive the strengths of their businesses, the owners of smaller manufacturing enterprises will decide whether they will or will not operate internationally in the future. Also, how owner-managers perceive the strengths of their business may determine whether they view entering international markets as an opportunity to extend the business advantages. At the same time, some enterprises try to utilize their perceived strength by offering their products at higher prices domestically and internationally. Some enterprises believe that their strengths almost automatically generate demand for their products, and that potential customers will take the initiative and seek out the individual enterprises instead of the individual enterprises needing to promote, sell, or undertake any other marketing effort. This is particularly the attitude of the craftsman or promoter managers responsible for smaller manufacturing enterprises. Since the position of strength was initially introduced by the owner-managers, it may in the future lead them into a false sense of security.

Depending on the background and managerial style of the entrepreneurs, some smaller manufacturing enterprises may have a real advantage that leads to a substantial competitive advantage in the market. For example, a medical doctor may perceive a need for a unique medical device to be used during a medical procedure. The medical doctor conceptualizes the device, develops a prototype, and, with external financing, starts a new venture and begins to successfully market the device. Perception of the need is thus translated into a real competitive advantage — being first on the market. In other words, the enterprise has introduced an innovative product to the market that customers then seek out and purchase. Because the enterprise becomes so well known for that product, they seldom need to actively market it. Enterprises that have introduced an innovative product or a new technology frequently become focused on their day-to-day operations. Because of the initially high demand for their products, they have a tendency to ignore what the competition is doing and quickly lose the advantage.

In some smaller manufacturing enterprises, a fine line exists between how the owners see their market advantage and how they implement marketing strategies and the reality of their market advantage. Unrealistic expectations of market performance that are not backed up by objective marketing research studies frequently lead to major disappointments. Some perceived advantages need to be actively marketed (or at least sold), but the owner-managers may not have the ability to do so; consequently, the enterprises quickly lose the advantage. The other extreme is if the advantage is significant and the market responds by generating a strong anticipatory demand for the product; unfortunately, enterprises often cannot provide sufficient quantities of the product to satisfy the high demand. For most owners who believe that their enterprise has a marketplace, it is important that they objectively know how to balance efforts between the enterprise's capability to produce and supply the product and its knowledge and skills in how to market the product. This is a difficult task for some smaller manufacturing enterprises.

Regardless of whether or not one can convert a perceived advantage into a marketable product with a strong competitive advantage, it remains a fundamental factor upon which many smaller manufacturing enterprises have been founded. Successful perceived advantages combined with sufficient financing and sound marketing can lead to strong competitive positions in the market. Many smaller manufacturing enterprise managers also believe that the stronger the competitive position, the less they need to be concerned about the future of their enterprises. This conviction became apparent in our follow-up interviews and in our observations during the study. In other words, as long as managers perceive an advantage that translates into competitive strengths for their enterprises, they tend to ignore the future. Some of the managers suggested that demand for their products is so strong that they do not have to worry about filling the potential demand for a long time; their enterprise will survive long into the future. This conviction leads to false expectations.

An examination of smaller manufacturing enterprises from this perspective also impacts their understanding of the concept of growth. For an enterprise that has been successful for a long period of time, demand for products increases. Since the enterprises have most likely grown, they are able to supply the products when requested. However, enterprises that cannot supply the products in a timely fashion have only a nominal chance to grow or, in some cases, survive. The key factor concerning perceived competitive advantage is the necessary knowledge needed to effectively and efficiently convert a perceived advantage into a real market-based competitive advantage.

For the purpose of this study, we asked the managers of smaller manufacturing enterprises to list the various perceived advantages they consider fundamental to their operations. The assumption was that these perceived advantages would represent real competitive advantages in the market. Ten perceived advantages were identified: adequate assets, competitive price, dynamic sales force, efficient distribution, efficient marketing techniques, efficient production methods, proximity to the market, strong management, technology, and unique product.

Over the period of the study, these factors were interpreted in the context of smaller manufacturing enterprises' operations and managerial know-how. Two important observations can be made. The first observation concerns the definition of the concept underlying each perceived advantage, which has changed slightly over the duration of the study. The second observation is concerned with the erosion of the meaning of each concept. Initially, each factor identified as a perceived advantage may have been competitively strong; however, as the factor was implemented, its competitive strength began to decay.

Adequate Assets

The definition of each perceived advantage is a concern to managers of smaller manufacturing enterprises. For example, *adequate assets* as a perceived advantage is defined by managers of start-up enterprises as having sufficient capital to found the enterprise and start manufacturing the product. The capital may be generated by the owner, borrowed from private sources, or received from commercial sources such as venture capitalists. For more established enterprises or those further along in their life cycle, the perceived advantage defined as adequate assets implies having sufficient operating capital and having the ability to maintain a line of credit at a bank. More mature enterprises view adequate assets as having a strong financial resource base available to the entire enterprise. As financial institutions change their financing practices, smaller manufacturing enterprises change their interpretation of what it means to perceive adequate assets as an advantage.

The concept of adequate assets as a perceived advantage has eroded significantly over time. In general, managers of smaller manufacturing enterprises suggest that the need for input of capital into manufacturing in general is increasing. At the same time, the availability of operational and investment capital is decreasing. In our study, smaller manufacturing enterprises that had their credit lines cut had to cancel some of their planned expansions. For some enterprises, the weakening of their capital base had continued for years; for others, such an experience was relatively new and resulted from the recent economic crisis.

Research indicates that a smaller start-up enterprise may experience its perceived advantage in the form of adequate assets that erode quickly, sometimes before the enterprise has had an opportunity to introduce the product to the market. For more established enterprises, the erosion results from inadequate sales or insufficient manufacturing capabilities. Such enterprises may begin to experience low sales and may need to expand their manufacturing capacity or modernize their manufacturing technology, but do not have the necessary capital. Banks will not lend the needed capital as a consequence of low sales. For the mature enterprises, the erosion of adequate assets as a perceived advantage results from poor competitive market performance driven by high fixed costs due to either obsolete manufacturing processes or fluctuations in the economy. Their entire financial resource base thus begins to erode and the enterprises find themselves in an unsustainable position.

Competitive Price

In general, smaller manufacturing enterprises perceive the *competitive price* for which they sell their products as one of their advantages. From their perspective, the definition is literal — it means that they can compete on the basis of their price or meet the prices of their direct competitors. However, this is not always the case. Some smaller manufacturing enterprises do not have the opportunity to compare their prices with the prices of their nearest competitors. Since some enterprises started out with the idea of having a unique product, they find it difficult to even identify their nearest competitor. Nevertheless, competitive price is one of the most frequently mentioned perceived advantages.

Smaller manufacturing enterprises point out that, when their markets expand and if competition plays a major role, the idea of competitive price as a perceived advantage rapidly erodes and the enterprises find it increasingly difficult to compete. However, the more mature enterprises tend to experience the greatest erosion with regards to competitive price as a perceived advantage. It is important to note that some small high-technology enterprises which are in their early stages of growth and have not yet experienced intensive competition still perceive that they have a competitive price advantage.

Dynamic Sales Force

The notion of *dynamic sales force* as a perceived advantage is also subject to different levels of interpretation. Some smaller manufacturing enterprises which have not yet reached the marketing orientation stage in their development simply suggest that they know how to sell their products and that the sales personnel are enthusiastic about the process of selling their products. This perception tends to suggest that these enterprises are still in the sales orientation stage. Enterprises that practice marketing highlighted by customer orientation define dynamic sales force as their perceived advantage in a more sophisticated manner — as a well-informed and motivated sales force that understands its customers. In this context, dynamic sales force as a perceived advantage is a marketing tool and is a part of the formal marketing strategy.

The erosion or decay of the concept of dynamic sales force as a perceived advantage also has different interpretations, depending on where smaller manufacturing enterprises are in terms of implementing a marketing philosophy. Enterprises in the production orientation stage generally do not employ a sales force. The owner-managers of such enterprises tend to be involved in product sales. Having a dynamic sales force becomes important in the sales orientation stage, when enterprises establish sales as one of the managerial functions and thus organize a sales force. As enterprises grow, they enter the distribution stage; the importance of a dynamic sales force usually decreases at the end of the distribution stage. In the final stage, the marketing orientation stage, the role of the sales force is integrated into all other managerial functions. The majority of enterprises in this study were found to be in the first three stages: production, sales, and distribution. Over the 35-year period, some of the smaller manufacturing enterprises progressed through all stages and can now be classified as operating in the fourth stage, the marketing orientation stage. This means that they have progressed from considering the perceived advantage, dynamic sales force, as their primary marketing tool to being simply one of the many tools integrated into the total promotional effort of their marketing strategy.

Efficient Distribution

The concept of *efficient distribution* as a perceived advantage among the smaller manufacturing enterprises has also changed dramatically over the span of this study. Distribution as a marketing concept evolved over the same period from a relatively minor managerial function of physical distribution to a complex system of logistics, and is sometimes viewed on the same level as marketing. Most enterprises in this study have upgraded their distribution services primarily due to customer demand or pressures placed on them by major providers of logistical services. Because of improvements in external distribution services, including logistics, the definition of the concept of efficient distribution as a perceived advantage has changed and does not carry the same importance as it did at the beginning of this study.

The above changes in the evolution of modern distribution and logistics have significantly contributed to the overall erosion of the concept of efficient distribution among smaller manufacturing enterprises. Most enterprises in the study suggest that their ability to distribute their products is closely connected with the efficiency and effectiveness of their distribution and logistical support providers.

Efficient Marketing Techniques

Efficient marketing techniques are another perceived advantage specified by managers of smaller manufacturing enterprises. The definition of this perceived advantage has changed only slightly over the span of this study. Initially, it was defined as a combination of sales and advertising of the product. The advertising efforts were closely related to the physical description of the product and a detailed listing of its technical specifications. Later, the concept of efficient marketing techniques was modified to include sales and suggestions for use of the product. As managers of smaller manufacturing enterprises gained a better understanding of markets and customer applications, they provided additional information about potential product advantages and potential applications as feedback to the marketplace. Product pricing, product improvements, distribution, or comprehensive promotion were not necessarily variables in marketing as efficient marketing techniques were defined.

Once marketing became more generally accepted among smaller manufacturing enterprises, it was slightly re-interpreted to encompass a more comprehensive set of factors that help managers of smaller manufacturing enterprises better understand the needs of their customers and deliver a quality product to them. The concept of efficient marketing techniques consisted of sales and marketing approaches that included a better understanding of product pricing and promotion. Promotion, at this point, consisted of providing less technically descriptive information and more examples of product applications. It also included being present at various trade shows and product demonstrations.

The interpretation of efficient marketing techniques as a perceived advantage has changed little over the span of this study. Even today, managers of smaller manufacturing enterprises differentiate between sales and marketing, although sales is an integral part of marketing. They believe that marketing supports sales activities, or that sales and marketing support each other. Approximately halfway into the study, marketing began to emerge as a strong competitive force among smaller manufacturing enterprises and the managers took on responsibility for marketing, although some of them had marginal understanding and knowledge of marketing. In reality, the sales managers frequently made decisions about markets, customers, and even product modifications.

Efficient Production Methods

Efficient production methods are another perceived advantage originally introduced by managers of smaller manufacturing enterprises.

The definition of this perceived advantage differs from its literal definition — having a method of production in place that enables the enterprise to cost-effectively manufacture a product.

Among more mature enterprises in the study, the perceived advantage of efficient production methods has lost its original meaning and has become integrated into the overall marketing performance of individual enterprises. In other words, efficient production methods have become part of the overall value creation process and are defined more broadly by managers of smaller manufacturing enterprises. This is partly due to the introduction of new approaches in manufacturing such as outsourcing the manufacture of parts and components, subassemblies, or even the entire manufacturing process.

Similarly, as the definition of efficient production methods changes, so does its interpretation. An efficient production method as a perceived advantage is important for those young enterprises that emphasize production in their managerial orientation. As an enterprise matures and its orientation changes, the notion of efficient production tends to become less important and more integrated into the overall managerial philosophy. Thus, the concept of efficient production methods as a perceived advantage loses its relevancy. This is especially true when the philosophy of value creation becomes the dominant philosophy in the entire enterprise. Value creation is also one of the philosophies which was introduced approximately in the middle of this study that had a major impact, especially on the more mature enterprises in this study.

Proximity to the Market

The concept of *proximity to the market* as a perceived advantage has also changed over the span of the study. At the beginning of the study, this concept was defined literally as being close to the enterprise's geographic markets. Today, this concept tends to express the idea that one can understand the market and have exclusive insight into the market by obtaining information not easily available to the competition.

The literal definition of proximity to the market was initially important for many of the start-up enterprises. Many start-up enterprises looked for a favorable geographic position that would put them physically close to the market. Today, proximity to the market has completely eroded from its original meaning of being physically close to the market. It is now accepted to mean that one has exclusive access or ability to gather information about the market, which today also has a different meaning. Markets today tend to be defined on the basis of product use rather than on a geographical basis. It is important to note that today even the smallest enterprise in this study defines its markets on the basis of how its products are used.

Strong Management

Another basis for perceived advantage is *strong management*, the definition of which has also changed from the initial study to the present. At the start of the study, managers of smaller manufacturing enterprises tended to define strong management as their own ability to manage. As the enterprises grew and the need for managerial functions increased, so did the number of managers in an enterprise. The owner-manager empowered other individuals within the enterprise to manage. As a result, the concept of strong management relating to a single manager or decision maker has shifted to the broader concept of multiple managers and decision makers. The term "strong management" now applies to having multiple managers of management teams.

It is important to understand how and why the concept of strong management has changed over the course of the study. During the study, the original managers — often the owner-managers — reached a point in their managerial ability when they could no longer make key managerial decisions and had to be replaced. Every time there was a change, planned or unplanned, the concept of strong management changed accordingly. In fact, when a new manager took over an enterprise, a new managerial style was introduced and the previous concept of management no longer applied. With these changes, the entire concept of strong management as it relates to perceived advantage has

been redefined; that is, the concept of strong management as a perceived advantage has been redefined in each stage of growth.

Technology

The definition of *technology* as a perceived advantage has not changed
much over the span of the study. Managers of smaller manufacturing
enterprises define technology as their knowledge and expertise to
design and manufacture a product that has a competitive advantage in
the market. In other words, enterprises have a method of converting
specialized technical knowledge into practical products.

The meaning of technology as a perceived advantage among smaller
manufacturing enterprises has not eroded; if anything, it has become
even more important over time. Many of the enterprises in this study
became sources of new technology. This appears to be due not only to
their size, but also to the close relationship between the managers and
the technical side of the enterprise. The smaller enterprises tend to be
more innovative with open, interpersonal communication channels,
which lead to the creation of new technology.

Unique Product

Managers of smaller manufacturing enterprises suggest that a similar
development to the concept of technology occurred for the concept
of *unique product* when presented as a perceived advantage. The definition of a unique product has not changed over the duration of this
study. Its importance has also not changed or eroded over time.

Conclusion

Our analysis of all 10 concepts of perceived advantages over the span
of this study has produced a number of important findings. Although
the managers who responded to the three surveys conducted in 1974,
1985, and 1995 initially identified the 10 perceived advantages listed
here, at the end of the study no statistically significant differences
were found among them. The enterprises that responded to all three

surveys perceived all advantages as equal except for one, the notion of adequate assets. All respondents to the three surveys perceived these advantages equally and they have not changed their perceptions over the 35-year span, although the definitions may have changed over time and their importance may also have eroded.

The importance of adequate assets increased significantly over the three surveys. Thus, over the span of the study, smaller manufacturing enterprises felt relatively confident that they were financially strong. The smaller enterprises represented in the sample reported that they had sufficient cash reserves. The larger enterprises felt that they had satisfactory lines of credit and they also believed that their financial resources were strong.

This is an important conclusion for the internationalization process. At the beginning of the study, internationalization was represented by export operations, and managers of smaller manufacturing enterprises considered involvement in export operations as a costly investment. When the concept of internationalization changed in the mid-1980s, the managers of these enterprises still considered internationalization to be an expensive investment, but they had the financial reserves for it. In the 1990s, when the internationalization process became even more competitively important, the enterprises perceived that they had the financial resources necessary to enter the process. In reality, the decision to internationalize was not necessarily a question of internal financial strength, but was due more to changes in the economy combined with a changing competitive climate.

The three perceived advantages that were most important to the managers of the smaller manufacturing enterprises in all three surveys were competitive price, efficient production methods, and strong management. The importance of competitive price as a perceived advantage increased only slightly in each survey, and its overall level of importance was approximately 68%. That is, approximately 68% of the managers who responded to the three surveys considered their enterprises to be price-competitive. Efficient production methods averaged a level of importance of approximately 57% in all three surveys. Strong management reached an average level of importance of approximately 55% for all three surveys, although there was a slight increase over the three surveys. It should be noted that strong management and efficient production methods switched ranking positions in the third survey: strong management rose from third to second, while efficient production methods fell from second to third.

The rest of the perceived advantages had mixed rankings. The concept of adequate assets was ranked sixth in the first survey but moved up to fourth in the second and third surveys, with an average ranking of approximately 47% for the three surveys. Technology as a perceived advantage changed slightly and was ranked fourth in the first survey, fifth in the second survey, and sixth in the third survey, with a response rate over the three surveys of approximately 44%. Perhaps the most interesting finding was that of the perceived advantage of a dynamic sales force, which was ranked last in terms of importance in all three surveys at the 30th percentile.

All enterprises in the study agreed that they were price-competitive and that price competitiveness was their most important perceived advantage. A deeper conceptual analysis suggests that all enterprises in this study are in some way very similar. They perceived themselves as being production-oriented enterprises, technologically advanced, and — to a degree — marketing-oriented. Efficient production methods and technology were relatively important for the enterprises in the study. The perceived marketing advantage was a composite of several marketing variables, specifically, unique product, proximity to the market, efficient marketing techniques, and dynamic sales force. When researchers discussed these conclusions with managers at the end of the study, managers suggested that they were still learning about marketing and its application in international competitive situations.

Finally, when these conclusions were compared to the findings from the six Wisconsin research cases collected at the end of the study, the results were similar. Managers representing the six enterprises pointed out that they were primarily price-competitive, had strong management, and considered technology to be important. Although they used marketing, it was not that important to them since they perceived that they had a unique product to sell.

The entire study suggests that the concepts perceived as advantages or strengths by managers of smaller manufacturing enterprises may also be their weaknesses. If all of the managers consider their products to be price-competitive, is this a perception or a reality? Since they have lost market position during the entire study to both domestic and foreign competition, can they rationally justify their position based on factual information? They probably cannot. This is also true for the second most popularly perceived advantage, efficient production methods. If this is a strength and not a weakness, how can smaller manufacturing enterprises relate to the overall phenomenon of domestic and foreign outsourcing? Based on the research cases, even some of the most successful smaller manufacturing enterprises outsource some of their manufacturing.

Similar conclusions can be reached about the other perceived advantages such as strong management and dynamic sales force, both of which, to some degree, address human resources. If only slightly more than half of the enterprises perceive that they have strong management and less than one third of the enterprises perceive that they have a dynamic sales force, perhaps these are not strengths but rather significant weaknesses. In addition, less than half of the enterprises perceive that they have the appropriate technology to compete. Yet, in today's internationally competitive climate, most enterprises compete on the basis of technology.

These findings suggest that, for purposes of both domestic and foreign competition, smaller manufacturing enterprises seem to examine their operations from very short-sighted perspectives. Most of the perceived advantages that were initially identified for this study, and to which survey responses did not significantly change over the span of this study, may not necessarily be the appropriate advantages to consider in today's internationally competitive world of global markets.

Chapter 4

Future Operations and Planning Processes among Smaller Manufacturing Enterprises

In order to decide whether or not to operate internationally, managers of smaller manufacturing enterprises need to be able to think about future operations. Doing so will help as they develop contingency plans and consider how to implement these plans. The assumption is that the enterprises will continue operating on the same growth path without any major unforeseen internal disturbances. In other words, the enterprises will continue doing in the future what they have done in the past unless external changes occur in the economy.

At various stages of involvement in smaller manufacturing enterprises, managers tend to think differently about future operations and planning options, including internationalization of operations. Craftsman managers are not prepared to look systematically into the future and think about planning options. They are too preoccupied with the daily challenges of managing their enterprises. Promoter managers weigh planning options differently and tentatively suggest some methods of dealing with them, often in cooperation with other managers or key employees by forming strategic planning teams or appointing committees. More experienced promoter managers may even contract with management consultants to assist them in identifying and exploring strategic planning alternatives. If the consultants suggest some viable planning alternatives, the promoter managers may recognize the importance of planning and take notice of the consultants' recommendations, but may choose not to implement them.

Rational managers tend to view the entire planning process as being an important component of their business models and, consequently, they provide organizational mechanisms to facilitate planning.

External versus Internal Growth

Managers of smaller manufacturing enterprises associate external growth with the general growth of the industry and the economy. A majority of these managers are concerned with internal growth, which they feel is achieved, in theory, through increases in various approaches to market penetration, product development, and (in a few cases) diversification. Their definition of "market" varies considerably, from a narrow geographical area to a broader scope of product uses. Within the marketing framework, planning for new markets, new products, or diversification is an integral part of many business models. Over the years, the concepts of planning for new markets, new products, or diversification have been refined in practice and have become integral components of many successful business models. However, most managers responsible for future operations and planning among smaller manufacturing enterprises view them differently.

Planning Factors

At the beginning of this study, we asked the managers of smaller manufacturing enterprises to identify planning factors that were important to them and to specify those for which they routinely planned. Six factors were identified: market share expansion, greater national distribution, new market development, development of foreign markets, new product development, and diversification into other businesses. These six planning factors differ from the three conventionally accepted planning alternatives — markets, products, and diversification.

The sequence in which these managers thought about their planning factors also changed. Planning for new products was first, followed by planning for new markets, and then planning for diversification. However, instead of planning for new products, the managers indicated that they planned for "new product development", which was consistent with the reality that they originally started as one-product enterprises. "Market factor" was interpreted by these managers as four discrete subfactors: expansion of the current market share, greater national distribution, new market development, and development of foreign markets. Planning for diversification simply suggested that the enterprise might in the future enter into another type of business.

Planning for New Product

The interpretation of each planning objective changed among the smaller manufacturing enterprises, depending on who managed the enterprise. Craftsman managers conceptually interpreted planning for new product development as an imperative to identify and develop a new product in order to replace or supplement the existing product on which the enterprise was originally founded. They indicated that in the future, when it would be absolutely necessary, they would have to start planning for the development of a new product, if the vital resources were available. In general, craftsman managers had a relatively low commitment to developing new products.

Promoter managers viewed the concept of planning for new product development from another perspective. They typically suggested that the existing products would no longer be competitive in the future and so the enterprise would need to develop new products to replace them. Developing new products could be done formally, according to a set of guidelines and procedures, or they could be developed informally. The promoter managers preferred an informal process but, because of their strong entrepreneurial tendencies, they needed time to formulate the approach to be used to informally develop new products. They tended to have limited commitment to formalizing the planning process for new product development. Nevertheless, promoter managers understood the need to plan for new product development.

Rational managers viewed the concept of planning for new product development literally — planning for new product development is necessary to grow and survive. They established formal new product development processes, where specific tasks and objectives were identified and assigned either to marketing or engineering specialists. Rational managers also frequently formed new product planning and development teams or committees, and worked very closely with them.

Planning for New Market

Planning for new market development was similarly interpreted by the various types of managers of smaller manufacturing enterprises as was planning for new product development. Craftsman managers conceived planning for new market development as planning for new geographical markets — markets where their products could be sold without undue effort and with relatively low risk. They generally did not consider new markets in terms of new applications for their products. The majority of craftsman managers were reluctant to seek new markets, since their existing sales volumes were sufficient. Any inquiries from markets outside the current, geographically defined market were frequently ignored. As with the process of planning for new product development, they noted that there might be a need to think about planning to develop new markets.

Promoter managers tended to be more concerned about planning for new market development. Regardless of how they conceptually interpreted the concept of planning for new market development, they set up the appropriate and necessary (formal or informal) guidelines. They worked closely with their sales personnel to formalize and implement the planning process for new market development. Depending on the nature of the product, they had a tendency to define markets either in a geographical or industrial context, but generally not on the basis of a product's potential applications. Actual implementation of the planning process for new market development was related to the level of current sales or the state of the economy.

Rational managers tended to consider the process of planning for new market development as an essential marketing tool. The process was guided by set policies and procedures, which were regularly reviewed by responsible teams or committees. Although these entities carried the responsibility for new market development planning, it was ultimately the managers who made the final decision as to which markets would be identified and eventually explored.

Planning for Diversification

It is interesting to note that all three types of managers responsible for managing the smaller manufacturing enterprises planned, to some degree, to diversify into other businesses. The nature of planning for diversification, however, differed by manager type. The concept of planning for diversification among craftsman managers was that when the enterprise — or, more specifically, the owner of the enterprise — had excess financial resources (generally cash reserves), those resources would enable the enterprise or the owner to purchase another venture. The venture that might be acquired in the future may be completely unrelated to the existing enterprise.

As far as promoter managers were concerned, planning for diversification as an alternative to planning for new product or market development meant acquiring a business that had some connection to their existing enterprise and their knowledge base. Or, the enterprise may have wanted to improve its technological competence level and needed to acquire a business that would provide the level of competence the enterprise needed for future operations or even survival. Among rational managers, planning for diversification generally implied taking the enterprise's marketing and technological competences and applying them to a new or existing business outside of its industry. This approach tends to be very common when smaller manufacturing enterprises join supply or value chains that service other industries.

The remaining planning factors were also important. Planning to expand market share was by far the most important planning alternative for smaller manufacturing enterprises, followed by planning for greater national distribution. The importance of planning for greater national distribution increased somewhat over the span of this study. The remaining planning alternative that became significantly important over the span of this study was the development of foreign

markets. However, it remained last in terms of its planning importance. It is this planning alternative that provided the foundation for
the internationalization of smaller manufacturing enterprises.

Conclusion

The long-term perspective regarding the six planning alternatives
specified by the smaller manufacturing enterprise managers at the outset of this study is important. The statistical analysis of the three sets
of data generated over the period of this study clearly indicates that
the smaller manufacturing enterprises, taken together, have not, in
any way, changed their perception of the importance of five of these
planning factors: planning for new product development, new market
development, market share expansion, greater national distribution,
and diversification into other businesses. The only planning factor
that has significantly increased in importance among these managers
is the development of foreign markets, which is important for their
internationalization.

It is important to realize that the necessity to plan for future operations has not significantly changed over the duration of this study.
One conclusion that can be drawn is that the enterprises are short-
term-oriented and they tend to act only when it is necessary to respond
to the market conditions or the economy. The fact that, over the years,
they somewhat reacted to the need to plan for the development of foreign markets is also important. However, it should be noted that this
reaction might be due more to the economy rather than the individual enterprises. The first time that the survey in this study was
completed, approximately 20% of the enterprises surveyed planned to
develop foreign markets. Ten years later, when the second survey was
organized, about 30% of the enterprises planned to develop foreign
markets. Another 10 years later, when the third survey was conducted,
just over 40% of the enterprises planned for the development of foreign
markets. When all six planning factors were ranked, the development
of foreign markets had the lowest ranking; that is, the lowest percentage of enterprises indicated that they planned for the development of
foreign markets over the span of the three surveys.

As suggested earlier, very few differences were found among the results of the three surveys. The only two exceptions were the responses to the planning for foreign markets factor, which increased from one survey to the next; and the small but consistent increases in responses to the planning for greater national distribution factor. When all six planning alternatives were ranked for each of the three surveys, only minor variations were detected from one survey to the next. The planning factor that consistently had the highest ranking was expansion of market share, with an average overall ranking of approximately 76%. Consequently, expansion of market share was their first planning priority, followed closely by planning for new product development and planning for market development. About 70% of respondents to all three surveys considered these two planning factors as important. Less than half of the managers responding to the three surveys combined considered planning for diversification and planning for greater national distribution as important.

These results suggest that smaller manufacturing enterprises are primarily sales-oriented. The sales orientation has not changed in more than 30 years. Furthermore, those managers who plan for future operations and growth are most likely to plan to expand their market share, and not necessarily to add new products or new markets. In addition, most managers do not consider international expansion to be a priority. Nevertheless, these managers tend to be aware of the reality that international competition and changes in the economy may create situations whereby they will have to consider international competition not only as a hindrance to their future operations, but also as requiring them to consider entering international markets in order to survive. When the results of these analyses were combined with information from the six Wisconsin cases prepared at the end of this study, we found that all of the enterprises interviewed operated directly or indirectly in foreign markets and were, to some degree, internationalized.

Part II

Decision to Internationalize among Managers of Smaller Manufacturing Enterprises

The objective in Part II is to examine the internationalization process among smaller manufacturing enterprises. The internationalization decision is considered from several managerial perspectives. Some fundamental questions are examined. Does the internationalization decision need to be supported with established policies and structures, or can the decision be made arbitrarily by the key decision maker? What obstacles does the key decision maker of the enterprise perceive as hindering the internationalization decision?

Chapter 5

The Internationalization Process

Deciding to internationalize presents a dilemma for managers of smaller manufacturing enterprises. Over the years, competition and other market forces have compelled managers of many smaller manufacturing enterprises to internationalize their operations. As domestic competition intensified, both domestic and foreign competitors offered similar products at lower prices. Customers changed their buying motives and became more price-conscious. Larger international customers asked smaller manufacturing enterprises to join their industrial networks, become active in their supply chains, or contribute to value chains. In some instances, the smaller manufacturing enterprises were asked by their large international customers to ship products directly to customers in foreign markets. Enterprises with innovative technology were sought after by large international corporations that wanted to purchase the technology or acquire the entire operation. Other profitable enterprises that served smaller strategic markets were bought out by their large foreign competitors. And, finally, many high-technology start-ups were quickly purchased by a variety of foreign investors.

Over the years, governments interested in exports as a form of internationalization have maintained programs to stimulate, promote, and develop export opportunities among smaller manufacturing enterprises. To governments, increased exports represent increased employment, higher tax revenues, and stability for their economies. Various governmental agencies provide direct training and educational assistance to smaller manufacturing enterprises. They also represent them on government-sponsored missions, trade fairs, and product seminars as part of governmental initiatives to help them internationalize their operations and thus compete more effectively and efficiently in foreign markets. Many managers feel strong pressure from export specialists who offer a range of services such as analyses of foreign markets, leads to export, or assistance in identifying potential distributors abroad. All of these services are typically available at both state and federal levels.

Service providers such as bankers, accountants, freight forwarders, shippers, and trade consultants also urge these smaller businesses to internationalize. These service providers have a vested interest in urging smaller manufacturing enterprises to internationalize. In order to increase their own business, they sometimes offer service packages that help managers of smaller manufacturing enterprises make the decision to internationalize. A trade consultant or a banker often helps expedite the first export order for a reluctant manager. Other types of service providers such as export brokers, international distributors, or sales representatives make it even less complicated for the reluctant potential exporter; they purchase products directly from smaller manufacturing enterprises and manage entire export operations themselves.

Challenges of Internationalization

Encouraging managers of smaller manufacturing enterprises to export products and thereby internationalize their operations has recently become even more complex. Occasionally, employees with more education and an understanding of international markets and cultures question why their employers have not been active in foreign markets. Employees such as engineers, managers, or even assembly-line employees and workers on shipping docks sometimes point out their employer's export potential. Many younger employees in the modern markets have had invaluable international experiences through education, travel, and residence abroad long before they accepted their first job, and they believe they have a fundamental understanding of foreign markets. They want to apply their experience to their jobs. Most managers consider these overtures helpful; unfortunately, some do not.

The challenges of internationalization have been a topic of discussion for many years. When considering all of the internationalization forces together, it is inevitable that some managers will finally decide to internationalize while others will postpone the decision as long as possible. Some managers eventually decide to internationalize because they have been confronted by external forces — either commercial or governmental. Commercial forces are usually due to growing competition, while governmental encouragements are due to repeated contact with trade specialists. Internally, managers need to personally confront employees who initiate questions of internationalization and who want the enterprise to grow and prosper globally.

Perspectives on the internationalization of smaller manufacturing enterprises have changed since the mid-1980s due to new business models and changes in competition. New business models have focused on issues such as leaner and faster manufacturing, just-in-time inventory systems, outsourcing, building of supply chains, and quality control improvements. Larger customers insist that their suppliers — the smaller manufacturing enterprises — join their supply networks which, in most instances, are predominantly international. Also, some high-technology start-ups are frequently asked to become part of highly coordinated value chains as sources of new technology. Many of these offers or invitations for smaller manufacturing enterprises to become active participants in value chains have been essential for them to remain competitive and, in many instances, to survive. The future of their manufacturing expertise and indeed of the enterprise was at stake. Managers were asked to give up their traditional markets, internationalize their operations, expand their capacity, and forge alliances in the new global marketplace. Some smaller manufacturing enterprises did just that and entered into the new global marketplace; others continued to operate in their own familiar marketplace, where they kept a close focus on their core knowledge and skills. Those enterprises that chose not to internationalize their operations survived only temporarily.

Outsourcing as a Form of Internationalization

In the mid-1980s, another facet of internationalization for smaller manufacturing enterprises also emerged. Smaller manufacturing enterprises began to experience domestic and foreign competition. They had innovative technology and offered unique products, but their material and manufacturing costs rose. The evolving concept was outsourcing, which partially or completely eliminated manufacturing facilities and thereby reduced overhead costs. Just as their large international competitors had done, the smaller manufacturing enterprises were eager to implement outsourcing with both domestic and foreign suppliers; this became another approach to internationalization.

Over the period of this study, smaller manufacturing enterprises became proactive as well as reactive recipients of internationalization. Those enterprises that opted for the proactive approach made the decision to internationalize relatively early. For some enterprises, this decision was somewhat spontaneous — they wanted to grow, compete, and survive. In a way, they had no other alternative but to internationalize their operations as quickly as possible. For others, it was a slow, cautious, and deliberate decision based on a number of considerations, plans, goals, and objectives. Even then, some managers made the decision conditionally, subject to future sales and market assessments. The managers who were reactive and reluctant to internationalize waited until competition was so strong that they had little choice.

Perspectives on Internationalization

One can view the decision to internationalize among smaller manufacturing enterprises from three perspectives. The first and traditional perspective focuses primarily on the output side of the enterprise, or, as known in the past, exports. Managers with this perspective had other options such as negotiating licensing agreements for their technological know-how, licensing the complete manufacturing of their products, or even licensing their business models. For example, a number of custom fabrication shops licensed their fabrication methods to foreign partners or they entered into joint ventures with partners in foreign countries. Some of the more mature enterprises invested abroad or purchased complete manufacturing operations similar to their own in foreign countries. Smaller manufacturing enterprises were also approached by development agencies of foreign governments to start subsidiaries or full manufacturing facilities.

Finally, smaller manufacturing enterprises could negotiate agreements with a foreign partner to cross-sell or market each other's products.

The second perspective on the internationalization of smaller manufacturing enterprises is from a public policy view. In the early 1970s, the preferred entry into foreign markets for smaller manufacturing enterprises was through exporting. International trade specialists from governmental agencies focused only on exports. From a public policy perspective, no other foreign market entry strategies were acceptable to governmental agencies. The import side of the enterprise was not sanctioned by state or federal governments until the late 1980s when, for example, importing became part of a trade-off consideration between domestic and international outsourcing at both state and federal levels. Government agencies wanted smaller manufacturing enterprises to maximize domestic outsourcing and minimize international outsourcing, and thereby reduce imports. This was particularly important for outsourcing the manufacture of final products, because government agencies wanted to keep manufacturing at home.

The third perspective is that managers of smaller manufacturing enterprises were not really thinking about internationalizing their operations until it became economically necessary to manufacture abroad. They looked for cost-efficient sources to produce their products. Some smaller manufacturing enterprises were introduced to aspects of outsourcing by their domestic suppliers. Suppliers gave enterprises that were faced with increasing costs of raw materials, component parts, and other supplies the choice to buy domestically or buy abroad. For many enterprises, it was an economic decision rather than a decision to internationalize. Managers who made this decision objectively and rationally considered the consequences in the context of their markets and competition, and not necessarily as a deliberate decision to internationalize.

Other Concerns

From the 1970s onwards, additional concerns forced the internationalization of smaller manufacturing enterprises. First, these enterprises were concerned with international mergers and acquisitions. Some smaller manufacturing enterprises were taken over by larger domestic and foreign competitors. Also, international enterprises searched for new technologies, products, markets, and other tangible and intangible assets to integrate into their operations or to purchase outright. Smaller manufacturing enterprises were attractive targets.

A secondary concern for enterprises included the rising cost of shipping. Fuel costs rose rapidly, especially in international shipping, which led to the restructuring of the entire transportation industry. Outsourcing abroad tended to increase market prices for smaller manufacturing enterprises. In order to maintain their competitive position, smaller manufacturing enterprises had to develop a fundamental understanding of the international transportation and shipping industry in order to maintain lower prices and remain competitive in the market.

If one examines the decision to internationalize from the framework of the input side of the enterprise, it is apparent that many smaller manufacturing enterprise managers had no choice but to internationalize. They had to develop substantial expertise and understanding of relevant issues in the global environment to remain competitive and survive. The more visible and dynamic enterprises had to learn not only how to outsource and ship economically, but also how to protect themselves from being taken over by larger, more internationally able competitors.

For some managers of smaller manufacturing enterprises, the decision to internationalize was also a question of resource allocation. For many managers, the forces that had an impact on the decision to internationalize were also directly related to their resources. Some enterprises were financially strong and did not have to consider the consequences of the decision on their employees or their physical resources. However, other enterprises had to train some current employees, hire new employees to deal exclusively with international issues, and ask some employees to travel, which considerably lengthened their time on a job assignment. Employees were concerned about job retention, since outsourcing manufacturing led to fewer jobs. The need for physical facilities also changed. Outsourcing required adjustments in storage, warehousing, equipment, and manufacturing lines. For some enterprises, these adjustments contributed to market and financial performance, but for others these changes were costly and unsuccessful.

Managers and Internationalization

Whether or not the decision to internationalize helped improve market performance and competition depended a great deal on the managers of the smaller manufacturing enterprises. Rational managers tended to approach these concerns objectively and systematically, not only in terms of resource allocation, but also in practical terms to determine if the enterprise would benefit from the decision to internationalize and to what extent. Promoter managers concerned themselves more about the survival of the enterprise and the benefits resulting directly from the decision to internationalize than about the actual decision. Most promoter managers were prepared to internationalize as long as it helped stabilize their markets and reduce competition.

Craftsman managers had the most difficult time deciding whether or not to internationalize. Due to concerns about product quality, craftsman managers were not willing to purchase parts and components from abroad unless they were of high quality and innovative technology. For the same reason, these managers were not likely to outsource manufacturing. Managers who exported their goods did so reluctantly because the products were manufactured by them in their own facilities. Consequently, for craftsman managers, the decision to internationalize was difficult and time-consuming.

Policy Makers and Internationalization

Many public and private organizations and institutions had a strong interest in the decision for smaller manufacturing enterprises to internationalize. They developed approaches and offered support for managers to make the internationalization process less complex. Not only did they try to have the internationalization decision based more on rational economic alternatives and outcomes, but they also offered support services to help managers successfully implement the procedures leading to internationalization. Government agencies provided decision models with hands-on assistance from trade specialists to help managers make the decision to internationalize. Consultants, bankers, and freight forwarders, among others, provided hands-on training for employees to learn the skills necessary to operate in international markets. Even universities and other educational institutions maintained support services for smaller manufacturing enterprises by providing much-needed information about market potentials, financial transactions, or foreign product requirements.

The objective of these services was to demonstrate to managers of smaller manufacturing enterprises that the decision to internationalize could be made rationally and that making such a decision made economic sense. For many managers, however, the decision to internationalize represented more than a positive economic outcome: it represented a decision that was partly rational and partly emotional. Since most managers were close to their customers and employees, they sometimes found it difficult to discuss the fact that they had to source abroad for materials, parts, and components, or even manufacture the entire product abroad in order to reduce costs.

Conclusion

Over the past 35 years, smaller manufacturing enterprises faced with the internationalization decision have operated in a highly changeable market and competitive environment. Initially, internationalization simply represented export operations. Managers of smaller manufacturing enterprises had to decide whether or not they would export. Even when managers decided to export their products abroad, some did so reluctantly and only when they received unsolicited orders, while others actively sought export orders and developed markets abroad.

Later, the market and competitive environments changed for smaller manufacturing enterprises. Foreign competitors entered the domestic markets and started to compete aggressively against the smaller businesses. Managers of smaller manufacturing enterprises had to change their business models; they had to consider their own survival potential as well as the foreign competition. To survive, the smaller manufacturing enterprises had to internationalize. At this point, the decision to internationalize had at least three distinct starting points: smaller manufacturing enterprises had the option of expanding their operations abroad by (1) changing their market orientation and market entry on the output side of the enterprise; (2) outsourcing their supplies or even manufacturing abroad on the input side of the enterprise; or (3) reorganizing their internal operations to focus on international opportunities.

For each option, managers had to make an implicit decision. Some managers made that decision with a strong commitment to their customers and their markets; others did not. Those managers who made the commitment and were successful often expanded their operations and became very successful in their markets. Those who did not make that commitment lost market share and faced liquidation.

More recently, managers of smaller manufacturing enterprises have found the decision to internationalize to be a necessity. In order to compete and survive, an enterprise must have its operations fully internationalized. It needs to service stable international markets, outsource its supplies and, in some cases, manufacture abroad. Internationally skilled employees who are capable of supporting a company's international operations are also necessary. Today, managers of smaller manufacturing enterprises are well aware of these realities.

Chapter 6

The Decision to Consider Internationalization

Over the years, managers of smaller manufacturing enterprises have confronted numerous external and internal forces challenging them to internationalize their operations. At some point, as a matter of necessity almost all managers of these enterprises had to consider internationalizing their operations. Changing market conditions, combined with strong domestic and international competitive pressures, forced managers of smaller enterprises to expand their markets beyond traditional markets close to their physical facilities.

Early on, these managers interpreted internationalization as simply a decision to export. Later, the decision to internationalize was interpreted as various foreign market entry options that would become integral parts of new and more competitive business models. Towards the end of this study, the decision to internationalize introduced major changes in the strategic and operational thinking of individual managers.

Some managers of smaller manufacturing enterprises considered the potential of internationalizing their operations early on and prepared their enterprises for the actual decision to internationalize. Other managers did not anticipate the need to internationalize their operations. Another group of managers who served only small regional markets had no connection with foreign markets at all. As the need to internationalize increased, managers realized that they had to consider internationalization as an alternative to growth and survival. Some managers tried to postpone the export decision to minimize risk for their enterprises by exporting only indirectly through international trade intermediaries. Those managers who entered the internationalization process early realized that they needed to adjust their organizational structures to accommodate export decisions and, subsequently, the future internationalization processes. All of these considerations were reflected in individual managerial styles.

This study initially focused on the decision to export as a means to internationalization. Therefore, among smaller manufacturing enterprises, the decision to export provided the basis for understanding the broader decision to internationalize. To sufficiently understand the decision to export, the study focused on the decision-making styles and approaches relevant to the export decision.

Craftsman Managers and Internationalization

Craftsman managers overseeing smaller manufacturing enterprises in their well-defined neighboring markets were reluctant to enter foreign markets, and were not interested in direct or indirect exports. Craftsman managers have an inherent need to know their customers, not necessarily to maximize their satisfaction with the product, but to communicate with them about the attributes and benefits of the product. For many craftsman managers, this appears to be the fundamental reason why they were reluctant to export their products into unfamiliar markets where they might not be able to speak the language. Although smaller manufacturing enterprises occasionally received unsolicited orders from abroad, they would ignore them and they would not actively solicit orders from abroad.

In the few rare instances when foreign customers approached craftsman managers and asked them to export directly, the craftsman managers would ignore the orders as long as possible. Frequently, they would not complete the orders at all. If they were at all curious about specific orders, they would most likely discuss them with their accountants or attorneys. When potential foreign customers inquired about the status of their orders, they were told that they had to wait, or that the enterprise's schedules were filled and it could not manufacture the product at that time. Craftsman managers were sometimes approached by local customers or international trade intermediaries to purchase products for shipment abroad. Some craftsman managers considered these orders as local or domestic sales, and they would fill the orders as long as they did not have to modify the products.

High-technology smaller manufacturing enterprises managed by craftsman managers initially approached exporting differently; they were more willing to discuss their products with potential foreign customers. Some craftsman managers who manufactured technologically advanced products received international attention because these products were innovative or patented. These additional benefits made the craftsman managers internationally known, and their products were in demand. Such a development complicated the craftsman manager's style and interfered with their ability to concentrate on products and manufacturing, which were their primary interests. When craftsman managers of high-technology enterprises agreed to export products, it was typically to known individuals with whom they had had previous professional contact or with whom they had pre-negotiated potential export orders.

Promoter Managers and Internationalization

Promoter managers, on the other hand, approached the initial export decision more openly. They were interested in both direct and indirect export orders, although they preferred indirect export orders to foreign customers. This preference was primarily due to their perception that domestic transactions carried less risk. Additionally, domestic intermediaries would expedite all of the necessary export documentation and payments. Promoter managers actively solicited export orders and frequently used professional assistance from sources such as banks, freight forwarders, and shipping companies. Some managers also relied on governmental sources for information and, occasionally, on leads for export opportunities that were received by governmental agencies or diplomatic services abroad. Other sources of information and leads concerning export opportunities were from banks, freight forwarders, and shipping companies that frequently called on managers of smaller manufacturing enterprises to inform them about exporting opportunities.

Promoter managers tended to be opportunistic in their decision to internationalize or, more specifically, to export. They would export their products directly or indirectly and would try to minimize any changes to their products, such as altering product specifications, translating installation and operating instructions, or modifying maintenance schedules to meet nonlocal conditions. Measurements such as local weight, volume, and length were frequently used rather than international measurements. Promoter managers were willing to change product specifications, issue instructions in foreign languages, and set up customized maintenance schedules, but at an additional cost. In other words, promoter managers considered these demands as unique requirements for special products that warranted additional costs but that added value to the products.

Among promoter managers of smaller manufacturing enterprises, the actual decision to export products was considered a discrete decision. Every time a new order was received, deciding whether or not to export was a new decision. For enterprises that did have guidelines concerning exporting decisions, these policies were tentative and subject to frequent review by promoter managers. Sometimes, promoter managers decided to seek export orders intended to fill excess manufacturing capacity or to reduce surplus inventory. In these situations, promoter managers advanced both their enterprises and their products. They tried to sell not only their products, but also the unique technological capabilities of their enterprise.

As smaller manufacturing enterprises managed by promoter managers grew, some managers confronted the formal decision to internationalize. This decision required them to develop policies and procedures concerning all international activities, including any options to enter a foreign market. Promoter managers appointed individuals responsible for foreign sales and other related activities, and selected technical personnel responsible for product modifications and technical documentation. Many promoter managers did not consider the decision to internationalize as final, and were reluctant to draft the policies and procedures necessary to implement it.

Rational Managers and Internationalization

Rational managers responsible for smaller manufacturing enterprises considered the decision to internationalize more systematically. Since rational managers control resources and delegate tasks and responsibilities, the decision to internationalize had to be internalized within the enterprise, and resources had to be set aside to implement it. Many rational managers initially considered export opportunities as integral components of their operations, but later were open to other approaches to internationalization ranging from exports to direct investments in foreign markets. For many rational managers, the decision to internationalize was not only about export opportunities; it also included long-term considerations of all potential entry strategies into foreign markets.

At the beginning of this study, smaller manufacturing enterprises managed by rational managers exported directly or indirectly. They relied on many sources outside of the enterprise for information, and assigned responsibilities for managing export activities. Managers involved themselves only when necessary. Marketing and sales personnel were available to assist with any required tasks to solicit and fill export orders. The technical personnel followed the necessary guidelines to modify products so as to fit the specifications of foreign customers. In order to stabilize and secure their export activities, managers were willing to organize sales and technical support abroad, either from their domestic location or by opening sales and technical support services in major export markets.

Although many rational managers were committed to making the decision to internationalize, they nevertheless perceived a number of operational or structural obstacles. Some managers were concerned with disproportional resource allocations. They wanted to operate in foreign markets, but only to have their products be visible or to be known for their technology. According to the managers, these expectations required minimum resources but also typically represented low sales volume. To maintain stable sales and not impact domestic market performance, managers sometimes allocated a percentage of their manufacturing capacity to foreign markets. All of these issues entered into their consideration of whether or not to internationalize.

Managers also needed to consider financial and pricing concerns. Rational managers of smaller enterprises wanted to get paid on time and in their own currency. At the same time, managers responsible for export orders were not experienced enough to price their products for foreign markets, and thus pricing products for foreign markets became the major concern for them. Although bankers routinely assisted them with collecting payments from abroad, they were not fully competent in quoting financial terms of sales and conditions of payment. Some managers even trusted their customers and sold against open accounts, which their bankers did not like. Bankers preferred confirmed letters of credit as forms of payment. In spite of all these concerns, rational managers expected the same profit levels from foreign markets as they realized from their domestic markets.

Towards the end of the study, all of these considerations in making the decision to internationalize had changed. Over the span of the study, all three categories of managers were involved with foreign markets through a variety of arrangements, ranging from indirect exports to becoming a subsidiary of a foreign enterprise. Those managers who considered making the decision to internationalize but did not make the decision in fact made it any way, because they exported indirectly. In the final interviews with the managers of smaller manufacturing enterprises which had survived, it became obvious to the interviewers that, at some point during the study, these managers had to make the decision either because of market demand or because of competitive pressures. Managers even suggested that they had not made a formal decision to internationalize, but in fact had considered all of the circumstances and obstacles necessary to make the decision.

Considerations to Internationalize

Considerations that provided a foundation for the decision to internationalize were somewhat complex for most managers. Managers searched for answers to questions such as whether the enterprise required a formal policy to consider every decision to internationalize separately, or if one policy for all decisions to internationalize would be sufficient. Specific structural changes were expected, since international operations such as exports required specialized knowledge. Additional functional areas had to be organized. Managers were most concerned about the potential contributions that the decision to internationalize would bring to individual enterprises. For example, would the decision to internationalize increase profitability, secure markets, or even contribute to the economy?

Fixed Policy and Formal Structure

We asked managers about these concerns at the beginning of the study. They suggested that it would be easier to make decisions to internationalize if a *fixed policy* concerning international operations were in place. Such a policy would also be useful in exploring the potential of individual export orders. In addition, any guidelines developed under such a policy would provide a clear understanding for the entire enterprise as to what tasks needed to be performed to satisfy foreign orders. At the beginning of the study, managers presented similar reactions concerning *formal structures* within enterprises designed to evaluate potential international opportunities. To most managers, such a formal structure suggested a well-defined process through which foreign opportunities were objectively evaluated. Both fixed policies and formal structures were typically found among the more mature smaller manufacturing enterprises; however, other managers agreed that they would also benefit from them.

Considerations

The considerations that made an impact on the decision to internationalize were important for managers of smaller manufacturing enterprises, and have changed little over time. When researchers asked managers at the beginning of the study which considerations would be important in making the decision to internationalize, they suggested five factors. The first important consideration was the impact of the decision to internationalize on the profitability of the individual enterprise, followed by the impact on the growth of the enterprise, security of investments, development and/or security of markets, and an external consideration — contribution to the development of the U.S. economy.

Past Performance

Responses to all five factors, along with the question of whether or not the individual smaller manufacturing enterprises had a fixed policy and formal structure concerning international operations, were analyzed for all three surveys (each survey being approximately 10 years apart). The results of the analysis offer interesting insights into managerial decision making among smaller manufacturing enterprises. Approximately 36% of smaller manufacturing enterprises exported their products in the mid-1970s, when the first survey was conducted. Over the next ten years, the number of smaller manufacturing enterprises that exported increased to 43%. When the third survey was completed in the mid-1990s, 55% of the same enterprises exported their products. The increase in the number of enterprises that exported their products is important because it illustrates not only the changes in markets and competition, but also the increasing awareness of how important foreign markets have become for smaller manufacturing enterprises.

Approximately half of the smaller manufacturing enterprises in the study made the decision to export when they sought their first order. The other half of the enterprises made the decision to export when they received an unsolicited order. A majority of the unsolicited orders were from customers abroad, while some represented domestic purchases. Enterprises that seek orders are labeled "aggressive exporters" and enterprises that wait for export orders are labeled "passive exporters". The first survey revealed about 40% aggressive and 60% passive exporters. In the second survey, during the mid-1980s, the percentage of aggressive exporters increased to 52%, while the percentage of passive exporters dropped to 48%. These findings reflected an increase in the intensity of international competition and the emergence of the global marketplace. In the mid-1990s, when international competition stabilized and smaller manufacturing enterprises learned how to compete more effectively and efficiently, they became less aggressive in seeking export orders. Findings in the third survey showed approximately 45% aggressive and 55% passive exporters.

The three surveys also suggest that, on average, there are more passive than aggressive exporters. In other words, more exporters are reluctant to make a clear decision to export their products and rely on more opportunistic approaches. Exporters who are reluctant to make the decision to export are primarily passive exporters. Aggressive exporters have included the decision to export as a part of their operational and strategic business models.

Although at the beginning of the study managers indicated that having a fixed policy regarding export decisions was important, only about 20% of these exporters had a fixed policy. The results of the three surveys suggest that more, but not all, aggressive exporters had a fixed policy regarding export opportunities. The results also indicate that no differences existed over the three surveys.

Even fewer exporters had a formal structure to evaluate the potential of export opportunities. At the end of the first survey, only 10% of the smaller manufacturing enterprises had any formal structure for evaluating export opportunities. When the second survey was completed ten years later, approximately 17% of the enterprises that responded had a formal structure for evaluating export opportunities. Ten years later, when the third survey was completed, the percentage of enterprises with a formal structure to evaluate export opportunities increased to 23%. These increases in the percentage of enterprises that had a formal structure to evaluate export opportunities are significant. Over the duration of the study, a relatively small number of managers who exported their products realized that they had to introduce a formal structure to deal with export opportunities.

These findings are important because they suggest that the actual decision as to whether or not smaller manufacturing enterprises will export their products, or internationalize, can be made with minimal consultation with their employees. However, if during the entire study enterprises were aggressively seeking export opportunities, they had to decide which opportunities were most advantageous for them. The findings suggest that it may be necessary to have a formal structure for evaluating export opportunities to gain input from other individuals within the enterprise. Sales personnel, accountants, and purchasing agents can help to decide if any opportunities under consideration could be realized. From the research findings, one can assume that formal structures within these enterprises ranged from a network of individuals within the company with whom managers would discuss export opportunities down to a single-page form or document that could be filled in by functional specialists within the enterprise. We could reach a similar conclusion regarding the passive exporters.

What is important to consider is that, at the beginning of the study, managers of smaller manufacturing enterprises suggested that both a fixed policy regarding exports and a formal structure would be useful for making the decision to internationalize. The findings from the three consecutive studies pointed out that only a minority of enterprises actually put in place a fixed policy regarding exports as well as a formal structure to evaluate them. Consequently, most decisions regarding export opportunities were made without either of them.

Similarly, findings concerning the contribution that the decision to internationalize could make to various factors produced important results. Respondents to the three surveys provided the following information. The decision to export products would first impact the growth of the enterprise. Approximately 75% of enterprises ranked this contribution highest over the three surveys. The second highest contribution from the decision to export was profitability. On average, more than 60% of the enterprises responding to the three surveys ranked this consideration. No significant differences occurred in the responses for the three surveys. However, a noticeable increase in the relative percentage of responses showed up in the third survey, which suggests in the mid-1990s that the decision to internationalize became more important to the enterprises. This change is reflected in the number of enterprises that had begun exporting products at the time of this survey.

The rest of the considerations ranked much lower in terms of their importance. On average, nearly 50% of the respondents over the three surveys indicated that the decision to export would contribute to the development of the U.S. economy; about 48% believed that the decision to export would have an effect on the development and security of their markets; and about 38% of the respondents indicated that the decision to export would affect the security of their investments.

These findings suggest that the majority of the smaller manufacturing enterprises that were already exporting at the time of the three surveys believed that the decision to export increased their growth and profits. However, this finding is interesting because managers who were interviewed at the start of the study and those interviewed at the end believed that they could expect lower profits from export operations. They also thought they would have to expand their operations to accommodate exports, a change that might lead to slower growth.

Conclusion

Based on both preliminary and follow-up interviews with managers, and on responses from smaller manufacturing enterprises that were exporting over the span of this study, the findings suggest that the decision to export is not necessarily dependent on policy and structural considerations within the enterprise. Whether or not enterprises have a fixed policy regarding exports or a formal structure for evaluating exports has little bearing on the decision to internationalize. One could also conclude that the consideration as to whether the decision will have an impact on such factors as profit and growth is important, but not essential. The additional factors that were introduced at the beginning of the study — the development of the U.S. economy, the development and security of markets, and the security of investments — are of minor importance to the managers of smaller manufacturing enterprises who made the decision to internationalize.

Chapter 7

Perceived Obstacles to Internationalization

The decision to internationalize is a difficult one for many managers of smaller manufacturing enterprises. Depending on their managerial style, they perceive varying obstacles to internationalization that hinder them from making a decision. Some perceived obstacles relate to marketing practices and others to financial transactions. The managers perceive fewer obstacles as they become more experienced with international practices. However, as they gain a better understanding of international practices, some of the perceived marketing obstacles become more important. Managers consistently complain about the need for marketing information and the cost of obtaining marketing information in international markets. This is particularly apparent when they try to market their products directly to end consumers in foreign markets and need to collect information about consumer behavior in those foreign markets. Some of the perceived obstacles to financial transactions are resolved relatively quickly after managers gain sufficient experience with such transactions. However, concerns about product pricing actually increase over time.

Later in the internationalization process, obstacles relating to product standards, approvals, and testing become major issues, especially for those enterprises that export high-technology products. These enterprises may require export and import licenses if their technology is classified. The managers of these enterprises also become aware of the laws and regulations concerning shipping practices, custom clearances, and other regulatory areas that control which products may enter a given foreign market and which may not. These types of obstacles usually become apparent only after an enterprise begins to operate in foreign markets, and typically are not a part of the initially perceived obstacles that managers identify when they first think about making the initial decision to export.

Whether solicited or not, first export experiences can be difficult for inexperienced managers. They ship their products to customers that they do not know, and are not certain if, when, or in what form they will be paid. Some managers do not understand the use of confirmed letters of credit, the role of bankers in export transactions, or the documentation needed to ship products abroad. These concerns are even more complicated because managers need to rely on intermediaries for assistance in completing export transactions. Managers need assistance from bankers, freight forwarders, and transportation companies, among other intermediaries, to make certain that customers receive their orders and pay their bills. Managers have to invest a great deal of time constructing a network of intermediaries to actually expedite their first export shipment. This is a relatively complicated and time-consuming process for managers of smaller manufacturing enterprises who export for the first time.

It is not unusual for managers whose enterprises have not exported and who have not had any experience with foreign customers to perceive a whole array of obstacles that do not make exporting practical for them. Managers of enterprises that attempted to export in the past and had difficulties because of customers' complaints or problems related to some part of the exporting process can become overwhelmed by these experiences, and turn them into reasons against (i.e. obstacles to) exporting in the future. Other managers find such experiences a challenge and learn from them; they also learn how to effectively utilize services offered by intermediaries and develop support networks for their export operations. All of these activities lead to the simplification of export operations and the elimination of most of the perceived obstacles to exporting or internationalization for smaller manufacturing enterprises.

Managerial Types and Perceived Obstacles

The three types of managers often perceive the obstacles to exporting in significantly different ways. Craftsman managers typically believe that their perceived obstacles to exporting make it uneconomical to export their products. They tend to ignore export orders that they receive because they do not know how to fill them, which becomes the greatest obstacle of all. Promoter managers tend to perceive fewer obstacles. The obstacles they usually perceive focus on the need for information about demand for their products in foreign markets and the complexities of financial transactions. They are not necessarily concerned with shipping the products to their foreign customers, but more with getting paid. Rational managers, on the other hand, tend to minimize the overall idea and importance of perceived obstacles in exporting. This is primarily because rational managers have greater experience with export operations and they perceive obstacles that are more specific to their products, customers, and markets.

Findings

At the beginning of this study, managers identified 10 obstacles that they believed would affect their decision to export their products. Six of these perceived obstacles were related to marketing: adequate representation in foreign markets is difficult to obtain; foreign opportunities are difficult to determine; shipping documents, export licenses, and other paperwork require too much time to complete; service is difficult (if not impossible) to provide in foreign markets; different product standards and customer habits make products unsuitable for export; and foreign business practices are difficult to understand. Four of the perceived obstacles were related to financial transactions: the high cost of doing business in export markets consumes any possible profits; it is difficult to collect money from overseas; start-up money is hard to come by; and the conversion of some currencies to U.S. dollars is difficult.

Some perceived obstacles can be interpreted as pre-entry obstacles and others as post-entry obstacles, depending on the management style and export experience of the manager. Pre-entry obstacles are typically those that preclude managers from considering exporting their products, such as questioning the suitability of products for foreign markets because of different standards or because the manager believes that it costs too much to get started in exporting. Post-entry obstacles are typically perceived by managers who are more experienced in exporting; they indicate that providing service in foreign markets is difficult or that it is sometimes difficult to collect payment for export shipments.

Perceived Obstacles

Managers with previous export experience were asked to indicate how important each of the 10 perceived obstacles listed above was to their decision to export. The first two obstacles were almost equally important. Approximately 40% of responses over the three surveys rated the difficulty in obtaining adequate representation in foreign markets and the difficulty in determining foreign opportunities as important. The perceived obstacle concerning adequate representation could be interpreted by many managers as a post-entry obstacle that became slightly more relevant as managers developed more experience with exports. The perceived obstacle regarding foreign opportunities could be considered by some less experienced passive exporters as a pre-entry obstacle and also became slightly more important over time. Neither factor could be considered a major obstacle that would potentially prevent managers from exporting or internationalizing their operations. The remaining perceived obstacles had an even lesser impact on the decision to internationalize.

Approximately one-fourth of the respondents to the three surveys indicated that three of the other perceived obstacles were equally important. Managers generally perceived the obstacle concerning the high cost of doing business in export markets and its propensity to consume any possible profits as a post-entry obstacle. In the mid-1970s, this obstacle was less important to managers than in the mid-1980s or the mid-1990s. Managers became slightly more concerned about doing business in export markets in the mid-1980s when foreign competition intensified, but they were slightly less concerned again in the mid-1990s when managers learned how to compete more effectively in foreign markets. Only after a series of export transactions were managers able to calculate the actual costs of such transactions as some of them realized that export orders were not profitable. Some less experienced managers may also have considered this obstacle as a pre-entry obstacle because of other financial considerations such as determining the appropriate export prices for their products.

Just less than a quarter of the respondents, over the three surveys, indicated that the perceived obstacle concerning shipping documents and other paperwork which required too much time to complete was important. This obstacle could initially be considered as a pre-entry obstacle by most passive exporters, but not for aggressive exporters. Early on in their export activities, they developed the policies and procedures required to complete any necessary documentation to accompany each export order, and they frequently asked for assistance from intermediaries that facilitated export shipments. The importance of this perceived obstacle appeared to be relatively stable over time.

Less than one-fourth of the respondents also perceived the difficulty of providing services in foreign markets as being an important obstacle in making the export decision. This could be considered a post-entry obstacle, since passive exporters may not have had enough experience initially to perceive such an obstacle. Only after they gained experience with export orders did passive exporters realize that customers were also concerned about service for the products they purchased. More experienced managers — that is, those interested in repeated export sales — also wanted to provide service for their foreign customers. Establishing an infrastructure designed to offer these services became more costly as exports increased.

Less than one-fifth of the managers in the three surveys indicated that the next three perceived obstacles were important for export decisions. The importance of the perceived obstacle concerning different product standards and consumer habits making a product unsuitable for export increased slightly over the three surveys. This obstacle was considered unimportant in the mid-1970s, when managers had a relatively low understanding of export operations. It somewhat increased in importance in the mid-1980s, when knowledge about export operations became more important for managers interested in foreign markets; and its importance increased more in the mid-1990s, when exports or international operations became essential for managers of smaller manufacturing enterprises. This obstacle intensified in importance as managers gained experience in the exporting business.

Another perceived obstacle that received less than one-fifth of responses was related to the high cost of getting started in exporting. This was considered a pre-entry obstacle by both passive and aggressive enterprise managers, and was more important to those enterprises about to consider an export order. The importance of this obstacle did not change over the three surveys.

The third perceived obstacle that received less than one-fifth of responses in the three surveys concerned the difficulty of understanding foreign business practices. Although it received relatively few responses, the response rate almost tripled in importance from the mid-1970s to the mid-1990s. Managers with export experience generally considered this obstacle as a pre-entry obstacle and only slightly important in the decision to export.

The last perceived obstacle involved the difficulty of converting some currencies to U.S. dollars. This obstacle received very few responses in all three surveys. The overwhelming majority of respondents indicated that this obstacle was not at all important in their decision to export.

Conclusion

The researchers concluded that the perceived obstacles identified at the beginning of this study play a minor role in the decision to export or internationalize. The findings suggest that managers of smaller manufacturing enterprises who decide to export their products, or to later internationalize their operations, tend to consider factors other than the perceived obstacles identified at the beginning of this study in making their decision.

The perceived obstacles used in this study were identified through initial interviews with managers represented in the sample of enterprises.

In the mid-1970s, smaller manufacturing enterprises were encouraged to export because of the impact on the economy and because managers had little (if any) export experience. The lack of export experience presented a distorted picture of the export process. Managers simply did not know what to expect; at the same time, they associated the encouragement to export with benefits to external entities rather than to their own enterprises. Only some more proactive smaller manufacturing enterprises managed by promoter or rational managers were willing to consider export operations.

When the international competitive climate changed in the mid-1980s and managers of smaller manufacturing enterprises realized that they would have to enter foreign markets, the decision to internationalize was not based on perceived obstacles but rather on domestic and foreign competition. It became a question of the manager's ability to generate foreign orders, to get to know foreign markets, and to be able to supply products that could compete. For many managers of smaller manufacturing enterprises, it was not necessarily a decision over whether to export but rather a decision on how to enter profitable foreign markets. Thus, the obstacles perceived in the mid-1970s were no longer relevant.

By the mid-1990s, smaller manufacturing enterprises had had experience with foreign markets through exporting and importing. Directly or indirectly, they gained knowledge about foreign management practices, market conditions, and competition. Those managers who had to make decisions about internationalizing their operations were not concerned about perceived pre-entry or post-entry obstacles. They were able to make internationalization decisions on much higher foreign market entry levels.

When the perceived obstacles are examined from the perspective of the internationalization of smaller manufacturing enterprises, only two perceived obstacles are somewhat relevant to the internationalization decision, both of which address marketing concerns: obtaining adequate representation in foreign markets, and determining foreign opportunities. These two perceived obstacles tend to challenge managers of smaller manufacturing enterprises, regardless of which approach they use to internationalize their enterprises.

Part III

Operations

The operational issues of internationalization among smaller manufacturing firms are explored here. The main questions are concerned with what motivates managers to make the internationalization decision and begin to operate internationally.

Chapter 8

Start of International Operations

For managers of smaller manufacturing enterprises, exporting is only one way to enter a foreign market and, in general, the most frequent method of approaching internationalization. Other ways for smaller manufacturing enterprises to enter foreign markets are to invest directly in the foreign market, to sign contracts with various entities in foreign markets as a way of combining or exchanging services, or to develop aggressive export activities. In this study, we focused on exporting as the basis for the decision to internationalize.

In deciding to export, managers of smaller manufacturing enterprises consider various factors. They weigh the consequences of such a decision on their operational goals, and examine their strengths and weaknesses in order to determine their potential in foreign markets. They assess their ability to compete and, formally or informally, start planning for the decision to enter a foreign market. A few managers also question whether or not they need a fixed policy regarding export opportunities or a formal structure to evaluate them. In reality, only a small number of managers decide to export based on the above factors. The decision to export tends to be more reactive and opportunistic rather than proactive and rational.

Some managers suggest they need to overcome certain obstacles to exporting. Such obstacles may be typically classified as marketing or financial barriers. However, in the overall context of exporting or internationalization, these obstacles play a minor role in a manager's decision to export. Managers of smaller enterprises also suggest that the decision to export is made based on their strengths and the advantages they perceive as helping them be competitive in their domestic market. However, the perceived strengths and advantages, such as having a unique product of high quality and competitive pricing, may not necessarily be realistic in a highly competitive international marketplace. It appears that, in deciding to enter foreign markets by exporting, managers tend not to emphasize the importance of perceived obstacles and they lose sight of their strengths and weaknesses because they lack sufficient marketing and financial information about foreign markets.

Among the smaller manufacturing enterprises in our study, the actual decision to export was made as a function of managerial style. Some managers made the decision to export systematically by examining all of their foreign market entry options; others did not. It was expected that not all managerial types in this study approached the export decision systematically; that is, they examined all of the factors, considered their strengths and weaknesses, evaluated the obstacles to exporting, and then made a decision. The fundamental issue seems to be this: how many rational managers made that decision formally, documented the decision by developing policies and structures to support future decisions, and communicated the entire process to others within the enterprise? How many rational managers simply made the export decision based only on their perceptions and experiences, and did not document the decision or discuss it with others? The same questions apply to craftsman and promoter managers. It is conceivable that some craftsman and promoter managers made the export decision in a systematic way, but most did not.

Final Decision to Export

The findings from this study suggest that the decision to export — or to internationalize — is made on the basis of how individual managers respond to situations in which they confront export opportunities or are competitively challenged to enter foreign markets. The findings also suggest that four situations cause all types of managers to arrive at an export decision. The first situation is when the decision to export is made systematically by exploring available options. The second situation is when the export decision is made because an unsolicited order is received from a potential customer in a foreign market, and the manager decides to ship the order. In the third situation, the export decision is made opportunistically. Managers obtain information from reliable external or internal sources about potential export orders that favorably coincide with internal events within their enterprise. These are typically one-time opportunities. In the final situation, the export decision is made based on exclusive information. Managers receive exclusive information from reliable sources that may be within or outside the organization. Internal sources may be sales persons, technical support specialists, or even engineers who are in close contact with their customers. External sources may include bankers, consultants, and attorneys. The managers must then decide whether or not to act on such information.

The first situation, systematic exploration of foreign market opportunities, requires that managers proactively or reactively examine all options and make a decision to export. A proactive decision to export may suggest that managers perceive inherent strengths in their enterprise to export successfully. A reactive decision to export may imply that the managers must consider some competitive challenges. If the first export experience is positive and if managers believe that their enterprise benefited from it, it is probable that a fixed policy regarding exports and a formal structure to evaluate export opportunities will be established. More mature smaller manufacturing enterprises have followed this pattern.

Unsolicited orders present a major dilemma for managers of smaller manufacturing enterprises. They can fill them or they can ignore them. Some managers decide to fill unsolicited export orders. If the first unsolicited export experience is successful, a manager may decide to accept other orders, thus requiring expansion and managerial changes to incorporate exporting into routine operations. If the first experience is not successful, managers may decide not to accept any future unsolicited export orders under any condition. Often, managers of smaller manufacturing enterprises do not know and do not attempt to find out the sources of unsolicited orders. The unsolicited orders may result from an advertisement in a trade journal, a product release announcement, attendance at a trade fair, or the enterprise's exposure through other media events.

Export decisions based on serendipitous export opportunities are often conveniently implemented if, when these opportunities materialize or are solicited, enterprises face lower sales volume, loss of market share, or unforeseen overproduction. Overproduction combined with high inventory levels can be the driving force for opportunistic exports. Managers of smaller manufacturing enterprises explore leads provided by governmental agencies, industry associations, and any other available sources of information that may generate opportunities to export until problems of overproduction or high inventory are solved. In the future, when similar problems emerge, managers of smaller manufacturing enterprises may look for additional opportunistic export orders.

Finally, export decisions made by managers on the basis of exclusive information reflect the risk propensities of various types of managers to make commitments to foreign markets and customers. Decisions made on the basis of exclusive information suggest that some individuals or entities are creditable and have information that virtually guarantees successful sales. Managers who make their decisions based on exclusive information tend to evaluate the credibility of the source first and the validity of the order second. Some managers maintain a network of associates, suppliers, and customers who they believe will supply them with exclusive information concerning potential export orders.

First Orders

There are additional considerations regarding the first export order, regardless of the basis on which the decision to export is made. If managers seek their first export orders systematically, they will search rather aggressively and eventually become proactive in searching both domestic and foreign markets for export opportunities. They will utilize governmental services to assist them in identifying export clients, distributors, and markets. They will join supply chains, and bid regularly on advertised and publicized export opportunities.

When first export orders are received but unsolicited, managers may have problems responding to them. Since such enterprises seldom have formal procedures to handle export orders, especially unsolicited orders, managers need to decide how to respond. Managers of smaller enterprises seldom question the orders themselves, but they do often question the motivation behind them. They begin to question why their enterprise was selected and who selected them rather than the size of the order or its importance to the enterprise. Most managers who are satisfied with the answers to their questions about the circumstances of unsolicited orders will fill them. However, if managers perceive uncertainties and risks associated with unsolicited orders, they will not fill them. Unfortunately, since the mid-1980s and with the greater exposure of smaller manufacturing enterprises on the Internet, most first orders are unsolicited.

First opportunistic export orders typically receive relatively low commitment from managers. Managers of smaller manufacturing enterprises tend to believe that opportunistic orders, in general, involve relatively low risk and represent only random export opportunities because these opportunities are frequently promoted by governmental agencies or passed on by domestic customers. Some managers successfully respond to first opportunistic orders and develop them into ongoing relationships. Managers also point out that tracking and obtaining opportunistic orders requires networks of professional contacts and relationships in both the public and private sectors. Most craftsman managers are not willing to invest their time into these activities; promoter managers are more likely to do so, and rational managers consider such activities to be a part of their managerial responsibilities.

Exclusive information provided by a reliable source is another way of receiving export orders. First export orders received on the basis of exclusive information provided by a reliable source are favorably accepted by most managers of more mature smaller manufacturing enterprises. A few managers tend to perceive such first orders to be important to their business. Since most orders based on exclusive information are typically conveyed by an individual known to both entities, the resulting seller–buyer relationship may lead to a long-term positive relationship. As a result, first orders based on exclusive information tend to be expedited more diligently than other first export orders, excepting only aggressively solicited first orders.

Solicited and Unsolicited First Orders

The three surveys conducted in this study illustrate that managers of smaller manufacturing enterprises base their export decision on systematic solicitation of export orders, unsolicited first export orders, export orders opportunistically received, or information received exclusively from reliable sources. However, a large majority of smaller manufacturing enterprises internationalized their operations by initiating exporting without systematically exploring any potential export opportunities. In the mid-1970s, less than one-third of the enterprises systematically explored opportunities to export. In the mid-1980s and 1990s, the number of enterprises that systematically explored export opportunities increased significantly but still represented less than half of the exporting enterprises in this study. These findings indicate that managers are reluctant to organize a systematic way for exploring export opportunities; they would rather wait until such opportunities materialize.

The significant increase in the number of smaller manufacturing enterprises that systematically explored export opportunities in the mid-1980s and 1990s is due to the intensified domestic and international competition and the loss of domestic market share. Had competitive and market conditions remained as they were in the mid-1970s, it is likely that the increase would not have occurred. Information gleaned from later interviews with managers who had survived for 35 years or more suggested that managers consider a systematic assessment of all foreign market entry strategies to be a necessary part of their ongoing internationalization process.

Similar conclusions can be reached about solicited versus unsolicited first export orders. The results of the three surveys are similar but less dramatic. Over the years, the first export order has been unsolicited for a majority of the smaller manufacturing enterprises. Approximately two-thirds of these enterprises started exporting because they received unsolicited orders, whereas only one-third of such enterprises actively sought their first order. Managers had to decide whether or not to fill the unsolicited orders, a choice that usually resulted in the internationalization process. During the time period covered by the three surveys, the number of enterprises that sought their first order increased slightly in the mid-1980s and decreased in the mid-1990s. When researchers examined the findings from the last 35 years, they concluded that the majority of smaller manufacturing enterprises did not seek their first order. Instead, they began their internationalization process of exporting due to forces external to the enterprise.

It is important to compare the three surveys' findings with information gathered from pre- and post-study interviews with the managers. The pre-study interviews were designed to collect information about factors used in the research document. The post-study interviews were held with the managers who responded to all three surveys and who were still operating these enterprises and had survived more than 35 years of internal and external challenges to internationalization.

Previous studies have suggested that there are two general perspectives on the export decision and, consequently, on the first export order. The first perspective focuses on the experiential or learning process by managers of smaller manufacturing enterprises, and is sometimes referred to as the *stage model*. Smaller manufacturing enterprises receive their first export orders, fill them, and learn from that process. The managers acquire knowledge about export markets and commit increasingly more resources to them. As the export activities increase and new export markets are added, managers become more comfortable in their decision-making skills and they become more proactive in the international marketplace. The stage model, however, is one-dimensional when it comes to the broad concept of the internationalization of smaller manufacturing enterprises. The stage model was appropriate for smaller manufacturing enterprises in the mid-1970s and, perhaps, in the mid-1980s; but it became less relevant in the late 1980s and 1990s, after smaller manufacturing enterprises accepted the use of the Internet as a way to distribute their products.

The stage model perspective on internationalization became less relevant because demand for products in both domestic and foreign markets changed and foreign competition intensified at home and abroad. Products lost their competitive edge. More significant to this change in the market was the introduction of the Internet, which gained wide acceptance from the late 1980s onwards. The Internet had a major impact on just about every smaller manufacturing enterprise. For example, the enterprises developed webpages to better communicate with clients and suppliers. They also developed internal networks to better communicate with employees and to more effectively coordinate commercial activities. The literature suggests that this perspective on internationalization is known as the *born global* perspective.

Although this perspective may be significant for many smaller manufacturing enterprises, it appears that the notion of "born global" mostly describes smaller, cutting-edge, high-technology software and computer manufacturers that began to emerge at the dawn of the information technology age — mostly after the mid-1980s. Many of these smaller high-technology enterprises invented and introduced new technologies being sought after by information technology innovators and early adopters. Examples of this pent-up demand were software developers. When they announced a release day for new software, orders would arrive over the Internet a few seconds past midnight on the release day itself.

Once managers presented their smaller manufacturing enterprises to the world via the Internet, they began receiving product inquiries, offers to merge, contacts from venture capitalists looking for investment opportunities, and attempts by large international enterprises for friendly (or sometimes unfriendly) takeovers. These situations became valuable learning experiences for a majority of the managers of smaller manufacturing enterprises. On the output side, they had to process market opportunities; on the input side, they had to deal with alternate suppliers; and internally, they had to be concerned about the potential knowledge drain — competitors trying to hire their employees. At the same time, the more successful smaller manufacturing enterprises were in danger of being acquired, taken over, or purchased and liquidated by their competition. The early stages of information technology placed tremendous pressure on smaller manufacturing enterprises from both domestic and foreign sources. Those enterprises that were able to adjust became much stronger and better focused both domestically and internationally.

According to managers of smaller manufacturing enterprises, all of the developments since the late 1980s have offered new options for internationalization. They now have more choices — export their products, license their know-how, merge, or find other means of entering foreign markets on their own or in partnership with domestic or foreign partners. The process of internationalization has become a multiple-decision process based on a portfolio of foreign market entry options. Depending on local market and competitive conditions, smaller manufacturing enterprises can enter several markets simultaneously using different modes of entry. Today, managers of smaller manufacturing enterprises consider the foreign market entry portfolio as a standard approach when making decisions to internationalize their operations.

Information Needs

To be successful in implementing the first export order or using the portfolio approach to internationalize, smaller manufacturing enterprises need information. The degree to which they need this information has not changed significantly over the past 35 years. During pre-study interviews, managers of smaller manufacturing enterprises suggested that certain information would be useful in helping them make the initial export decision. Managers were interested in information concerning the actual export process, including export financing and shipping. They were also interested in marketing information such as market share potential, product pricing, product design, and packaging for foreign markets. Managers were also concerned about domestic and foreign competition, economic and political conditions in foreign markets, and export quotas and tariffs. They judged such information to be useful but not essential in making their first export decision.

The most important information for internationalization initially identified by managers was about consumers, economic conditions in foreign markets, market sales potential, product pricing and design, export shipping, and foreign competition. Questions about these sources of information were included in the three surveys, and only managers who exported responded to the three surveys. The responses were consistent for all three surveys.

A minority of managers who exported in the mid-1970s indicated that they found information about their potential market sales useful. This response was followed by information about pricing, and information about economic conditions in foreign markets. A small minority also indicated that information about shipping exports to consumers was useful. During that time period, managers who found these types of information useful were typically less experienced with export operations than were other managers in the study.

Information became more important in the mid-1980s, when more managers started exporting and realized that they needed more information to export products. Still, only a minority of exporting managers indicated that they could benefit from additional information. They continued to be concerned primarily over market sales potential and product pricing information; a concern for foreign competition and economic conditions in foreign markets followed closely behind. Information about product design also began to be an issue. Managers at this time were more knowledgeable about export operations, and they realized that they needed more specific information.

By the mid-1990s, information needs had changed again. A slightly larger minority of smaller manufacturing enterprise managers now indicated that product pricing information was useful to them, followed by information concerning the potential of market sales. Information about foreign competition, economic conditions in foreign markets, and export shipping was also considered useful. Although the information considered useful for managers making decisions about exports remained about the same over the span of the three surveys, foreign competition intensified and export operations became increasingly important for growth and survival.

In the interviews conducted at the end of the study with managers who had survived for more than 35 years, the information most of the managers found useful was relatively general and of limited importance to export decisions. They suggested that since most orders were unsolicited, they contained most of the information managers needed to ship the order and receive payment. Managers who were more aggressive about seeking orders typically looked for additional information to help them reduce any potential risk in their export transactions.

Managers interviewed at the start of this study perceived as useful information about all kinds of factors related to making decisions about exporting. However, after many years of experience, managers indicated that information only about certain factors might be useful. Furthermore, experienced managers interviewed at the end of the study discussed the possibility that the information needed to successfully fill an export order is directly related to that particular order. This means that each export order is unique and requires specific information to fill it. That is the main reason why only a small number of managers found information about a limited number of factors to be useful.

Conclusion

Beginning export operations and deciding to fill first export orders — or internationalizing in a broader contemporary context, such as joint ventures or direct investment, among others — are relatively difficult decisions for managers of smaller manufacturing enterprises to make. The nature and urgency of the decision has changed considerably over the years. In the mid-1970s, the decision was made by forward-looking, proactive managers who perceived the potential of foreign markets, or the decision was made out of necessity. The decision was most likely motivated by outside forces and made on the basis of an unsolicited order.

In the mid-1980s, managers decided to internationalize because their domestic markets were changing. Those markets were frequently invaded by foreign competitors, and customers were looking for more competitive and better-performing products. Smaller manufacturing enterprises had to search for alternative sources of supplies and had to look in foreign markets to find them. They became experienced in international operations by purchasing abroad, which encouraged them to begin exporting or to use other foreign market entry initiatives.

Later in the 1980s, first export orders or first contacts with foreign entities took on a new character. The Internet opened up unexpected options for smaller manufacturing enterprises to internationalize. The webpage became a two-way entry point into the global marketplace. Unsolicited orders from unforeseen potential customers placed pressure on managers to decide for the first time to export products, be subjected to takeovers, or join various evolving arrangements (such as supply chains, industrial networks, or value chains). Managers in the late 1980s again decided to participate in international operations because of unsolicited inquiries.

By the mid-1990s, managers of smaller manufacturing enterprises had little choice but to internationalize. Foreign markets and competition had changed and, in order to compete and survive, these enterprises also had to change. Those enterprises which began exporting, or became involved in international operations in any other way, entered a system that was already organized and that managed to accommodate a variety of international operations. Managers who began international operations in the mid-1990s entered a relatively predictable world of international operations.

The managers who have survived the past 35 years suggest that it is commonly accepted today that their enterprises will participate in as many foreign markets as possible, and that the first export order is now viewed in the same way as an order from a domestic customer.

Chapter 9

The Motivations for Internationalization

Managers of smaller manufacturing enterprises can choose to actively look for opportunities to export their products, or they can respond to unsolicited orders from abroad. Either option requires a decision. The decision to actively search for export opportunities can be either formal or informal. Either type of decision represents the first step in the internationalization process for that enterprise. A formal decision implies that a fixed policy regarding exporting has been put in place along with a formal structure to evaluate each export opportunity. Managers make informal decisions about export opportunities along with advisory input from employees when needed. Smaller manufacturing enterprises making formal or informal decisions can search aggressively or passively for export opportunities.

Aggressive versus Passive Exporters

Managers of smaller manufacturing enterprises who aggressively search for export opportunities believe they have strengths or justifiable reasons that motivate them to compete in foreign markets. The strengths underlying these beliefs can be the knowledge base of the enterprise or the managerial ability to understand markets abroad and successfully compete in them. The level of commitment to internationalization may vary, depending on the managerial style of the individual decision maker. Even craftsman managers may have some commitment to internationalizing their enterprises, and to some degree they may want to participate in markets abroad. Promoter managers often believe that international exposure is good for their domestic market exposure. They want to promote their international exposure and point out that they are internationally known. It is the rational managers who choose to balance their marketing strategies between domestic and foreign markets.

Smaller manufacturing enterprises that passively identify and accept export opportunities wait for export orders. When receiving general inquiries from abroad, leads on export opportunities, or even unsolicited export orders, passive exporters evaluate them separately from their domestic opportunities; and if they have available manufacturing capacity or time to respond to inquiries, evaluate leads, or fill unsolicited orders, they do so. Passive exporters are reluctant to communicate with potential customers abroad. They need time to decide how to deal with each inquiry, lead, or unsolicited export order. Craftsman managers generally have to be convinced by reputable professionals to even consider unsolicited orders. Enterprises that respond passively to inquiries from abroad, leads, or export orders tend to have promoter managers who try to manage demand for their products over a relatively short-term period. If faced with the need to fill manufacturing capacity, they will then accept an unsolicited order. Promoter managers follow up on general inquiries from abroad and on leads on export opportunities. Occasionally, when confronted with a high inventory level, they will also consider unsolicited orders. However, promoter managers evaluate unsolicited orders on the basis of perceived risk: if the perceived risk associated with a specific export order is too high, they will not accept the order. Rational managers typically use a functionally based process to evaluate general inquiries from abroad, export leads, and unsolicited orders, and they manage each in the same way that they manage domestic orders.

Differences Between Aggressive and Passive Exporters

It is important to examine what motivates smaller manufacturing enterprises to become either aggressive or passive exporters. Aggressive exporters tend to consider their strengths and weaknesses as motives. More specifically, they judge export activities in terms of their managerial abilities and functional advantages such as marketing, finance, or technology. They also consider external motives such as exclusive information, competition, or domestic market conditions. Both internal and external motives drive aggressively run enterprises to actively solicit export opportunities and to use their own initiative to compete in foreign markets by relying on their proprietary know-how and managerial skills.

Passive exporters tend to rely more on external forces that motivate them to rationalize or justify why they should accept unsolicited export orders. They believe that foreign customers will find them because of their unique products or technology. They anticipate that general inquiries and export leads from abroad will produce unsolicited export orders. Channels of distribution and distribution networks are additional sources of potential export opportunities for passive exporters.

A fundamental difference between aggressive and passive exporters is reflected in the amount of managerial effort necessary to obtain and complete an export order. Aggressive exporters are prepared to invest resources into aggressively soliciting export orders, while passive exporters are more comfortable waiting for export orders to come in. Another fundamental difference is the willingness to invest in sources of information that will produce contacts and information about potential foreign market opportunities. Unlike aggressive exporters, passive exporters simply are not willing to invest in developing such information sources.

Internal and External Motivating Factors

At the beginning of this study, researchers asked the managers in the sample what internal and external factors had motivated them to begin exporting. Managers identified 13 factors they considered as internal motivators and 11 factors they considered to be external motivators. All factors listed were used in the three surveys and revisited at the end of the study. The internal factors were classified into five types: marketing, finance, management, technology, and competitive pressure. The marketing factors were responsible for most internal motivation leading to export operations. Managers also listed five types of external factors that motivated managers to export: government agencies, competition, distribution channels, banks, and general inquiries from abroad. Members of distribution channels such as distributors, wholesalers, or manufacturers' agents were named as strong external motivating forces.

Internal Motivators

The five types of internal factors identified by managers at the beginning of the study were perceived as strengths and weaknesses. Marketing factors included strengths and weaknesses such as unique products, product patents, price advantage, marketing know-how, efficient distribution network, proximity to ports, exclusive information about foreign customers, declining domestic sales, and overproduction. The financial factor represented the financial strength of the enterprise — the financial ability of an enterprise to profitably develop export operations. The managerial advantage suggested a positive attitude toward export operations, and the technological advantage indicated a technological superiority over competitors. Increasing pressure from competitors was considered a weakness and became a motivating factor to start export operations.

Only a minority of managers responsible for the smaller manufacturing enterprises which exported and responded to all three surveys indicated that internal factors were important in initially motivating them to export. The responses were consistently low for the three surveys. However, approximately one quarter of respondents suggested that the primary motivator for them to export was the uniqueness of their products. Both in the mid-1970s and mid-1980s, technological advantage became the second most important motivating factor leading to exports. These findings suggest that managers of smaller manufacturing enterprises offered unique products and perceived their enterprises to be technologically advanced in domestic markets, and were able to extend their strengths into foreign markets.

By the mid-1990s, they still believed that their products were unique, but their technological advantage had deteriorated significantly and had been replaced by competitive pressure as the second most important motivating factor for starting export operations. Managers who were exporting began to experience domestic competition and needed to decide whether or not to enter export markets. Over the span of the study, strengths such as unique products and technology confronted competitive pressures in both domestic markets and abroad, and many smaller manufacturing enterprises had no choice but to enter foreign markets. Strong internal motivating forces to enter foreign markets turned into competitive weaknesses and necessitated that they enter foreign markets.

The other internal factors that were initially identified as motivating smaller manufacturing enterprises to export were only marginally significant. In the mid-1970s, these factors were marketing know-how, financial advantage, and exclusive information about foreign markets or customers. In the mid-1980s, the order of importance of these factors changed slightly: marketing know-how along with competitive pressure, efficient distribution, and lastly financial advantage. Financial strength became less important in motivating enterprises to begin export operations, and the competitive pressure on the decision to export became more important. In the mid-1990s, financial strength became more important, along with declining domestic sales as a weakness and exclusive information about markets or customers abroad and marketing know-how as strengths. Those factors were again followed equally by price and technological advantages. It is important to note that less than a quarter of the respondents to the three surveys indicated that internal factors listed as motivators in the initial interviews were important.

External Motivators

External factors that motivated managers to start export operations were first identified in the initial stages of this study and classified into five types. The largest classification centered on distribution channels and included domestic distributors, wholesalers, manufacturers' agents, export agents, and foreign distributors. Two governmental entities were also initially identified: the U.S. state of Wisconsin's export expansion effort and the U.S. Department of Commerce.

Competitive factors included competition from domestic as well as foreign sources. Two external motivators that managers identified as separate types were banks and general inquiries from abroad. All external motivators were initially identified as having a positive impact on the decision to export and on the export process.

Managers considered external motivators as relatively positive, as they offered useful information concerning potential export opportunities. During periods of domestic market growth, some managers considered certain external factors as intrusive and time-consuming. When representatives of governmental agencies provided leads for potential export orders, managers preoccupied with the domestic market or competitive issues tended not to respond. Similar situations developed when bank representatives called on these managers. Leads or inquiries provided by distributors, wholesalers, or manufacturers' representatives were also frequently given a low priority.

Slight differences occurred between aggressive and passive exporters, and how each related to the external factors motivating smaller manufacturing enterprises to export. Enterprise managers who aggressively sought export orders tended to cooperate with government agencies much more frequently than those who responded passively to such orders. Government agencies became components of enterprises' order-seeking networks, and they used the offered export development services. Aggressive exporters also cooperated with banks and relied on their connections and corresponding banks for export opportunities, whereas passive exporters tended to use banks only to clear payments. Aggressive exporters used motivating sources such as distribution channels more often than did passive exporters.

Findings from the three surveys suggest that general inquiries from abroad were by far the strongest motivator for smaller manufacturing enterprises to enter export operations. Approximately half of the respondents to all three surveys indicated that they were motivated by general inquiries from abroad to start exporting. Responses were relatively uniform over the three surveys. It appears that for some smaller manufacturing enterprises general inquiries from abroad represented potential opportunities, while for others they presented time-consuming dilemmas. The latter was especially true for enterprises that did not have a fixed policy or formal structure in place to evaluate inquiries from abroad. General inquiries need to be converted into leads, and leads in turn need to be changed into export orders. This type of transformation is a major challenge, particularly for passive exporters. Apparently, the rate of conversion of general inquiries from abroad into actual export shipments is much higher for aggressive exporters.

Responses to all three surveys indicate that the importance of the individual factors, with the exception of general inquiries from abroad, changed over the duration of the surveys. Some factors identified at the beginning of the study received extremely low responses and were not included in the final analysis; these factors included banks, government agencies, and wholesalers. Other factors were of marginal importance.

Responses to the first survey in the mid-1970s indicated that manufacturers' agents, followed closely by domestic distributors, were important to export orders. The next two categories that were of equal importance in motivating smaller manufacturing enterprises to develop export operations were export agents and foreign distributors.

By the mid-1980s, foreign distributors were more important motivating forces for smaller manufacturing enterprises than were manufacturers' agents. Managers of such enterprises started to develop major contacts abroad, some by way of foreign distributors. Export agents also became important to this process. However, domestic competition had also become an important motivating force by the mid-1980s. By the time the second survey was completed, managers of smaller manufacturing enterprises were more aware of external pressures to expand their export operations.

At the end of the third survey in the mid-1990s, general inquiries from abroad were still the dominant motivating force to expand export operations. Foreign distributors and manufacturers' agents also played an important role in motivating these smaller manufacturing enterprises to increase their involvement in markets abroad. Even export agents assumed a greater role in export expansion among smaller manufacturing enterprises. A new motivating force also emerged: foreign competition. Foreign competition in domestic and international markets forced smaller manufacturing enterprises to export more products and to become more active in markets abroad.

In the final interviews with managers, researchers posed several questions about which external factors motivated them to expand their exports and other international activities abroad. Managers agreed that increased use of information technology in the late 1980s and the creation of Internet websites by the mid-1990s substantially increased the number of inquiries from abroad. When the number of inquiries began to increase, some managers considered the increase less than favorable and did not always respond to inquiries. Other managers considered them essential to expanding their foreign market involvement.

Another issue that emerged from the follow-up interviews that concerned the external motivation to expand export activities involved government agencies. Managers pointed out that they received minimal assistance from either state or federal agencies motivating them to increase their export activities. The information that managers received from government agencies was either too general or incomplete, or it did not effectively connect the buyer and the seller. For example, leads provided by U.S. commercial attachés in foreign countries were considered too exploratory.

Conclusion

A number of internal and external factors play an important role in motivating smaller manufacturing enterprises to export their products, increase their export operations, and become more active in markets abroad. Managers of these enterprises weigh such factors, and decide how much credibility or importance they have in implementing export processes and in becoming internationalized. Most of the managers responsible for smaller manufacturing enterprises believe that they offer cutting-edge technology and unique products to their customers, and those are their main motivations for entering foreign markets.

Most passive managers of smaller manufacturing enterprises have begun exporting, or have expanded their export activities, by converting general inquiries from abroad into viable export orders. Some managers consider this a normal sales development process. Others consider general inquiries from abroad as unsolicited orders.

When considered together, all internal and external factors only partially explain the reasons for export expansion among smaller manufacturing enterprises. Although managers of these enterprises insist that they rely on many sources of information, when actually deciding to export their products, they tend to make the decision based on a personal perception of the risk-to-payback ratio emanating from each export opportunity. Managers may consider information from many sources, even from their own employees, but ultimately the final decision is based on their own personal motivation.

Part IV

Decision to Internationalize and Integrate

In this part, the main internationalization aspects of European smaller manufacturing enterprises are compared with those of Wisconsin. First, the six research cases representing the Wisconsin smaller manufacturing enterprises are presented and summarized. These cases represent enterprises that have been a part of this study from its beginning, and illustrate the changes in approaches to internationalization that they have experienced. Next, the experiences of smaller manufacturing enterprises from the Czech Republic, Denmark, and Sweden are compared on the basis of their internationalization process. The unique features of each enterprise are presented and compared to the other enterprises in all three countries. The major differences in international experiences are noted.

Chapter 10

Summary and Overview of Research Cases: A Wisconsin Perspective

Smaller manufacturing enterprises in Wisconsin have a long tradition of contributing not only to the local economy, but also to the national economy. Many such Wisconsin enterprises have grown into major players in the global marketplace. Some large Wisconsin international enterprises began as small family operations. Many of these enterprises survived numerous domestic and international economic, social, and technological challenges, and they adjusted by changing their business models and finding more effective and efficient ways to compete and become internationally engaged. Some smaller manufacturing enterprises in this study have followed a similar path.

Wisconsin Cases

The following six cases illustrate some of the challenges and opportunities that managers of Wisconsin smaller manufacturing enterprises have faced during the last 35 years. These cases represent enterprises that have survived several economic, social, and technological challenges. These businesses were randomly selected from those enterprises that have functioned over the last 35 years and that are still successfully competing domestically and internationally. They also represent enterprises managed by dynamic managers with broad perspectives of their operations and growth potential.

Researchers conducted a series of in-depth structured interviews with key managers in 2008 and 2009 at the conclusion of the study. The objectives of these interviews were to learn more about how managers view internationalization, which we reported on earlier, and how they manage international operations today. The findings from these interviews generally reinforce the earlier findings. Based on these results, we made a series of comparisons. It is interesting to note that all six of the enterprises began as small, locally oriented enterprises with no substantial involvement in foreign markets, yet 35 years later they are all directly or indirectly involved with international operations.

The oldest enterprise among the six was established in 1919 as a family business. The youngest enterprise was established in 1974 as an owner-managed enterprise. All six enterprises were started by individuals who also became the top decision makers of the enterprises, and who have changed owners or top managers or are in the process of doing so. The current managers whom we interviewed can be classified as two craftsman managers, two promoter managers, and two rational managers. Five of the enterprises are still Wisconsin-owned and Wisconsin-operated, and one became a subsidiary of a large British engineering enterprise.

Two of the enterprises believe that they are primarily job shops, although one is managed by a craftsman manager and the other by a rational manager. Two others are classified by current managers as primarily manufacturing enterprises managed respectively by a craftsman manager and a promoter manager. The remaining two enterprises focus on sales and marketing, and are managed respectively by a rational manager and a promoter manager. No relationship appears to exist between the primary focus of the enterprise and its current style of manager.

Wisconsin Managers

In order for enterprises to succeed and grow, managers need to make decisions, and one would expect that the three types of managers would approach decisions differently. In the six cases studied, decisions about new products and markets, including international markets, are typically made by the managers, sometimes with input from teams of employees appointed by the key decision maker.

The exception to this finding is the foreign subsidiary, where decisions are made by relevant managers according to policies and procedures. For all six enterprises, an advisory group reviews and presents pertinent information to the key decision maker.

Each enterprise began by offering a product perceived by the original owner-manager to be unique. Reflecting on the history of each enterprise, the current managers pointed out that the founders recognized an opportunity in the market and proceeded to fill it. They attributed their growth and market expansion to the single unique product that they manufactured. Through systematic product improvements and innovation, they managed to maintain their growth and market expansion. Even today, all of the managers interviewed believe that they offer a unique product of relatively high quality to their customers. In fact, all managers pointed out that their primary competitive advantage is centered on the manufacturing of a high-quality product which is based on innovative technology and supported by superior customer service. Two of the six enterprises also suggested that they charge relatively high prices for their products.

Today, all six enterprises serve international markets to some degree. Three of the enterprises export indirectly; that is, they sell their products to local customers who export those products directly, or those products become part of final products that are marketed in international markets. One enterprise exports directly and also maintains a sales and distribution center abroad (including a large warehousing facility). Another enterprise owns subsidiaries abroad and actively markets its products internationally. The remaining enterprise became a subsidiary of a foreign enterprise.

The Initial Step in the Internationalization of Wisconsin Enterprises

The initial involvement in international operations differed substantially among the six enterprises. The three enterprises that are considered indirect exporters suggested that they never formally conduct any international operations. Two of the three enterprises simply deal with local customers who export their products, and the third enterprise initially had an unsuccessful exporting experience and will no longer export directly. One of the six enterprises started exporting almost from the beginning of its operations. The remaining enterprises used the services of a representative to enter their first foreign market. Five of the six enterprises interviewed have no policies to evaluate international opportunities; only the enterprise that became a foreign subsidiary has a policy to search for new geographic markets and new opportunities. Managers of the five enterprises that do not have a formal policy to evaluate foreign opportunities have an ongoing process whereby they consider new opportunities as they arise, sometimes without making any real commitment.

Enterprises active in international markets generate somewhere between 25% and 50% of their sales volume from exports. Most of the managers in the six cases presented here believe that profits generated from international sales are less or equally as profitable as those generated from domestic sales. They believe there are significant obstacles to international operations. Most obstacles are not major; for example, collecting payment and pricing products for export are typically perceived as minor obstacles. According to the manager of the foreign subsidiary, one major obstacle to international operations is a lack of understanding of foreign cultures.

Decision-Making Process of Wisconsin Enterprises

Researchers also asked the six managers how they examine and assess international operations in relation to their enterprises. Do they systematically examine their international operations? Only the Wisconsin-based foreign subsidiary has done so. It is part of a broader, enterprise-wide system that evaluates and assesses international markets and opportunities. Even though the other enterprises do not have a systematic process for examining and assessing international markets, neither do they have a way of assessing domestic operations. All of them expect that in the next five years they will grow, develop new products and markets, and perhaps diversify. How the growth and the other objectives will be realized is not clear. It appears to be an unstructured day-to-day process, except for that of the foreign subsidiary.

These six cases represent strong smaller manufacturing enterprises that have survived over the span of this study in the Wisconsin economy. They are not presented in any predetermined order. They are examples of the types of firms included in the overall study that have managed to operate successfully over the past 35 years and, to some degree, enter into international operations (even if somewhat reluctantly). They illustrate how current managers of smaller manufacturing enterprises view their present and potential growth options as well as their domestic and international operations.

Closing Comments

The six smaller manufacturing enterprises have contributed significantly to their local, regional, and national economies and, to some degree, to the global economy. They also maintain substantial market segments. Over the years, they have survived many changes in their markets and growing competition. The important question is this: what is unique about these enterprises, and can other smaller manufacturing enterprises be stimulated to grow domestically and internationally to become better global competitors? A second important question is this: how different are smaller manufacturing enterprises operating in the U.S. state of Wisconsin from those operating in other states or countries?

10.1 Alpha Technology Corporation

Company Background

Alpha Technology Corporation (ATC) is a medium-sized, privately held engineering and manufacturing corporation, and is located in a large industrial city in Wisconsin. As a strategically important high-technology market player, it operates from the well-established, sheltered, and inconspicuous location. Once inside, the visitor has an impression of seeing a large laboratory rather than an engineering and manufacturing facility. In addition to its Wisconsin headquarters, ATC operates in two other locations in the U.S. and two abroad, along with its European operations in the U.K. ATC is considered to be one of the leading international suppliers of electronic systems for air, space, land, and sea applications. ATC has been active internationally since its founding, first as an exporter and later as a major player in the international marketplace. ATC was established in the late 1950s by two siblings. One sibling had a degree in engineering and long R&D experience; the other had a law degree. Both came to Wisconsin for professional reasons, and ATC was established in Wisconsin as a matter of convenience.

Products

Initially, one of the founders and several employees developed ATC's first product. Today, ATC is involved in several layers of engineering and manufacturing, ranging from product design and development to manufacturing. All products are supported by the necessary software systems. ATC offers extensive support services for all of its products and customer maintenance services for a variety of clients.

Aside from its engineering and manufacturing services, ATC is also known for high-quality customer service and wants to be known for single-source service in its industry. It maintains a worldwide staff of technicians, all trained in the U.S., and local support personnel. It maintains several strategically located walk-in or mail-in service depots in the U.S. and in two foreign locations. In order to support such a high level of service, ATC conducts ongoing training for its service personnel.

In today's highly competitive world, ATC offers a high level of product and service technology domestically as well as through its subsidiaries abroad. Over the years, ATC has made numerous developments in flat panel displays and digital avionics. ATC not only supplies military aircraft worldwide with its highly sophisticated avionics, but also supplies airlines and cargo carriers with the Electronic Flight Bag and the latest technology in airborne servers. ATC also provides Inertial Navigation Systems for space, satellite, and sea applications.

Although ATC products are used in the newest aircraft, ATC manages to maintain a relatively low level of market visibility at the same time. This approach to its business transactions projects its reputation for stability and reliability. A high level of exclusivity and confidentiality are especially important with large international clients. One of its subsidiaries abroad is dedicated to high-technology defense systems and is known for highly innovative products. The U.S. subsidiary is recognized for its design, development, and ability to manufacture entire systems from beginning to end.

Focus

In our interview, Mr. John Black, CEO, suggested that ATC is primarily an engineering organization that focuses on technology and product more than anything else. He sees himself as a professional manager managing a craftsman manager-type job shop. Most of his employees are technicians involved in designing, developing, and assembling customized products for the clients. ATC does not conduct research activities on its own. Most of its products are retrofits based on other companies' research and designs. Its products are fabricated according to specifications provided by its clients and, in many cases, are retrofitted into existing applications. If research would be needed for any reason to support its own products, it is likely that ATC's personnel would conduct such research. According to Mr. Black, this is why ATC must remain flexible: in order to compete.

Competitive Advantage

ATC's ability to adapt to changing market conditions is its most important competitive advantage. ATC's U.S. competitors are much larger and more rigid, and thus are unable to respond quickly to market conditions. There are other reasons for ATC's agility. Mr. Black believes that, since ATC is privately owned, he has an easier time making decisions. He does not have to worry about shareholders or spend time preparing quarterly financial statements. Being a privately held company has not limited its ability to borrow capital from financial institutions. Mr. Black believes that ATC's relationship with financial institutions has been very strong over the years and does not foresee any changes in the coming years. He also believes that ATC does a lot for its customers and makes sure that its products meet the needs of its customers.

Importance

When asked what is important to the enterprise, Mr. Black replied that, in his opinion, ATC is not always concerned with profitability. The main concern is long-term sales. The emphasis is on maintaining a positive cash flow and increasing sales growth. Making cash flow the first priority is a matter of survival, but it is not fun, he says, because at the same time he cares more about the employees and the business than the profit.

Impact of Current Economic Conditions

ATC is fully committed and looking forward to delivering products and services to its customers. However, due to the challenges of the current economic environment, ATC has started to detect a decline in its overall business. Demand for its products and services is down, especially in the commercial market. Yet, as economic conditions deteriorate, ATC's clients tend to retrofit their older equipment rather than purchase new equipment. Retrofit remains a contributing driver of avionics sales in the air transport category, particularly in the cargo sector. Some overcapacity in airline medium- to narrow-body airplanes will set in motion the transfer of these aircraft to the cargo market. Older airplanes used by cargo and charter operators, and in parts of the world outside the U.S. and Europe, will require upgrades within the next five years to meet government standards.

Since retrofitting new technology into older equipment is very much a part of ATC's business, this may have a strong positive impact on ATC's balance sheet in the future. At the same time, retrofitting is also an international phenomenon from which ATC can benefit. Mr. Black expects that revenue will continue to grow even under declining market conditions. The concern is over profit. For the reasons above, ATC is not hiring new personnel but rather replacing some personnel in one of its U.S. locations.

Future of the Company

Because of its market duality, with both commercial and military markets for its engineered electronic systems, ATC has a solid potential in future domestic and international high-technology markets. In 2008, ATC generated approximately US$235–US$240 million in sales volume and employed approximately 1,800 employees. Throughout its history, ATC has remained committed to pushing the boundaries of technology to create outstanding products. With the advent of integrated avionics in defense and commercial systems in the late 1980s, ATC recognized the importance of providing a technical and management sounding board for this emerging technology domain. This should provide the company with a bright future.

Systematic Decision-Making Process

A systematic decision-making process helps the company address the critical elements that result in a good decision. By taking an organized approach, it is less likely to miss important factors and can build on the approach to improve decisions. ATC, however, does not have a systematic decision-making process for developing new products and evaluating new markets. ATC's strategy is to constantly monitor market trends, assess what courses of action its competitors are taking, and follow what military developments laboratories are focusing on and, of course, what new products are actually reaching the market. In reality, ATC's role in the market is to find applications for its own core know-how — to introduce its own products in products introduced by others. Mr. Black suggests that ATC is not a sales and marketing-driven organization. Its engineers and managers are responsible for constantly looking for market opportunities. Meetings with clients, attendance at international trade fairs, and corporate visits are sources of new market opportunities for ATC.

Initial Markets

ATC is heavily dependent on international business. About 50–60% of its products are sold abroad. Its largest commercial and military markets are in Western Europe, the Middle East, and Asia. The rest of its market is in the U.S., mostly to large commercial and military clients such as Boeing and Lockheed. One way or another, ATC's products end up in products that are used extensively in international applications.

According to Mr. Black, ATC's involvement in international markets began when it started exporting in the early 1960s, shortly after ATC was established. His guess is that the first orders came from Western Europe or Japan. Although ATC continues to export, it also operates two subsidiaries abroad. One of the wholly owned subsidiaries, which was established in 1970, is engaged in research, development, production, and logistical support for products that are comparable to those made in the U.S. Another subsidiary, a joint venture that was established in 1993, is responsible for joint engineering, development, and software verification. Both subsidiaries serve a range of international clients.

Export Obstacles

What seems to be the greatest obstacle for ATC in the highly integrated international markets for electronic systems, particularly in the large commercial and military markets, is getting paid by its commercial clients. Military clients sometimes pay late, but they do pay. Public airlines, on the other hand, are not only experiencing major downturns, but some airlines are also entering bankruptcy, which makes payment collection even more difficult.

ATC occasionally faces a more complicated and somewhat high-technology obstacle in the international marketplace, and that is the dual use of its products. Since most of its engineered electronic systems can be used for commercial as well as military applications, the U.S. government sometimes restricts the export of its technology to certain countries. Although some of the restrictions are being eliminated, they do present a formidable problem. ATC must work closely with the proper agencies to obtain the necessary export licenses required under regulations in place at the time of export.

Future Markets

Because of the nature of its products and services, ATC has an interesting perspective on future markets for its electronic systems. When looking at a particular international market, it needs to consider both its commercial and military potential. A country's commercial and military potential is very much connected to its level of prevailing technology. The higher the prevailing level of technology, the greater the potential for ATC's products and services. Based on these conditions for assessment of future markets, ATC believes that India will offer substantial potential for purchasing its products and services.

China, as a potential market for ATC's products and services, is more complicated. The level of prevailing technology in China is increasing for many commercial applications, but from a strategic perspective, the U.S. government restricts the sale of high-technology electronic systems to China. The justification for this regulation is, in fact, one of the obstacles of dual use of technology discussed by Mr. Black. The concerns of the U.S. government are strategic: the systems could be shifted from commercial to military applications.

Systematic Exploration of International Business Opportunities

Although ATC is active in international business operations, it does not have a specific policy or process to evaluate international opportunities. However, according to Mr. Black, ATC plans for other business activities such as new products and markets by watching the marketplace to see what new products are being introduced so that ATC's engineers can improve the performance of these products by using its core competencies. Its planning horizon is five years.

A specific example of a source for information and an input into the planning process is the U.S. Federal Aviation Administration, which frequently introduces new regulations for the airline industry. The airline industry then needs to meet these regulations by retrofitting electronics into existing equipment. This is an ideal niche for ATC.

As part of the planning process for market opportunities, ATC's engineers and managers also closely monitor the requirements of its clients both as inputs into the development of clients' new products and as retrofitted supplements or component parts into existing products. Participation in the development of clients' new products tends to be a longer-term process as opposed to providing retrofit solutions for clients' existing products.

Mr. Black also indicated that ATC has a five-year growth plan. If, however, it is necessary to modify the growth plan for various reasons such as major developments in technology or economic reasons, changes may be made informally to adjust for any positive or negative growth opportunities or challenges.

When the profit levels of domestic and international operations are compared, it appears that there is no difference in the levels of profitability. This is primarily due to the types of ATC's clients. Most of its clients are large international entities with operations abroad. Depending on how the invoicing and payments are structured, the margins might be equal for both domestic and foreign billing. The actual prices for ATC's products and services tend to be the same in both markets.

Summary

ATC is a privately held, dynamic, medium-sized engineering and manufacturing corporation specializing in engineered electronic systems. It is located in a large industrial city in Wisconsin. More than half of the demand for its products and services comes from abroad. It is a strategically important player in the international marketplace. As an engineering job shop, it appears to be centrally managed by its CEO. Some top-level engineers and managers are responsible for assessing and evaluating potential product and service opportunities and strategic developments in both commercial and military markets. ATC has the advantage of operating in both new high-technology markets as well as in old-technology markets, where it retrofits new high-technology electronic systems solutions.

Over the time ATC has been studied, it was considered to be a solid exporter. This is the case even now, since over half of its sales revenue is generated from abroad. However, over time, ATC has become more active in the international marketplace. Today, ATC operates from several foreign locations. It entered into a joint venture, and set up engineering and development capabilities abroad. These capabilities have moved ATC from the realm of an exporter into the realm of a major international player.

ATC remains a privately owned corporation. It is centrally managed and controlled financially. Its growth potential is carefully managed, depending on market conditions. It also does not seem to have any major problems operating in the international business environment. ATC's engineers and managers tend to be comfortable operating in the broad international business environment. Finally, ATC appears to have close ties with all of its clients and maintains long-term relations with them.

The main characteristics of ATC are as follows: (1) a centrally managed, privately held corporation managed by a dominant decision maker; (2) successfully operating in a high-technology, internationally strategic environment; and (3) positioned for growth with new products and services matching the needs of its clients.

10.2 Bio-technology and Horticulture Unlimited

Company Background

Bio-technology and Horticulture Unlimited (BHU) is a smaller manufacturing company located in a relatively rural part of Wisconsin. It is located in a comparatively unassuming headquarters and unpretentiously sophisticated engineering and manufacturing facilities. It operates well-designed warehousing and distribution facilities at the same location. BHU represents a classic, entrepreneurially based company. Its founder, James G. Green, started solving horticultural problems over 60 years ago when he opened his operations as a result of comments received from growers suggesting that they had problems with specific horticultural applications. The growers came to the founder of BHU because he was an entrepreneur interested in solving horticultural problems.

Products

Today, BHU is a formidable competitor in the horticultural and biotechnology industries. BHU is primarily known for its lines of horticultural equipment. Its products are sold around the world. In addition to its headquarters in Wisconsin, it also manages a Canadian sales office and distribution centers in Australia, Europe, Japan, and South America. A new facet of business development at BHU is its BHU Liquid Fish Fertilizer. Liquid Fish Fertilizer is environmentally appealing because it is 100% organic. The low-impact fertilizer utilizes chopped-up fish, something considered waste and formerly disposed of in landfills, which are now made into a useful and highly effective product. BHU's Liquid Fish Fertilizer contains naturally occurring amino acids as well as a complex of minor elements (especially B vitamins). Many professional gardeners recommend combining it with liquid kelp to enhance performance. A clean, state-of-the-art factory was newly completed in Wisconsin to produce this fertilizer.

Focus

From its beginning, BHU has been a family business. Family values remain very much a part of its entire operations today. When the founder died, his older son, Peter J. Green, worked closely with his mother to grow the business and develop new products. Although educated as a marketing specialist with a strong self-educated engineering focus, he introduced a number of innovations and initially made a major impact on the horticultural industry. When the founder's younger son, Kenneth W. Green, later purchased a part of the business from his mother, the family involvement continued. The younger brother was educated in horticulture. Early in his professional career, he acquired strong sales skills in the horticultural industry. The older brother operated the manufacturing company, while the younger brother managed the sales company. As a family business, both companies operated as one entity. When the older brother died, the two companies merged.

Competitive Advantage

BHU maintains a low profile in both the horticultural and biotechnology industries. It is known for highly innovative products sold in both commercial and consumer markets. BHU is in tune with both industries and follows their rapid development. It reviews new methods and applications, and relates them to its engineering and manufacturing capabilities.

Importance

The quality of products and services has been the hallmark of BHU since its inception. In a recent interview with the current owner-manager, Kenneth W. Green, it became apparent that the focus on quality and a strong emphasis on sales and marketing have brought the company into a better and more stable market position. At the same time, he pointed out that both commercial and consumer markets consider BHU's products as being of high quality but rather expensive. High-quality personal service is designed to offset the higher prices, and fast responses to technical questions are clearly an important component of BHU's domestic and international customer focus.

Over the past 25 years, there has been a massive shift in the geographical distribution of production from developed to emerging economies. Companies are constantly looking for ways to lower their labor and raw material costs. Emerging economies have become parts suppliers to the global economy; this has given rise to global commodity chains. Facilitated by increasingly efficient, low-cost transportation, it has become cost-effective to distribute the production of individual components of a given product across several geographically distant locations, and then have the parts assembled in another country and re-shipped for sale to markets around the world. While this globalization of production may increase the profits of companies, it also increases the amount of competition.

Impact of Current Economic Conditions

For almost a decade, greenhouse manufacturers such as BHU rode the wave of a good economy. Home gardeners and retailers alike spent money, and lots of it, on all things green. To meet the increased demand for plant material and floral products, growers retrofitted, expanded, and built to keep up with the demand. As a result, greenhouse manufacturers and equipment suppliers had more orders than ever before. But over the past couple of years, the economy has taken a turn for the worse — consumers are spending less and retailers are more cautious.

Reflecting on the current economic conditions, Mr. Green suggests that there is still a need to respect BHU's relationship to the U.S. economy and protect its employees as much as possible from the economic slowdown. He realizes that there is a more fundamental reason why some companies continue to be successful and some bite the dust. In his opinion, BHU follows three market disciplines: product quality, efficiency, and customer service. He believes that BHU must be great in at least one of these and at least good in the other two to succeed. Mr. Green believes that BHU makes top-quality products and is well known in the industry as one of the suppliers with the best customer service. At the end of the day, he acknowledges, it is all about satisfying the needs, wants, and desires of customers, giving them a reason to come through the door in the first place and then come back to buy again. The trick, he says, is to understand the company's strengths, know who its customers are and what drives their purchase decisions, and understand its competitors and what their compelling business propositions are. If BHU does these with consistency, he believes that BHU will survive the current economic conditions.

Future of the Company

According to Mr. Green, BHU intends to continue to grow in the future. There are opportunities for new complementary products for both its commercial and consumer product lines, in addition to opportunities for diversification into other biotechnology and horticultural markets. This growth agenda is very much based on BHU's innovative capabilities and clear view of the future. In order to implement its growth strategy, it needs to be strong financially. Over the years, it has experienced satisfactory financial growth to support its new marketing activities; however, the recent economic slowdown has somewhat affected its growth potential. Nevertheless, even in the depressed markets, the demand for BHU's products seems to be relatively strong.

Mr. Green believes that BHU will grow considerably in the next five years, primarily due to its diversification into a line of biotechnology-based commercial products. As an innovator, he believes that BHU has a strong competitive advantage in the new emerging line of biotechnology-based products. It is also likely that, as competition sets in, BHU's margins will somewhat erode in the biotechnology market. As a processor of organic raw material that is the base for its biotechnological products, BHU may, in the future, have to compete more aggressively for raw material. More intense competition will reduce its market share, even though it currently holds a dominant position in this market.

Systematic Decision-Making Process

In order to increase its efficiency, BHU maintains flexible working hours and allows its employees to structure their jobs to suit their own personal preferences. For example, each employee can design his or her own workstation to more efficiently and effectively accomplish the tasks. This, according to Mr. Green, helps employees to be more interested in their work and more productive.

Involvement in day-to-day operations by employees is visible not only in the way they organize their workstations, but also in their suggestions for product improvements, inventory control management, and the configuration of warehouses for more efficient distribution. Even if the employees are empowered on some levels, they are not empowered on other levels. Their input into corporate decision making is not noticeable. In a discussion with Mr. Green, he pointed out that in recent years he has tried to include his sales and marketing personnel in corporate decision making, but it is not working as he would like. He is still the primary decision maker.

There are apparent signs that Mr. Green's role as the key decision maker is changing. For example, his marketing director is allowed to introduce new product ideas that would complement BHU's current product lines. If, as a team, they decide that the new product would contribute to BHU's bottom line, they will start manufacturing the new product. Also, his son, who has an MBA from a major university, is taking over the finances, and may in the future assume a major part in the decision-making process.

BHU is a typical owner-managed family business that has been innovative and competitive in relatively specialized markets. Its centralized decision-making propensities tend to limit its view of the future. Many of the decisions are made without substantial input from marketing research or publicly available formal sources of information. Personal knowledge and direct feedback from customers tend to determine the potential market opportunities. According to Mr. Green, BHU does not systematically and regularly plan for such activities as new products, new markets, or diversification into other businesses.

Initial Markets

The shroud of gloom and doom that hangs over the U.S. economy has not completely lifted yet, but BHU executives have realized that now is not the time to complain. Mr. Green considers these challenges as a new opportunity to make changes and become smarter in order to prevent an undercurrent that could drown his business. Both horticultural and biotechnological market conditions are favorable for BHU. About 80% of its combined retail and commercial sales revenue is derived from domestic sales, and the rest is from international sales. Retail sales are strongest on the U.S. coasts, but commercial sales are nationally dispersed with heavy concentrations in California, New York, Michigan, and Texas. Its international sales revenue is high in Canada and the Netherlands. The sales revenue is high in Canada primarily due to the location of its sales office, and in the Netherlands because of its distributor and warehousing operations.

BHU is also an active Wisconsin exporter. It exports aggressively to China, Ecuador, Israel, Germany and, in various amounts, to the rest of Europe and South America. The value of its exports has increased over the years. According to Mr. Green, BHU initiated exports to Canada in the 1950s, followed by exports to Germany in the 1960s. Steady expansion has followed since then.

While globalization is a direct threat to BHU, it could become an asset. BHU outsources the production of much of its equipment overseas, as do many industries. Today, BHU is an active importer of supplies for its manufacturing from countries such as Switzerland, Taiwan, and Japan. It has developed strategic relationships to bring in lower-cost products and to pass savings on to its customers.

Mr. Green believes that domestic sales are more profitable than international sales. In his opinion, exporting involves extra costs due to, among other factors, market research, adaptation of products to local regulations, and transport costs. These extra costs are one reason BHU earns more profit from its domestic sales than from exports. Although the international activities are rather substantial for a smaller manufacturing company that employs approximately 50 employees and generates about US$13 million annually, he suggests that the sales revenue derived from its international sales activities contributes positively to its corporate growth, investment, and security of its markets. He also believes that international sales contribute only marginally to the U.S. economy. During the discussion with Mr. Green, it was pointed out that at least some of the 50 employees make products destined for foreign markets. At that point, he agreed that BHU's exports partly secure his workers employment.

Export Obstacles

Even though BHU has been exporting for many years, it has not yet encountered any major obstacles in its exporting operations, and it is not aware of any problems with other international operations. With its development of biotechnology-based products, BHU currently faces certification obstacles from the U.S. Department of Agriculture concerning the content of its products relating to mad cow disease. This certification process, however, is not directly related to obstacles concerning the exporting process.

World markets are diverse, dynamic, and competitive. To successfully export its products, BHU should systematically examine foreign markets through research. It is apparent that BHU pays a great deal of attention to its international operations. Nevertheless, many of the international product and market opportunities somehow emerge spontaneously. They are not subject to systematic assessment processes, nor are they part of a well-developed growth strategy. Although this type of selling is valuable, the company may discover even more promising markets by conducting a systematic search. BHU does not systematically examine an array of international opportunities. However, BHU's representatives regularly attend domestic and international trade exhibitions relevant to its industries, especially in the Netherlands. Attendance at such trade exhibitions is an important part of its information-gathering procedures to keep a pulse on the markets and to maintain contact with customers. Occasionally, international trade exhibitions are also used to contact potential customers.

Future Markets

When BHU looks, rather informally, at the future and attempts to speculate about future geographic markets, it judges its market potential by key indicators in its industries. For example, in the horticultural industry, the key indicator is the growth in the number of greenhouses. Using this indicator, Mr. Green believes that, in the next 10 years, Ecuador and Saudi Arabia have the best market potential of any of the other countries. Saudis, for example, are increasing their efforts to achieve self-sufficiency in as many farm products as possible and to "turn the desert green." Greenhouse vegetable projects are expanding in most regions of the country. New irrigation and harvesting equipment as well as a growing replacement for pivot machines offer continued sales opportunities for BHU.

Systematic Exploration of International Business Opportunities

BHU operates in two very important and environmentally sensitive industries. Both of its product lines — horticultural equipment and biotechnological products — are, to a great extent, part of environmental concerns and may contribute to global warming. Mr. Green emphasizes that his company is environmentally conscious and, in fact, indirectly contributes to the reduction of global warming. BHU has gained a competitive advantage and created a sustainable business by adopting good environmental practices. For example, many greenhouse operations would score poorly in terms of energy and water consumption. BHU can help growers reduce their waste. It also helps growers capitalize on the interest in organic and locally grown produce. It is trying to make the green industry as green as it can be. Growers have the desire to reduce their carbon footprint; they just need to be shown how it can be done cost-effectively.

This conviction is clearly presented in an official statement on the company's website, where its environmental concerns are interpreted in the context of sustainability. It states, "It is trendy, now, to be sustainable. Companies market their sustainability and consumers look for sustainable products." It further maintains that "sustainability has been a way of doing business since our founding." For a smaller manufacturing family business, the sustainability philosophy expresses a particular perspective about its domestic as well as its international business. The following is a direct quote taken from BHU's website regarding its statement about sustainability:

> ... We have always thought of it (sustainability) more as simple frugality and basic environmental stewardship. It is central to our business model to offer products that reduce waste for our customers. At the same time, we have always looked for ways to manufacture and package these products in ways that are responsible, not only to the environment, but to our bottom line and to the bottom line of our customers. Excessive packaging or poor manufacturing methods only cost more for both [BHU] and the consumer.
>
> We at [BHU] pride ourselves on the ability to produce world class products that are durable and functional while keeping the input costs reasonable. If a watering tool purchased by a consumer breaks within months, it is thrown away, wasting these materials and filling a landfill. [BHU] produces tools to last.
>
> When packing products, we seek to use as little material as possible while still protecting our product through shipment and sale. Since our early days, [BHU] has used recycled newspaper as packing materials. Often brought from homes of our employees, this offers us a low cost, frugal way to ensure our products arrive safely at their destinations. Boxes for many items are reused from shipments we have received. Finally, when we purchase boxes for packaging, they contain at least 85% post-consumer waste.
>
> When merchandising our products for retail, we offer little or no packaging, saving expenses and materials. Instead, we utilize durable, reusable displays, maximizing the space needed to merchandise while still making an attractive, informative presentation.
>
> From a product standpoint, we have always offered tools for growers and gardeners designed to make work easier and to reduce waste. The original nozzle was born out of the need to water plants more efficiently in greenhouse operations. Every product since then has had the same goal: to increase efficiency and reduce waste.

This philosophy regarding sustainability is unique. BHU believes that, over the 60 years of its existence, this business model has helped it to succeed and be "right for both of us and our customer base." The sustainability statement goes on to state, "Going forward we accept the increasing demands on society to change practices for the benefit of the environment and future generations. We will continue to look for ways to improve both our products and our processes to meet these challenges." At the end of its statement, BHU welcomes any comments from its worldwide customer base on ways to improve its products and procedures "for the betterment of the industry we serve and the environment as a whole", as stated on the company website.

Family involvement has always been an integral part of the company's growth and success, and is still a vital ingredient today. Throughout the history of the company, both Kenneth and Peter Green's children have had roles in BHU. The company has moved from a basement operation to a multi-million dollar global corporation. This past decade has witnessed explosive growth. Combined with the firm footings of a strong family heritage, Kenneth Green expects his company to survive and thrive even after he passes the company to his children. He says that his company is prepared and confident to prosper in the 21st century.

For BHU to remain successful, however, it needs to continue its product quality improvements, genuinely understand what is important to its customers in the context of the current economic environment, and identify the areas in which it wants to excel. Once identified, all of the company's resources must be marshaled consistently to deliver its core-value messages. BHU must treat this as an ongoing process, and needs to constantly re-evaluate and reinvent itself as the markets in which it operates change. Mr. Green realizes that this is not going to be easy, and in today's environment it is tougher than ever. But the history of the company shows that it knows how to manage its businesses both financially and operationally. It also knows what is important to its customers, and focuses on exceeding or at least meeting their expectations.

Summary

BHU is a successful family-owned and family-operated smaller manufacturing enterprise that employs approximately 50 employees.

Located in a rural part of Wisconsin, it operates a profitable business consisting of mostly domestic sales, but it also carries out both exporting and foreign-based sales and distribution operations. BHU operates in two industries and two markets: one traditional market, the horticultural market; and another very modern market, the biotechnological market. Although the traditional market provides the business base, the new modern market offers growth and expansion. Yet, the owner-manager in his decision-making framework emphasizes the traditional market as the one that is more important.

Over the period that BHU has been studied, it has been viewed as a steady exporter and market innovator. Over the years, it has supplemented its exporting operations with sales and distribution activities abroad, intensifying its internationalization efforts. It has consistently felt financially adequate and views itself as having unique products. Although it does not see itself as a very innovative company, it has diversified into a new and significant technology — biotechnology.

Even after this significantly long time period, BHU still considers itself a family business, managed by an owner-manager, with a strong market base responding to increasing growth and competition, especially in the horticultural industry. While there appears to be input from the family members concerning some of the growth and diversification issues faced by BHU, the owner-manager remains the main decision maker.

The main characteristics of BHU are as follows: (1) an owner-manager-operated family business; (2) ownership of innovative products with unique applications; (3) operating successfully in domestic and international markets; and (4) positioned for dynamic growth in a new industry.

10.3 Outdoor Advertising Company

Company Background

Outdoor Advertising Company (OAC) is a manufacturer and installer of a variety of outdoor signs, ranging from large neon signs to store signs and banners. OAC is a privately held company operating from three Wisconsin locations. All three locations are in a relatively industrialized part of Wisconsin with a wide customer base. The company was established in 1935 in the original location, when the use of neon sign technology was emerging and outdoor advertising was in vogue. The company's focus on neon sign technology was reflected in the original name of the company; however, additional sign-making options were added over time in OAC's efforts to diversify and establish a strong competitive base in the sign-making industry. In 1998, the present owners, Tom and Mary Day, purchased the original company; and two years later, they purchased an additional sign-making business and opened an office in the second location.

The background of OAC and its owners is somewhat complex and interesting. Tom and Mary Day purchased a franchise in 1984, specializing in providing signs for automotive dealers and restaurants, from a well-known sign franchisor. Their operation soon became one of the top 10 in the U.S. In 1992, they sold their franchise and started their own graphics and sign company. The business grew rapidly, mostly due to good management practices and well-trained employees. Given their strong customer focus, their customer base expanded and made it possible to diversify even further. In 1998, they purchased the original neon sign business from its owner and the two entities merged. In 2000, OAC purchased another outdoor sign business, one of its competitors. The three companies were consolidated and OAC emerged as a strong competitor in the Wisconsin outdoor sign market.

An additional expansion came in 2006 when OAC purchased another outdoor sign company in the largest industrial city in Wisconsin. In 2008, with the growth of its customer base for both products and services, and as a part of its territorial expansion, OAC relocated from its most recent location to a new location north of the major industrial city in Wisconsin, where it maintains additional facilities for its sales representatives in order to provide better and faster service for its customers. OAC believes that its competitive edge is based on the fact that it is the only sign manufacturer in Wisconsin whose award-winning designers have university degrees in graphic arts. In addition, OAC is active professionally in various industry associations and community organizations. Currently, the company employs 26 employees in three locations with annual sales of US$2.5 million.

OAC is a company with an interesting mission and slogan. Its mission statement declares, "Our mission is to work together and value one another as partners for the purpose of designing and producing a product and service that exceed our customers' expectations." This mission statement is supplemented with the following slogan: "Your Identity Professionals." Both of these statements are prominently displayed on the company's website.

Products

OAC is primarily in business to manufacture, install, service, and maintain outdoor signs such as neon light signs. The neon sign was first created in France in 1910. After this initial model, the neon sign went on to become extremely useful and advertising companies began competing with one another with regard to their creativity, design, and presentation. Neon-lit signs are now considered a very effective form of advertisement, as they usually attract immediate attention and have a wonderful impact on customers and travelers.

OAC has a dedicated design team that works closely with clients in designing the final product. As a manufacturer, OAC has over 30 years of experience in fabricating all types of outdoor signs using state-of-the-art technology and environmental precautions. Much of the fabrication process is computer-driven. Its installation business is performed by highly trained, skilled specialists. Because most outdoor signs have electrical components, installation services must comply with appropriate laws and regulations and need to be approved by reputable electrical appliance testing laboratories such as Underwriters Laboratories (UL) or Underwriters Laboratories of Canada (ULC). The service and maintenance business is subject to municipal and state laws and regulations, and requires service and installation permits. OAC can secure these permits for its customers.

Focus

Although OAC is a relatively small company generating about US$5 million in annual sales volume with a total investment between US$2 million and US$2.5 million, Tom Day believes that his company is managed professionally and rationally. He does not perceive himself as a salesman or a craftsman manager, but more as a rational manager. His objective is to systematically grow the company and remain competitive. For example, in the past OAC fabricated all of its products, and this was one of its competitive advantages. As the business became more cost-sensitive, however, he needed to rationalize its overall cost structure. The only alternative was to subcontract some of the fabrications and installations.

Competitive Advantage

Tom Day suggests that one of OAC's competitive advantages is its flexibility to reinvent itself. Without this flexibility, he believes that his company could not survive. Mr. Day also believes that another competitive advantage is that the jobs get done to the satisfaction of customers. This requires high product standards and superior service. Mr. Day perceives his company to be the dominant competitor in the outdoor sign business in Wisconsin.

Importance

During the interview, Mr. Day suggested that his original operational philosophy was to sacrifice short-term profits for the sake of long-term growth. Under the current circumstances, that is no longer possible. Today, profit is more important. His new business model suggests a more rational selection of financially stronger customers. He points out that some of his accounts receivable are due over 90 days. He also points to customer loyalty and complains that customers today are not as loyal as they were in the past. Competition in the industry is increasing — even Chinese competitors are entering the Wisconsin market at less than competitive prices.

Impact of Current Economic Conditions

The current state of the economy has impacted OAC greatly. The company recently made redundant 20 employees from its manufacturing facilities. A decision was made to subcontract about 10% of its sales volume. As a countermeasure, OAC plans to hire two sales persons in order to increase sales. Although attempts are being made to increase sales, the general tendency of the market for outdoor advertising points to a sales decline over the next two-year period or longer.

Two major obstacles in Mr. Day's overall business model are increasing insurance costs and taxes. He calculates that the insurance premium he pays for workers' compensation, health, liability, and unemployment accounts for 10% of his sales volume. He also has a problem with taxes, especially sales tax. According to Mr. Day, he has to pay sales tax as soon as he sells the product, regardless of whether or not he eventually collects the money from the customer. Since his recent accounts receivable have increased substantially, the sales tax obligations have become a burden to his small business.

Future of the Company

What will be the future of OAC? What will the next five years bring for OAC? Mr. Day hopes that his company will generate additional profitable sales. He has purchased a new computer program that gives him more flexibility in pricing products and services. This allows him to control costs more effectively. This might only be a partial solution to his problems, though, since the entire market for outdoor advertising is stagnating. Additional steps may need to be taken to stabilize the business in the short term and grow the business in the long term.

Systematic Decision-Making Process

Mr. Day is the top decision maker in the company. His responsibilities include not only decisions concerning the strategic direction of the company, but also decisions concerning new products and sales strategies. At the same time, he is trying to change the culture within the company and involve others in his decision-making process. An example of this effort is his attempt to introduce strategic planning into the overall management process by organizing a strategic planning team. One recent issue considered by the team was a decision on whether OAC ought to remain a manufacturer of neon lights or update its technology and introduce signs containing light-emitting diodes (LEDs). The decision was necessary because OAC is not able to manufacture LED lights in signs, but needs to purchase LED lights from other manufacturers. The decision was made to purchase LED lights from suppliers and offer them in its products. This was a good decision that is beneficial for OAC's future competitiveness.

Changes in corporate culture as well as the introduction of new technology require not only decisions concerning financial and human resources, but also major shifts in the decision-making process. Empowering lower-level managers to make decisions in smaller companies such as OAC requires supervision and open channels of communication. In addition, the primary decision maker, frequently the owner-manager as in this case, needs to open the company records, including policy and strategy statements, and provide the necessary inputs for lower-level managers so that they have the necessary information on which to base their decisions. This change in corporate culture represented by decision-making empowerment is frequently threatening to the owner-manager. Consequently, the owner-manager finds it difficult to let go of the responsibility to make decisions.

The introduction of new technology often requires that the owner-manager hires a specialist who understands the technology and can guide its integration into corporate products and services. The new technology may be too complex for the primary decision maker to understand and requires interpretation. In fact, the owner-manager may lose control by not understanding the new technology being integrated and may be reluctant to accept it. Strategic planning teams in smaller manufacturing enterprises may frequently serve as sources of interpretive knowledge for the owner-manager; but the ultimate decision concerning the acceptance of new technology still lies with the owner-manager, not with the strategic planning team.

Initial Markets

OAC serves a geographically homogeneous market. Approximately 80% of the sales volume comes from an approximately 50-mile radius of its primary location. The rest of the sales volume is generated from a variety of geographic market segments. The surrounding states also provide market opportunities. OAC has also exported products to Canada. These sales were to Canadian subsidiaries of American firms such as PDQ and Burger King. Exports to Canada were very disappointing for Mr. Day, as the banks charged him too much for conversion fees from Canadian to U.S. dollars, thus reducing his profit on the export orders. Mr. Day did not initiate these orders in the first place; he was contacted by the American companies on behalf of their Canadian franchises. Perhaps one reason for Tom's disappointment with the Canadian experience was his lack of company policy to evaluate international business opportunities.

Export Obstacles

Chinese competitors are not the only problem for outdoor sign companies such as OAC. There are also environmental issues. Many municipalities, state and federal governments, and even countries are enacting restrictive laws concerning outdoor advertising. Light and sound environmental pollution, especially in big cities, is becoming a concern to environmental advocates. Safety issues concerning inattentive driving, obscured vision, or lack of ambient visibility are frequently cited by police departments as causes of accidents. Energy conservationists question the social value of energy-consuming outdoor signs. The combination of these issues and concerns may, in the future, dramatically change the outdoor sign business. Companies such as OAC need to be aware of these developments and integrate them into their future business models.

Future Markets

For many smaller manufacturing companies such as OAC, international business remains an unsolved puzzle. The primary decision makers are not certain how to benefit from international opportunities; they speculate about the profitability of international sales and frequently do not follow up on international orders. Mr. Day indicated in his interview that, on two Canadian orders, he charged the same price as he would charge domestic customers. Since OAC has only filled two foreign orders, it is difficult to speculate as to what impact international business would have on its sales and profitability, and in turn what impact international business would have on the U.S. economy.

As a business owner, Mr. Day is not very happy that the U.S. economy has shifted from a manufacturing economy to a service economy. In his opinion, this shift provided the initiative for increased competition from foreign suppliers, especially the Chinese. He finds it difficult to compete with Chinese suppliers. In his opinion, the only reason why he remains competitive is the superior quality of his products and services. He adds that many of his customers do not recognize competitive issues related to product quality and service. He fears that he may lose more business in the future to his Chinese competitors.

Systematic Exploration of International Business Opportunities

Policies for new product development, market growth, or internationalization are frequently problematic for smaller manufacturing companies and often non-existent. Since their current businesses are viable and growing, there is no need to plan for the future. The assumption is that the business will continue to be viable and grow, as is the case with OAC. The primary decision maker will be faced with strategic decisions only when there is a market option or competitive challenge. One response to such decisions is the formation of a strategic planning team, as occurred with the technological change from neon to LED lights for OAC.

In addition to all of these developments, Mr. Day believes that he cannot compete with foreign manufacturers, especially those from Asia. He simply cannot produce products at the same price levels. Even though OAC does not systematically examine foreign opportunities, Mr. Day understands that foreign competitors are the main reason why OAC will not be able to export its products in the future. Today, quality products and services are not necessarily the critical variables in international business; rather, price is the most important factor. This is a difficult lesson for small manufacturing companies such as OAC to learn.

Summary

OAC is characteristic of a smaller manufacturing company operated by an owner-manager who is completely in charge of its entire strategic as well as day-to-day operations. Although he attempts to delegate decisions and empower employees in his management style, he is still in charge. In this particular case, the owner and the owner-manager, who manages the business, were able to purchase and consolidate several businesses into one in order to become more efficient and effective competitors in a geographically defined market. However, external issues such as international competition, environmental concerns, and economic downturns ultimately hindered the company's market position and expected growth.

Although the owner-manager perceives himself as a rational manager, his management style does not reflect this perception. The company does not plan for future products or markets, does not consider international opportunities, and is not willing to face foreign competition. In fact, the same foreign competition has forced the owner-manager to reduce the size of his workforce and subcontract portions of his fabrication business. For some smaller manufacturing companies, these are clear signs that competitive, market, and/or technological changes are coming.

10.4 Packaging Container Services

Company Background

Packaging Container Services (PCS) is an established, privately held packaging container company located in the largest industrial city in Wisconsin. It offers both products and services to a variety of customers. According to Mike Smith, the current owner, the original company was established in 1974. It consists of 12 employees, generates slightly over US$3 million in sales volume annually, and values its assets at around US$0.5 million.

Mr. Smith purchased the firm in 1984 and moved it to its present location. He is now semi-retired and lives part of the time in Florida. Although semi-retired, he is still involved with his firm and its customers. He has over 40 years of experience in the container industry, and has been the current owner and president of PCS for over 20 years. Mr. Smith believes in his management team and is an avid supporter of his sales team. He also considers his employees his friends; he points out that they encourage him to develop new ideas to grow the firm for the benefit of all.

When Mr. Smith is in Florida, the firm is managed by John Black, the general manager. Mr. Black has been working for the company for about 10 years and has over 30 years of industry experience. The additional members of top management include Steve Wood, the sales team leader (sales manager), and Jim Long, the customer service representative (manager of customer service). There is an understanding among Mike Smith, John Black, and Steve Wood that, when Mr. Smith fully retires, the other two will take over the company. As general manager, Mr. Black directs all plant, office, and sales functions. He is a strong team player. Mr. Wood manages the sales team and has been with PCS for close to 20 years, which is as long as he has been in the industry. As sales team leader, he is responsible for the entire sales effort, including coordinating field sales and designing the packaging container. He believes that PCS stands for excellent quality and practices a responsible attitude to problem solving. Jim Long, who is responsible for customer service, has over 30 years of industry experience and has been with PCS for over three years. His responsibilities include entering orders, quoting, and purchasing, and he is in direct contact with customers.

Products

PCS primarily services the automotive aftermarket, manufacturers of medical equipment, and manufacturers of pest control equipment. Several packaging container case histories taken from these industries are displayed on PCS's website. PCS also services other clients in a number of industries in Wisconsin. PCS's products are tested by industry associations such as the International Safe Transit Association (ISTA), and its packaging complies with the U.S. government HAZMAT standards concerning the transport of hazardous materials. Also, all of its products are tested for compression and edge crushing. The results of these tests are made available to customers. The main focus of the company, according to Mr. Black, is on customer service, order fulfillment, and product safety.

Focus

As general manager, John Black is PCS's principal decision maker. During our interview, Mr. Black indicated that ultimately he runs a lean manufacturing process. In order to be able to manage a lean manufacturing operation, he needs to cut overhead wherever possible. He subcontracts a portion of production to a local contractor, who provides him with additional production flexibility. The subcontractor employs skilled and knowledgeable workers, and supplements PCS's quality requirement. Subcontracting as a tool is viewed by Mr. Black as a very positive experience: it significantly reduces PCS's labor and health care costs, and keeps it competitive.

Mr. Black also believes that, as general manager, he manages the company in a logical and rational manner. In spite of its small size, he believes that PCS is creative and innovative in keeping its customers satisfied. PCS delivers orders on time. Most of its customers demand delivery within 24 hours, and he makes certain that they receive their orders in that time period. In other words, as general manager, Mr. Black assists in expediting orders. Both he and Mr. Smith believe that PCS ought to treat its customers the same way they themselves expect to be treated. Mr. Black also suggests that PCS expects its suppliers to ship orders in a timely fashion.

When PCS participates in a value chain, it attempts to improve the value chain's performance as much as it can and frequently serves as a packaging container consultant within the value chain. Two years ago, PCS purchased new software that allows its regular customers to log into PCS's computer, check its inventory of required material, place an order, and arrange for shipping. Even occasional customers can place custom orders and PCS will fill the order within 24 hours. These experiences suggest that PCS's services are more important than the actual products that it custom designs and produces for its customers and clients.

Competitive Advantage

The product container industry is highly competitive. Mr. Black believes that PCS's competitive advantage is the speed with which it responds to any customer's request. Office employees are trained to respond to any telephone call; telephone calls ought not to be left unanswered. Customers can reach Mr. Black, Mr. Wood, or any other sales person directly to request price quotes or information. Price quotes are typically expedited within two hours. This strategy is in contrast to PCS's closest competitor, who takes three days to prepare a price quote. According to Mr. Black, since most of PCS's customers expect 24-hour delivery, they will not wait three days for a price quote. Also, due to the present state of the economy, most customers are not willing to place large orders. PCS is willing to accept smaller orders than its competitors which, according to Mr. Black, gives PCS an additional competitive edge.

Another competitive advantage appears to be the flexibility of PCS's employees. Every employee has been trained to operate every piece of machinery and is willing to perform every operation neces- sary to complete an order, even if it is not in the employee's job description. As an example, Mr. Black pointed out that sometimes he even cleans the factory floor. Employee flexibility is considered an important competitive asset for PCS.

Impact of Current Economic Conditions

Even though the future of the economy is uncertain, Mr. Black and Mr. Wood will own the company in five years. During the interview, Mr. Black was not very optimistic about the future of PCS: "It all depends on the general economic recovery." PCS may grow slowly at first, but recover over time. According to Mr. Black, several competitors have already gone bankrupt. He pointed out that the biggest packaging container company in the U.S. with several plants in Wisconsin, including one close by, has filed for Chapter 11 bankruptcy. Furthermore, due to the current downturn in the economy, many larger customers are placing smaller orders for packaging containers. This trend is not economical for PCS's larger competitors but, he believes, is good for PCS.

Future of the Company

Mr. Black believes that PCS is well positioned to grow. It is willing to sacrifice short-term profitability for the sake of long-term growth. He indicated during the interview that, on several occasions, he has foregone profit on an order because he knew that the customer also had several large orders that could potentially generate additional profit. He also believes that by reducing his fixed costs by outsourcing, PCS can grow and compete more effectively.

Over the last two years, PCS has been able to raise its prices twice. The price increases did not result in any reduction in the number of orders. However, Mr. Black indicated that, in meetings with his customers, most have mentioned a 10–20% drop in sales during the recent economic downturn. He expects some decrease in PCS's sales revenue. Nevertheless, he expects that PCS will recover after the current economic downturn. He did not want to speculate as to how quickly the economy will recover.

Systematic Decision-Making Process

In spite of the somewhat pessimistic outlook, Mr. Black suggested during the interview that PCS has a systematic decision-making process for the identification and introduction of new opportunities. Every Wednesday, Mr. Black, Mr. Wood, and the sales force meet to discuss current and future market opportunities. Every potential customer is identified and contacted. The new sales software allows sales personnel to screen potential customers in each sales territory. Each potential customer is contacted either by the sales manager (Mr. Wood) directly or by one of the sales personnel.

Initial Markets

PCS's market is geographically defined. It is spread over a 100-mile radius. PCS has never exported any products abroad. It services several foreign customers who need PCS's services for their Wisconsin subsidiaries. Presently, PCS is negotiating with a broker from Georgia who is trying to purchase products for a foreign customer who operates a subsidiary in Wisconsin. During the interview, Mr. Black emphasized that PCS has not exported its products outside of the U.S. Although PCS is willing to sell products to foreign customers with subsidiaries in Wisconsin, it does not have any specific policy to evaluate international opportunities.

The purchase of the new sales software was also meant to help with the planning of new products and markets. Aside from the sales software, however, PCS does not have a formal planning process for new products or markets. Moreover, the sales software does not help PCS plan for the exploration and development of international opportunities.

Mr. Black believes that domestic sales are more profitable than international sales. His belief is based on several "cut-throat pricing" experiences among international customers. In addition, foreign customers cannot be trusted as long-term customers. Mr. Black points out that, as soon as foreign customers find another packaging container company that offers them a slightly cheaper price (even at lower quality), they change suppliers. Consequently, PCS would rather develop long-term relationships with reliable domestic customers. Quoting on tenders (bids) from large multinational corporations is perceived as the biggest obstacle for PCS.

Export Obstacles

From an international perspective, Mr. Black points out that the current economic recession, or "depression" as he calls it, will potentially impact PCS's business. Several of PCS's customers, especially in the health care industry, have significant international businesses. As the demand for their products will decline, he expects that the demand for PCS's products and services will also decline.

Packaging container companies serve a special niche in the value chain. Their products and services are essential in making certain that manufactured consumer products arrive safely and undamaged. They frequently have to engineer for their customers the containers (packages) in which the finished products are shipped. This combination of engineering services and fabricated products makes the packaging container industry extremely competitive. Membership in supply chains, or in entire value chains, may depend on the ability of packaging container suppliers such as PCS to cut overhead, develop new technologies, and find less expensive and more durable materials. In reality, packaging container companies must be flexible, knowledge-based innovators and agile competitors. They must constantly look into the future and anticipate what the value chain and its members will need to serve the ultimate consumer or business-to-business customer. Smaller packaging container companies lack both the flexible knowledge base and competitive agility.

One of the major deficiencies of smaller packaging container companies is their inability to anticipate the development and growth of future markets. Packaging container technology is changing rapidly. Environmental forces are placing heavy burdens on packaging containers. Users are demanding a lower weight of packaging containers to reduce the cost of shipping; environmentalists demand that recyclable and biodegradable material is used in shipping; and municipalities legislate less waste and more recycling. All of these requirements point to new challenges and options for the packaging container industry. The entire industry, along with its individual members, needs to look into the future and think about new packaging container solutions. In order to remain competitive, the individual firms need to examine every option, including international markets. Future markets for the packaging container industry will be a combination of domestic and international markets.

Future Markets

PCS does not export, but is involved to some degree in international operations. It does not plan for future markets either. Its future intentions are toward what Mr. Black calls "fulfillment work", in which PCS not only makes the packaging containers (boxes) but also packages and ships the products on behalf of its customers. Customers send their products to a fulfillment expeditor and the expeditor handles the entire shipping process, including the documentation. PCS suggests that this would provide additional value-added business with little additional fixed costs and without dramatically changing its core strategy.

Systematic Exploration of International Business Opportunities

Although fulfillment work opportunities are increasing both domestically and internationally, it is difficult for smaller packaging container companies to take advantage of these opportunities. Depending on the characteristics and physical configuration of both consumer and business-to-business products, major processing adjustments typically need to be made by a fulfillment expeditor. These adjustments include modification of existing production lines, retraining of employees, and investment in specialized equipment. A small packaging container company such as PCS may find it difficult to make the transition from offering packaging container products and services to becoming a fulfillment expeditor.

Summary

PCS is a typical small product and service company located in a large industrial city in Wisconsin. Its top management believes in logical and rational decision making, combined with a strong customer focus. The strong customer focus in PCS is driven by its customers and their need for fast service. Customers have direct access to the management team and sales personnel. In order to expedite orders faster, individual employees are trained to perform all necessary production operations within the plant.

A willingness to sacrifice short-term profit for the sake of long-term growth is one of the outstanding features of PCS. This philosophy is reflected in its order-taking and pricing practices. At the same time, PCS is attempting to reduce its fixed costs by subcontracting some of its operations.

The current owner/president of PCS is expected to retire in a few years, and the business will then be owned by the present general manager and the sales manager. This change is expected to have a minimal impact on the future of PCS, since the current general manager already manages the company, develops its strategy, and, with his entire team, identifies future opportunities. Systematic decision making is embedded in the general manager's day-to-day management style; meetings are scheduled regularly and sales opportunities are discussed.

PCS is not an internationally positioned company; rather, it exports indirectly through Wisconsin subsidiaries of foreign-based customers. The entire international environment seems to be perceived as a burden rather than a field of opportunities. If PCS does make the transition from a strictly domestic and regional product and service company to a viable player in the field of international business, it will most likely depend on the competitive nature of its customers.

10.5 PJ Manufacturing Inc.

Company Background

PJ Manufacturing Inc. was established in 1919 in Southern Wisconsin as PJ Machine Company. Initially, it provided counting machines for movie projectors to keep track of the amount of film that had run. However, in the early 1950s the company was inherited by Mr. W.P. Schneider, who started cutting gears and changed its name to PJ Manufacturing Inc. Mr. Schneider moved the company into its existing facility in 1960. In 1962, Mr. Schneider decided to retire and sold his company to two brothers from the Milwaukee area, John and Michael Johnson.

The Johnson brothers were not very active in managing their company. They hired managers to run their business. Sales were flat for the first couple of years, but the company gradually became more efficient and profitable. Then, sales started to grow and profits were reinvested in the company. Additions to the company's facility were made in 1973, 1979, 1984, 1990, and 1995. The facility has grown from 15,000 square feet to 68,000 square feet, and investment in new, modern machinery has been continued on an annual basis.

Since 1962, whether in good or bad economic conditions, employees of PJ Manufacturing have had steady work. There have been no layoffs and no short hours. As a result, the company has succeeded in maintaining a seasoned and loyal workforce. In fact, the employees disassociated themselves from their union in the early 1990s and the union withdrew in 1994. However, in 1991 the family patriarch, John Johnson, sold his half of the company to his younger brother, Michael, and his two sons, Karl and Ethan. Later, Michael Johnson also sold his shares to his sons.

Products

Today, PJ Manufacturing produces gear shafts and blanks in its state-of-the-art facility. It also provides an extensive range of services such as assembly, gear grinding, machining, gear shaping, gear shaving, thread milling, and thread grinding. PJ Manufacturing gears can be cut from many kinds of materials, including ferrous and non-ferrous metals as well as plastics, nylon, and Bakelite, among others. It also produces gears from customer-supplied materials. In addition, PJ Manufacturing's Inspection Department utilizes quality control methods to ensure uniform compliance with customers' specifications.

PJ Manufacturing has made its utmost effort to meet the gear requirements of a wide range of industries: medical, agricultural, construction, oil, printing, and recreational, to name a few. Applications of its gears include electric motors and controls, pumps, snow throwers, winches and gearboxes, hoists and jacks, outboard motors, machine tools, speed reducers, and many more. Other capabilities at PJ Manufacturing include an engineering advisory service for customers' gear problems, an experimental department for customers' gear development, and on-time delivery assured by in-house production control.

Focus

Mr. Karl Johnson, who manages the company today, considers PJ Manufacturing as a job shop that focuses on the production of high-quality short and long run gears, custom gearboxes, and gear assemblies that meet or exceed customer requirements. He stressed in his interview that "we understand and share our customers' commitment to quality. Our standards exceed the norm; that's why we inspect the parts we manufacture using the most sophisticated equipments available. Our computer numerical control (CNC) gear inspection capability assures compliance with customers' specifications." PJ Manufacturing considers sales and marketing as secondary, as its customers approach the company with requests.

Competitive Advantage

PJ Manufacturing aims to be the vendor that is the easiest with which to do business. Any time customers call during business hours, their calls will be answered by a real person who will direct them to the proper party. If a customer's call requires it, senior management is either immediately available or will call back promptly. According to Karl Johnson, customers do not need to go through different layers of management in order to get to him. He believes this gives the company a competitive advantage compared to its bigger competitors. Also, the quality of its products is far superior to that of competitors; and any business that it has lost due to lower bids by other firms has come back shortly, as customers realized they get much better quality for their money from PJ Manufacturing.

Importance

The primary goal of the company is profit maximization. PJ Manufacturing is unwilling to sacrifice profit for sales growth or for any other reason. Regardless of the long-term profitability of a contract, the company will not accept it if it is not profitable in the short term. Karl Johnson believes that the company is working at full capacity for the long term and does not foresee a lot of slowdown in the near or long term, and therefore does not believe he should sacrifice short-term profitability for the sake of growth.

Impact of Current Economic Conditions

Economic growth in the U.S. has slowed down dramatically in the last two years. However, this slowdown varies by industry and by economic sector. The adverse conditions experienced in the manufacturing sector in the second half of 2008 were expected to continue in 2009. On the other hand, the non-manufacturing sector foresaw marginal growth during the same period. While the U.S. economy may have been experiencing its worst economic downturn since World War Two, Karl Johnson predicted a good year in 2009 for his business. In 2008, PJ Manufacturing achieved its best year ever in terms of sales (US$11.6 million), but not its best year for profit.

Contrary to the general trend in the manufacturing sector, PJ Manufacturing has been working overtime to meet customer demand. Currently, the company employs about 70 workers. Although the company has not terminated any employees, it has recently lowered the number of hours worked from 60–65 hours per week to 50–55 hours per week. Currently, PJ Manufacturing is not hiring any new employees to expand its operations, but if it needs to replace a retired or departed employee it would consider hiring for replacement purposes only. Karl Johnson actually believes that now is the time to spend money on training and marketing. He stresses that business owners are reading news headlines claiming doom and gloom on a daily basis and, understandably, their natural reaction is to tighten their belts and prepare for the worst. But if the majority of businesses are cutting back on training and marketing, then logically the few who train their staff and market their products and services effectively will grow their market share and profit.

Karl Johnson acknowledges that the biggest challenge manufacturing firms such as PJ Manufacturing face over the long term — beyond the current recession — is not how to bring manufacturing jobs back, but rather how to improve the earnings of America's expanding army of low-wage workers who are doing personal service jobs in hotels, hospitals, retail stores, restaurants, and all other businesses that need bodies but not high skills. According to him, it is very beneficial for the U.S. economy to replace its low-wage manual labor jobs with higher-skill, higher-tech, and higher-education-content jobs. Therefore, in order to confront these unprecedented challenges to the U.S. global economic leadership, the nation's manufacturing competitiveness needs to be strengthened.

Future of the Company

In our interview with Karl Johnson, he could not picture where his company will be in five years, but he emphasized the fact that it has not seen any slowdown in its sales yet. He also mentioned that, due to the company's well-diversified customer base, it will survive the current economic crisis. It does not have a customer who accounts for more than 9% of its total sales. He also emphasized that, in order not to depend on certain industries with a history of "cut and run" for their orders, it avoids the automobile, aerospace, and government sectors. Furthermore, he thought that the fact that the company has no debt would put it in a much better position to be around in the next five years.

According to Karl Johnson, manufacturing is the backbone of any industrialized nation. Recent worldwide advances in manufacturing technologies have brought about a metamorphosis in industry. Fast-changing technologies on the product front have created a need for an equally fast response from the manufacturing industry. In order to meet these challenges, manufacturing companies such as PJ Manufacturing must select appropriate product designs, manufacturing processes, and equipment. The selection decisions are complex, as decision making is more challenging today than ever before. Decision makers in manufacturing companies frequently face the problem of assessing a wide range of options and selecting one based on a set of conflicting criteria.

Systematic Decision-Making Process

Since PJ Manufacturing is a job shop, Karl Johnson does not think there is a need for any systematic decision making for any new product or market. However, later in the interview, he mentioned that the company is looking into other areas of business such as gear grinding, powdered metal gears, and nylon gears, which compete with its products. As a matter of fact, it has already begun producing nylon gears to make sure that it will remain competitive.

Initial Markets

PJ Manufacturing's domestic market is mainly in the Upper Midwest of the U.S. Although in recent years the company has expanded its domestic market to other parts of the country, the management is very content with PJ Manufacturing's market position. Karl Johnson emphasized that the company does not need additional growth for the sake of growth. As mentioned earlier, if any contract does not make a profit, the company will turn it down regardless of potential additional sales in the future.

Currently, PJ Manufacturing does not export to any foreign country. However, on a few occasions it has exported to Canada and China mainly on behalf of domestic customers, with very poor results. In the case of the Chinese transaction, Karl Johnson was angry as the Chinese did the reverse engineering of the part and never ordered again. In fact, the company's experience with collecting money and shipping was so bad that he does not want to consider exporting again. Karl Johnson does not believe that foreign market expansion is very critical for PJ Manufacturing. He even mentioned that one of its biggest customers has asked the company on several occasions to export parts to its foreign subsidiaries, but he has refused and has offered the customer the option of accepting the delivery of the parts in the U.S. and exporting them itself. He also thought that, in the near future, that customer may not be a big customer of PJ Manufacturing's products, since it has bought several lawn mower and snow blower makers and its orders for PJ Manufacturing parts have declined dramatically.

Export Obstacles

There have been substantial efforts by federal and state agencies throughout the U.S. to stimulate export activities of smaller companies. An increase in the exports of small firms can generate broad benefits for both the companies themselves and the general U.S. economy. Although these firms have the capacity to export, many do not fully maximize their potential gains from exporting.

One of the biggest problems faced by would-be exporters is obtaining the information necessary to enter the export market. Smaller manufacturing firms (both exporters and non-exporters) need help in locating foreign markets. Poor knowledge of potential markets hinders the export activities of both exporting and non-exporting firms. Getting concrete information on prospective foreign markets is essential before exporting can occur. Indeed, Karl Johnson acknowledged that this problem is more severe for smaller firms like PJ Manufacturing because they often lack the internal resources to research essential information. While large firms frequently have special departments geared toward gathering information and promoting their products overseas, most small firms lack the workforce or financial resources necessary to explore foreign markets.

There are other obstacles facing smaller firms which intend to enter foreign markets. For example, pricing and competition, both foreign and domestic, are consistently seen as serious obstacles to expanding exports. Karl Johnson agreed that the pricing of products is very important to PJ Manufacturing. The few times that PJ Manufacturing has attempted to export, it has invoiced its customers in U.S. dollars. Karl Johnson insisted that his company cannot afford to use any other currency because it does not have the human resources and expertise to manage the currency risk. He believes that the currency risk could easily eliminate any profit margin from the sales of his products.

Advertising and promotion in foreign markets, although not the most difficult barrier to overcome, could be another inhibiting factor. Furthermore, finding a reliable distributor who will represent the company adequately is also considered a difficult barrier to exporting. Although PJ Manufacturing has never advertised in foreign journals or promoted its products by attending foreign trade shows, Karl Johnson believes that the costs of those activities would be beyond what his company can afford.

Exporting requires certain knowledge and skills about export procedures and handling of export documentation. For PJ Manufacturing, one of the most noted obstacles to exporting is the expense, time, and paperwork required to comply with foreign and U.S. regulations. For many smaller firms which are not yet engaged in export activities, not knowing how much or what type of paperwork is required is an obstacle in itself. Besides the cost and time factors involved in complying with various regulations, the paperwork is generally viewed as intimidating and confusing. Overall, the perception of complexity in dealing with export procedures acts as an obstacle to export activity.

Cultural differences and languages are another group of obstacles facing smaller firms interested in export activities. Smaller firms fail to enter international trade due to their inability to understand foreign languages and adapt to foreign cultural and business practices. Karl Johnson showed some inquiries he received from Jordan that were written in Arabic. Since he has no knowledge of Arabic nor knew anyone who could read the inquiry, he never responded to them. This inability to communicate with foreign customers may be partly due to the strong ethnocentric orientation of some managers (which can be controlled by the firm, to some degree, by training).

Finally, financing problems, such as getting payments, honoring letters of credit, dealing with banking inefficiencies, and having inadequate capital, are potential obstacles to smaller firms exporting. Karl Johnson named several practical, everyday business problems such as getting payments, obtaining credit, and dealing with banking inefficiencies as obstacles PJ Manufacturing faced on the very few occasions that it exported. Even when it sold parts to a foreign subsidiary of one of its domestic customers, it had a hard time collecting the money, as the customer's parent company headquarters in Milwaukee refused to pay and asked PJ Manufacturing to collect directly from the subsidiary. Therefore, the main obstacle in dealing with foreign customers, in Karl Johnson's opinion, is the lack of assurance of being paid.

Future Markets

The competitive positioning of a company in the global environment must be a concern of any company's executives. Management's positive view that exporting is an attractive opportunity for increasing sales or profit is the most significant internal stimulus to initiate an export decision. Most research studies on international business agree that international activities are more risky, but they are compensated by higher profits than domestic ones. Many smaller manufacturing enterprises source their supplies in the global marketplace; few, however, return their products to the global marketplace. Managers operating these companies need to learn more about successful export operations in order to modify their operations and become more effective and efficient competitors in the global marketplace. Therefore, understanding export operations among smaller manufacturing firms — and, more specifically, understanding the differences between exporting and non-exporting manufacturers — is critical to both public policy and management perspectives.

The management at PJ Manufacturing is not convinced that engaging in export activities will help the company's long-term survivability. Also, Karl Johnson does not think that international business is necessarily more profitable. Considering that the last time the company exported it took several months to collect the money, the time spent is not worth any additional potential profit. In the past, PJ Manufacturing has had several setbacks but, in Karl Johnson's opinion, any such impact was temporary. For example, he mentioned that several times in the past it lost business to foreign competitors (as they bid lower than PJ Manufacturing for a contract), but the customer came back shortly thereafter because the quality of the parts manufactured (by Chinese competitors) was so poor. He thinks the superior quality of PJ Manufacturing's products protects it against foreign competitors.

In terms of future market penetration, PJ Manufacturing will mainly concentrate on the U.S. market. Karl Johnson is hopeful that his company can find customers outside the Upper Midwest of the U.S. He realizes that market diversification is very beneficial to his company's survival, especially in the current economic environment. Indeed, the company has started importing steel from a foreign manufacturer, although he makes sure to be invoiced in U.S. dollars. The downside of this strategy is that PJ Manufacturing's production cycle has become longer. Karl Johnson mentioned that many purchasing agents do not know how long it takes for each piece to be manufactured. He mentioned that, in some cases, it takes his company seven weeks to buy the metal from New Zealand. Many purchasing agents think the company should be able to make the completed parts in a very short period of time. When told that it is not possible, the agents are disappointed.

Today's gears are made from new materials, resulting in more durability and lower cost. Karl Johnson anticipates that future trends to lower costs while increasing quality will lead his company to use new production materials. Furthermore, the recent stringent requirements for higher precision prompt companies such as PJ Manufacturing to improve their processes such as gear grinding and honing. This has led the company to produce new gears using different materials, such as powdered metal and nylon gears.

Systematic Exploration of International Business Opportunities

In today's increasingly integrated global marketplace, the need for a systematic evaluation of international business opportunities and selection of foreign markets has become essential. Unfortunately, many smaller firms including PJ Manufacturing have not completely realized the importance of such an evaluation. PJ Manufacturing has no specific policy or process to evaluate international opportunities. Its past international business experience was so disappointing that the management of the company does not want to consider going back into the export business. When asked if PJ Manufacturing has ever sold products through freight forwarders that might have been exported, the answer was negative. Karl Johnson indicated that he always deals with the customers, as they provide the blueprint and they know the type of products for which the gears are used.

In recent years, there has been an increased emphasis on the development of a competitive position among smaller manufacturing firms. As a result, smaller manufacturing firms have changed considerably with respect to how they respond to their environmental conditions and how they react internally to their own operational preferences such as planning or not planning for new product and market development. Some smaller manufacturing firms are perceived as successful if they systematically plan for new product and market development, and are thereby assumed to reason strategically with respect to their future. Other manufacturing firms do not systematically plan for new product and market development, and find it difficult to adjust their operations to changing environmental conditions. Although they still might grow and increase their share of the market, they are less preferred by many of the organizations interested in stimulating smaller manufacturing firms' growth and competitiveness. Unfortunately, many smaller firms in the U.S. are short-term-oriented in their operational and strategic philosophy.

They tend to concentrate on their existing customers. Production backlogs are considered measures of success. In addition, smaller manufacturing firms have a tendency to perceive their own advantages as being significantly different from those of their competitors. Yet, they seldom objectively compare their perceived advantages to market realities.

Although Karl Johnson suggests the importance of continual improvement in cost, quality, and cycle time, and to this end he encourages his employees to submit their suggestions for improvement, PJ Manufacturing does very little planning for any of those activities. It is very content with its current market position. Usually, such perceptions give a firm a false sense of security and tend to reflect a level of technical and marketing expertise which frequently leads a firm to ignore its own ineffectiveness in developing and marketing products. One of the most disturbing issues in examining the operations of PJ Manufacturing is its approach to defining and setting goals. PJ Manufacturing is still reluctant to consider the importance of setting even the most fundamental goals.

Summary

Since its humble beginning as a provider of counting machines for movie projectors 90 years ago, PJ Manufacturing has turned into a world-class producer of gears for a variety of industries. The company now occupies more than 68,000 square feet under one roof in the southeastern part of Wisconsin and employs approximately 70 people. Inside its manufacturing facility, a full host of capabilities are present, including a wide range of gear-cutting capabilities, complete gear finishing, and gear grinding. According to Karl Johnson, the president of the company, "PJ Manufacturing offers very broad capabilities under one roof." In addition to standard gears (such as spur, worm, and helical), PJ Manufacturing provides custom gear design and manufacturing which are engineered for specific applications. This ability can be extremely valuable to original equipment manufacturers (OEMs) by eliminating the need to devote their resources and time on in-house design, or to spend money for design consultation and assembly of a complete unit. Instead, OEMs can focus their efforts on the end machine as a whole, rather than on one specific component.

Even as PJ Manufacturing expands its production focus to other lines of production and new materials, it continues to provide exceptional service to its traditional sectors. All of these evolving markets require the highest level of quality as well as technical expertise and experience. PJ Manufacturing also prepares for the future with investments to ensure that it is ahead of the growth and needs of customers. Continuous investments have positively impacted efficiency and quality in all aspects of its manufacturing. PJ Manufacturing's leadership does not stop there. The company plans to continue leading the way in gear manufacturing, working with its customers to advance the craft and meet the rapidly expanding needs of industry.

The main characteristics of PJ Manufacturing are as follows: (1) a small company managed by a dominant decision maker; (2) aggressively pursuing growth in domestic markets; and (3) positioned for growth with new products and services matching the needs of its clients.

10.6 Process Controls International

Company Background

Process Controls International (PCI) is a British engineering company that in 2002 purchased a well-established smaller manufacturing company located in Milwaukee, the largest city in Wisconsin. It is the Milwaukee subsidiary of PCI (PCI-1) that is the focus of this case. It was established in 1955 and moved from its original location to its present location about 40 years ago. Today, PCI-1 is managed by Chris Brown, a professional manager educated in the U.K. The Milwaukee subsidiary manufactures process controls used in the oil and gas industries to control the flow of gases or liquids. The markets for such process controls include oil and gas, chemical, power, and water treatment industries. Currently, the company employs 50 workers with annual sales of US$20 million.

Products

With more than 50 years of extensive knowledge and experience, PCI-1 has manufactured actuators for virtually every industrial application worldwide. Actuators are used to control and regulate a large number of technical processes today. There is a steady increase in demand for high-precision, dynamic, and system-capable miniaturized drives, particularly in high-tech sectors such as automation and medical technology as well as in numerous other industries. With the unquestionable ruggedness of its actuators, PCI-1 can meet any actuator requirement for any industrial application. Along with the durability come accuracy and reliability, to ensure the precision necessary for critical applications by customers. PCI-1 supplies proven solutions to numerous industries in the U.S. and overseas. Its actuators — both rotary and linear — have been used extensively in serving the process control, power, oil and gas, and other industrial markets worldwide. They are used on control valves, dampers, and slide gates, and for many other industrial applications. Whatever the application, no matter how difficult and demanding the conditions, PCI-1 knows that accuracy and efficiency are essential at all times.

Its actuators are designed and built to perform perfectly under the most exacting requirements.

PCI-1 maintains a comprehensive website for its customers; the website is also tied to its parent company in the U.K. The website contains sales and marketing information, and technical specifications on all of its products for design engineers. In addition to providing the address and contact information, PCI-1 is identified on its website as the worldwide headquarters for process controls.

The website also indicates that PCI-1's products comply with quality standards in accordance with ISO 9001. According to the website, the quality system that is in place involves all employees and reinforces the company's core values of trust, integrity, teamwork, and customer commitment. Its strong commitment to quality improvement is regularly communicated, monitored, and reviewed for effectiveness. The actual ISO certificate is also displayed on the website. PCI-1 is a member of the American Society for Quality.

Focus

From his perspective as the key decision maker and manager of PCI-1, Chris Brown pointed out in his interview that his main focus is on sales and marketing. Although PCI-1 designs its individual products and product lines, the manufacturing of parts and components is subcontracted to companies throughout the state of Wisconsin. The final assembly is carried out in the Milwaukee location, where the products are tested and shipped to customers throughout the U.S. and abroad. The entire sales and marketing effort for the process controls is controlled by the Milwaukee subsidiary.

Competitive Advantage

According to Mr. Brown, PCI-1 derives its competitive advantage from the superior quality of its products and services that meet or exceed the requirements of its customers. He emphasized that its products are not the cheapest on the market, but the quality and superior technology of its products attract many satisfied returning customers. PCI-1 has achieved this through a quality system focused on prevention and continuous improvement in quality, cost, delivery, and technology.

PCI-1's emphasis on product quality, combined with ownership of superior technology, is also reflected in the certifications displayed on its website. The website states, "Our core values of trust, integrity, teamwork, and customer commitment involve all employees in the quality system." PCI-1's commitment to quality improvement is communicated, monitored, and reviewed for effectiveness. It is important to note that both factors, product quality and superior technology, are frequently identified as the main sources of competitive advantage among smaller manufacturing enterprises.

Importance

During the interview, it became obvious that Mr. Brown spoke for PCI-1. As the general manager, he is responsible for top management decisions. However, management of PCI-1 is a team effort, and marketing and engineering decisions are made on several levels — mostly about sales efforts. In the context of moderately diversified decision making, Mr. Brown stated that sales growth is important to the company. The company is willing to sacrifice short-term profitability as long as it guarantees future sales growth.

PCI-1's Chinese experience is profound. Mr. Brown gave an example of selling in the Chinese market. Competition is fierce, but his company is willing to cut prices and take lower profits simply because of the large volume involved and because of the fact that PCI-1 wants to gain a significant market share. In order to accomplish the objective of gaining a significant share of the Chinese market, a smaller manufacturing entity such as PCI-1 typically needs an innovative and dynamic marketing strategy. Mr. Brown believes that PCI-1 has already confronted these challenges.

Impact of Current Economic Conditions

PCI-1 is a business-to-business company. Mr. Brown believes that it is not very much affected by the current state of the economy. The products produced by PCI-1 are not discretionary, according to Mr. Brown, and the economic slowdown does not impact the company as much. However, he underscored the fact that some of the biggest and most profitable industries are oil and gas. PCI-1 generates approximately 25% of its sales from oil and gas. Any change in oil or gas prices has an effect on oil and gas exploration and, in turn, on the demand for PCI-1's products. At the same time, according to Mr. Brown, the current discussion about moving towards cleaner energy (including cleaner coal-fired power plants) would help PCI-1.

Future of the Company

Demand for actuators has increased as a result of huge investments and expansion in various process industries. The Asian and other world markets are expected to see good growth compared to their European and North American counterparts. Among the various end-user criteria, aftermarket service assumes the highest importance.

PCI-1 expects an increase in sales and profits in the next five years, regardless of the current economic slowdown. According to Mr. Brown, being part of an international company has given the Milwaukee subsidiary access to numerous sales offices and sales personnel in the U.K. and elsewhere in the world. Through these entities, efforts are made to find new markets and customers for PCI-1's products. He believes that the Milwaukee subsidiary is well positioned and will be in a better financial position in the next five years.

Systematic Decision-Making Process

As the general manager, Mr. Brown pointed out that PCI-1 does not have a formal systematic decision-making process to evaluate new products and market potential. However, a new product development process is in place and it will introduce new products shortly. There is also an implied new product development process in place on the engineering side of the business. Engineers have a natural tendency to think about new products. Furthermore, the company is also looking for new market opportunities. One promising new market potential might be the solar power industry. Although there is no formal decision-making process in place, there are individuals within PCI-1 who are encouraged to think about new products and markets.

Initial Markets

PCI-1's markets consist of North America and the rest of the world. Approximately 75% of sales volume is generated from North American markets, and about 25% from the rest of the world. There is a company effort to increase international sales to a higher level in the future. Mr. Brown explained that the majority of domestic markets are east of the Mississippi River, where most of the power plants are located, and in Texas, where most of the oil and gas industries operate. International markets are scattered over several parts of the world. From a historical perspective, the original company — before PCI-1 became a subsidiary of the parent company — made its initial entry into international markets via the combination of a distributor and a manufacturing representative in Venezuela.

PCI-1 has a policy for evaluating international business opportunities. The policy is formulated to supplement the future international expansion effort as indicated above. In addition to all of the sales personnel operating in the U.K. and from various sales offices around the world, PCI-1 employs two sales specialists — one in Singapore and the other in the U.K. — for the sole purpose of finding new markets and new customers for its products. The emphasis relating to future markets and increased sales volume seems to be more from the sales perspective rather than an overall marketing strategy. This approach may not be unusual for an engineering, high-technology-oriented business.

The above approach is also reflected in PCI-1's planning process. PCI-1 does not formally plan for new products or markets; however, it does set sales objectives and budgets. Planning sessions are held every September to determine what products will be sold and in which markets. At the same time, budgets are set to support these objectives. The set objectives are then reviewed quarterly to determine how closely each objective was achieved. Both positive and negative corrections and adjustments are made accordingly.

International sales are not necessarily more profitable, according to Mr. Brown. He believes that profitability in international markets depends on the industry in which products are sold. He points out that, generally, sales in the oil and gas industries are more profitable regardless of location, with the exception of China. As mentioned above, the competition in China is fierce and PCI-1 has been forced to cut prices substantially for the sake of large volume sales. This is primarily because it wants to gain a greater market share in China. PCI-1's sales to water treatment plants, mostly owned by local governments, are not very profitable.

Mr. Brown believes that international business is important not only for the U.S. economy, but also for the local Wisconsin economy. PCI-1 employs approximately 50 individuals in Wisconsin, and Mr. Brown suggests that an additional 100 individuals are employed by Wisconsin suppliers contracted to supply some of the parts and components for PCI-1's products. Since approximately 25% of PCI-1's sales volume is derived from international sales, the importance of international business for the economy is obvious.

Export Obstacles

Mr. Brown was educated in the U.K. and manages the Milwaukee subsidiary for its U.K.-based parent company. His perspective concerning obstacles encountered in managing international business represents a different point of view than a typical Wisconsin-owned and Wisconsin-operated entity would provide. He believes that the major obstacle that affects PCI-1's international business is the lack of knowledge of different cultures by his employees.

According to Mr. Brown, most of his American employees are ignorant of other cultures. To improve or even remedy the situation, the U.K. parent company has developed a program of sending employees to foreign locations so that they can become familiar with different cultures where the company does business. One of the Milwaukee workers is presently visiting in Brazil. But, more appropriately, the Wisconsin subsidiary has hosted many workers from the parent company to make certain that they are familiar with business and cultural issues in Wisconsin and in the U.S. These are excellent educational and cultural opportunities for individuals from all company levels. Because the future of many smaller manufacturing enterprises is closely aligned with international operations, companies must overcome cultural obstacles in order to survive.

Differences in cultural environments typically present major obstacles to international business for many smaller manufacturing enterprises. PCI-1 is not an exception, as clearly perceived by Mr. Brown. However, owner-managers of smaller manufacturing enterprises do not frequently recognize that the future of their international business opportunities also concerns their regular employees. They typically recognize the obstacle for themselves and are unwilling to do anything about it. In this instance, it is the foreign entity — the parent company in the U.K. — which has actually implemented a corporate policy to do something about it.

Future Markets

Where and in what industries will future markets for PCI-1 be? Mr. Brown believes that PCI-1's future domestic markets will still be east of the Mississippi River and in Texas simply because that is where the oil and gas industries are located, unless other supplies of oil and natural gas are discovered. For example, California's oil and gas industry is emerging and offers some interesting business opportunities for PCI-1. Other sales opportunities are not evident west of the Mississippi. Future international sales opportunities seem more promising. There are potential opportunities in Eastern Europe that look promising. New opportunities are possible even in Germany. Both Latin and South America offer interesting potential for future international sales. Whether these opportunities have been systematically and objectively identified is not clear.

Systematic Exploration of International Business Opportunities

Nevertheless, Mr. Brown suggests that PCI-1 systematically evaluates international business opportunities because it has a set process for the evaluation of international business opportunities. The parent company in the U.K. has 14 factories scattered around the world. It has 60 sales offices — one in almost every developed country in the world. The main objective of the manufacturing facilities as well as the sales offices is to systematically search for new markets and business opportunities. The Milwaukee subsidiary is well integrated into this wide international network.

PCI-1 employs about 50 workers and last year generated approximately US$20 million in sales volume. It has a relatively good profit margin of about 15% and a very positive cash flow. Its total capital investments are not available.

Summary

Although the original company was a well-established manufacturer of process controls in Wisconsin, it was sold in 2002 by the previous owners to a British engineering firm. Management of the engineering firm re-established the original company as its subsidiary and appointed a managing director who was educated and trained in the U.K. The current general manager has been managing the subsidiary since its acquisition. How much of the information provided by the general manager represents the original Wisconsin entity is only speculation. The original company was established in 1955; it operated for almost 50 years as an independent, free-standing business.

As a subsidiary, PCI-1 has a sales and marketing focus within the oil and gas industries. It assembles its proprietary products from parts and components manufactured by Wisconsin subcontractors. A heavy emphasis is placed on quality control and testing of all its products. Products are shipped domestically and internationally from the Milwaukee subsidiary. The high quality of its products and its superior technology are reflected in the higher prices charged for its products.

According to the general manager, PCI-1 is willing to sacrifice short-term profits for the sake of long-term growth. This strategy is especially apparent in international markets; the Chinese market is one example. The same strategy is used to gain market share. Most PCI-1 sales are domestic, mainly east of the Mississippi River and in

Texas, but a significant percentage of its sales volume is generated from international markets. It is expected that, over the next five years, its overall sales volume will increase. Growth in clean energy generation will also positively impact its sales volume. The current economic decline does not affect its current sales volume.

PCI-1 is constantly searching for new market opportunities. It does not have a systematic decision-making process for new products and markets, but the process is implied in its day-to-day management style. The parent company PCI and its subsidiaries around the world are charged with identifying new market opportunities for all of its products. PCI-1's management, including its sales force, meets once a year to discuss sales performance and new market potentials.

PCI-1's international operations are important for the economies of the U.S. and Wisconsin, since it generates about 25% percent of its sales volume from international operations. PCI-1 is committed to international business operations and attempts to remove major obstacles to international business operations as much as possible. The greatest obstacle to international business operations, according to the general manager, is the lack of knowledge of different cultures by its employees. Employee exchanges appear to be overcoming this obstacle.

Chapter 11

Summary and Overview of Research Cases: A European Perspective

Smaller manufacturing enterprises have contributed to the economic development of not only individual countries, but also the whole of Europe. Smaller manufacturing enterprises in Europe are typically older and well established in domestic as well as foreign markets. Many European enterprises faced the need to internationalize their operations shortly after they were established due to the size of their domestic markets. The decision to internationalize was generally made by accepting the first export order judged to be convenient for growing the enterprise rather than through a systematic evaluation of market options. In most instances, managers were not concerned with developing strategic business models. As the demand for all types of consumer and industrial products grew in response to economic development throughout Europe, an increasing number of smaller manufacturing enterprises internationalized their operations.

Although the European market is not homogeneous — there are many social, cultural, economic, and technological differences — sufficient similarities exist in markets for a variety of products. In particular, industrial markets tend to be relatively similar and stable. Only in countries where the political system has recently changed is it possible to detect major changes in market demand. Political changes in Central and Eastern Europe in the early 1990s created a new environment and greater opportunities for establishing and growing smaller manufacturing enterprises. Managers responsible for smaller manufacturing enterprises in that part of Europe have a great deal to consider in their recent attempts to compete with their more established counterparts in the rest of Europe. This situation is the primary motivation for comparing several smaller manufacturing enterprises in Europe.

Most published studies dealing with the internationalization of smaller manufacturing enterprises and comparisons of initial decisions to export focus on Europe and, more specifically, on the Nordic countries. Comparisons between European smaller manufacturing enterprises and those in North America are also common. To better understand how the internationalization of smaller manufacturing enterprises in Europe has evolved, we selected two Czech research cases, three Danish cases, and three Swedish cases. All eight cases represent the types of smaller manufacturing enterprises that have evolved in Europe over time, and that are still evolving in the Czech Republic.

Smaller manufacturing enterprises have been well established in Denmark for centuries. Most Danish enterprises evolved from individual initiatives and were managed primarily by craftsman managers at their founding. Smaller manufacturing enterprises in Sweden also have a long tradition. Many such enterprises evolved in remote parts of Sweden, and yet they were able to get their products into far distant rural and urban markets. Their management styles at the outset also indicated that the founders of smaller manufacturing enterprises in Sweden would have fallen into the craftsman and promoter types of managers. The Czech environment for smaller manufacturing enterprises is relatively new. Before the political changes in the late 1980s, private ownership of smaller manufacturing enterprises was illegal. A few outlaw entrepreneurs produced a small offering of consumer products such as furniture, clothing, and food items. It was only after the political changes in Eastern Europe that smaller manufacturing enterprises had a chance to grow. To this day, the growth of smaller manufacturing enterprises in the Czech Republic is relatively slow. Those enterprises that are successful are doing well and can be compared to start-ups in other parts of Europe.

The oldest enterprise among the eight cases was established in Sweden in the early 1870s as a cheese producer, and the most recent enterprise was established in 1997 in the Czech Republic. All enterprises were started by individuals who also managed the enterprises. The

Danish and Swedish enterprises have changed managers several times since they were established, and have progressed from the owner-manager style in most instances to a team-management style. Of the two Czech enterprises, one is still managed by the original owner-manager and the other is managed by a professional manager recently hired to grow the enterprise. All Danish and Swedish enterprises are well integrated into European and international markets; the Czech enterprises are not.

From a managerial perspective, Danish and Swedish enterprises focus on well-developed lines of products and accompanying services. They believe that they offer high-quality products suitably priced for domestic and foreign markets. Although they have a tendency to view their operations as job shops, they represent highly advanced and technologically sophisticated manufacturing operations and are well endowed with financial resources. The Czech enterprises focus on what they can produce and sell. Managers of the Danish and Swedish enterprises believe that their competitive advantage is embedded in technology, product quality, and service. The Czech managers believe that their products are price-competitive and also of superior quality.

All enterprises represented in these eight cases look for growth and market expansion. However, the Danish and Swedish firms are concerned about technology and the role that cutting-edge technology plays in growth and market expansion. The Czech managers are concerned with the physical growth of their enterprises and with expansion into new geographic markets in Europe and elsewhere.

The domestic and international economies do not seem to be important for the Danish and Swedish smaller manufacturing enterprises. The Danish and Swedish managers believe that they are sufficiently diversified in foreign markets such that changes in local or regional economic conditions can be offset by expansion in other markets. They feel confident that their advanced technology and aggressive sales can help stabilize any economic downturns. On the other hand, Czech enterprises perceive economic instability at home and abroad as challenges. One enterprise is concerned about the fluctuating demand for its products, while the other faces potential currency fluctuation. The Danish and Swedish managers believe that their enterprises are not vulnerable to changes in economic conditions. Czech managers, on the other hand, believe that their enterprises are weak when faced with changing economies.

Although the eight cases were developed over a span of approximately five years, it is interesting to note that all of them look for growth in the near future. All managers are optimistic that they will have market opportunities both domestically and internationally. The Danish and Swedish enterprises tend to evaluate future options systematically using a team approach, while the Czech enterprises are still learning how to make systematic and consistent decisions. Team decision making is very much embedded in the Scandinavian model of decision making, and was more or less invented by the Swedes. Czech managers tend to be much more individualistic and normative in their managerial decision making, and they anticipate that growth will happen merely because they are involved in foreign markets.

The eight smaller manufacturing enterprises discussed here started international operations by exporting their products shortly after start-up and mostly into neighboring countries; this finding is consistent with conclusions from studies presented by European researchers. Later on, the Danish and Swedish enterprises established or purchased subsidiaries or sales and marketing organizations abroad. The Danish enterprises entered into contractual agreements with partners abroad. They systematically evaluate international business opportunities and select those that are likely to contribute to the growth and profitability of their own enterprise. Although they perceive that obstacles exist to international operations, these obstacles are on relatively high operational and strategic levels. For example, training subsidiary managers is an obstacle for one Danish enterprise, and product standards specific to an export market may become an obstacle for one Swedish enterprise. The Czech managers perceive obstacles differently: to them, obstacles relate only to financial issues, such as whether they will get paid or whether they might face an unfavorable exchange rate.

Managers of smaller manufacturing enterprises represented in the eight following research cases all believe that future markets for their products are growing in Europe and internationally. They have a strong international perspective and, with the exception of the Czech enterprises, they regularly explore the potential of international markets and plan for such potential. The Czech enterprises do not have the same knowledge base to examine international market potential in the same way.

Finally, these eight enterprises employ from approximately 35 employees in the case of one of the Czech enterprises to more than 900 employees in one of the Danish enterprises.

Closing Comments

The Danish and Swedish smaller manufacturing enterprises have a long tradition of operating in foreign markets; it is not possible to determine how the initial decision to internationalize was made. From a long-term perspective, managers of the Czech enterprises are just getting started in systematically and rationally evaluating foreign opportunities and internationalizing their operations. However, all eight enterprises included in this sample believe that they will be well integrated into the global marketplace in the future.

11.1 Czech Cases

11.1.1 *ABC Plastic Limited*[1]

Company background

ABC Plastic Limited is a successful family-owned company in the Czech Republic with experience in manufacturing plastic products through hot press molding and hot air welding. The company was established in 1997 by the founder of the company, Mr. Milos Karel, and his two sons, Kamil and Milan. Mr. Karel is a trained chemical engineer who used to work for a state-owned chemical factory during the communist regime. After the collapse of the communist regime, Mr. Karel decided to open his own company. Originally, the company made polyvinyl chloride (PVC) pipes only for the construction industry; however, over the years ABC Plastic has been able to expand its business into other types of plastic products.

Due to his prior training as a chemical engineer, Mr. Karel is a "hands-on" manager. He explained that initially he saw himself as a craftsman manager focusing on production capabilities. But as his business started growing and relationships with other businesses both in the Czech Republic and overseas became more complicated, he found a need to manage his company in a more logical and rational manner in spite of all the problems. Although he has delegated some of his tasks to his sons in recent years, he is still the ultimate decision maker in the company. All new product development projects or new market expansion decisions are ultimately made by Mr. Karel.

The globalization of the world economy has provided a great opportunity for many family-owned businesses to expand their operations to other markets around the world. The internationalization of family-owned businesses, however, is a very challenging task. Due to their small size, these businesses face many impediments when they

---

[1] Professor Hamid Moini of the University of Wisconsin-Whitewater developed this case. The name of the company has been changed at the request of the owner-manager. This case cannot be copied or electronically reproduced in any form without written permission from the author.

venture into foreign markets. For example, certain characteristics of family-owned businesses, such as concentration of power and delays in or lack of succession plans, hamper their efforts to internationalize.

The recent European Union (EU) expansion and the relatively rapid economic growth in some Central and Eastern European countries, such as the Czech Republic, are generating great interest among small- and medium-sized enterprises (SMEs) in the region. According to Mr. Karel, the Czech Republic has to fulfill certain obligations before and after joining the EU. From a positive point of view, these obligations entail a lot of new projects for improving the country's infrastructure. Therefore, there are numerous opportunities for ABC Plastic to benefit from government projects. On the other hand, joining the EU requires Czech companies to meet certain regulatory requirements, such as safety standards which could be costly for them. Meeting different product standards and procedures, in Mr. Karel's opinion, might eliminate any competitive advantage that his company has in conducting business in other EU countries. Unfortunately, this is a fairly common perception among smaller firms in the Czech Republic. As soon as they learn that their products have to be modified to meet foreign health and safety standards, they lose interest in exporting. Smaller companies perceive different product specifications as an important factor in preventing them from exporting.

Products

ABC Plastic operates several plastic processing units. Plastic piping systems are a sustainable and environmentally responsible choice that will serve generations to come. Advantages of plastic piping systems include low absorbability, low weight, high chemical resistance, and sufficient steadiness. They are energy-efficient during manufacturing and provide peak protection from contamination during service. Strong, durable, lightweight, and flexible, these piping systems require significantly less energy to fabricate, transport, and install than metal or concrete alternatives. With superior resistance to corrosion and abrasion, plastic piping systems also offer a long service life, excellent joint performance, and leak-free protection — all adding up to exceptional value. Since most of the materials used in their production (even in standard design) are stabilized against ultraviolet (UV) radiation, customers can use them for exterior projects without any problem. Due to these advantages, plastic piping systems have numerous applications in many industries such as chemical, pharmaceutical, food, and other manufacturing operations. Pipes made of different types of plastic are routinely used for water, sewer, storm sewer, and drainage systems; for transporting natural gas and petroleum products; and for buried ducts and conduits in which telecommunications and electrical cables are placed.

ABC Plastic is able to supply the complete delivery of pipes, bends, sound dampers, exhausting heads, exhaust covers and slots, and plastic fans and grills. Its products are mainly manufactured from PVC, flammable polypropylene (PP), non-flammable polypropylene (PPS), and high-density polyethylene (HDPE). As a standard, ABC Plastic pipes are produced for a pressure between −1,500 pascal (Pa) and +2,000 Pa; however, ABC Plastic is also capable of manufacturing pipes for higher-pressure jobs using stronger or reinforced materials. ABC Plastic's air conditioning pipes from plastic, for example, have a lower aerodynamic resistance and lower noisiness without vibration risk as compared with metal piping. The smooth-surfaced inner walls of pipes and piping fluency also provide a steady flow of air for higher operating speeds. ABC Plastic also manufactures air distribution hoses. These hoses, with a smooth-surfaced inner wall, can connect a customer's air piping system with their machinery and production lines. They can be designed as antistatic, which can distribute clean air throughout a customer's air distribution system. ABC Plastic is capable of manufacturing these hoses according to customers' requirements.

Plastic fans are ABC Plastic's other line of business. ABC Plastic has developed a wide range of plastic fans for a variety of industry applications where aggressive media must be moved. The current users of such corrosion- and chemical-resistant fans include universities, medical research institutions, defense laboratories, fume hood original equipment manufacturers (OEMs), and pharmaceutical laboratories. ABC Plastic's fans are the finest-quality blowers available for efficient movement of corrosive, humid, or polluted air, gases, and fumes. These fire-retardant and corrosion-resistant plastic fans are specially designed and suited for hostile applications where coated metal blowers typically corrode. ABC Plastic's fans are distributed thoughout the Czech Republic and parts of Europe, and are clearly recognized for their superior quality, reliability, and efficiency.

Currently, ABC Plastic offers fans with exhaust volumes ranging from 50 to 140,000 square meters per hour (m^2/h), and pressures of up to 6,000 Pa. They have been designed for exhausting aggressive substances from non-explosive and explosive materials. High-efficiency impellers result in low power consumption, low operating costs, and quieter operation. All metal hardware is completely sealed from exposure to corrosion by encapsulating it into fiberglass-reinforced plastic (FRP) or plastic; the steel support frame and motor base are powder-coated with a corrosion-resistant finish. In addition to being highly resistant to chemical corrosion, PP fans are self-extinguishing and will not support combustion. Since removing aggressive substances with various concentrations and temperatures is very complicated, ABC Plastic offers technical assistance to its clients. ABC Plastic offers complete delivery of exhaust (EX-type) fans or whole distribution systems made of materials which guarantee the electric conductivity.

Focus

To maintain its market share, ABC Plastic has no choice but to make high-quality plastic products which are competitively priced. Mr. Karel is proud of the fact that his company is making very high-quality products, and is willing to guarantee long service and chemical resistance against common acids for his products. As Mr. Karel mentioned in his interview, "ABC Plastic wants to make sure that its customers know that it will remain a solid supplier of top-quality and diverse plastic products with competitive pricing, and promises to meet any delivery deadline that customers have."

The launch of new products is a major element of ABC Plastic's strategy and one that Mr. Karel believes will succeed even amid difficult economic times. Mr. Karel believes that ABC Plastic's level of technological superiority in the design and quality of its products gives it a competitive advantage which his company cannot afford to lose. According to Mr. Karel, since ABC Plastic has a large number of multinational companies such as Samsung, Kia Motors, Coca-Cola, Sony, and Volkswagen as its customers, it has to continue to be innovative and make sure it produces top-quality products at highly competitive prices; otherwise, these multinational companies can easily replace ABC Plastic with other Czech or overseas suppliers.

Competitive advantage

Although the market for plastic pipes and fittings is growing, it is strongly competitive and there is a lot of pressure on prices. ABC Plastic has realized the competitive environment in which it operates. ABC Plastic's strategy is dependent on sales growth and diversification. It plans to continue its diversification into other production lines. For example, the introduction of plastic fans with applications in numerous industries has enabled the company to expand its customer base, while the new generation of pipes with blowing slots for the production of car chassis for Škoda — a subsidiary of Volkswagen — has allowed the company to become a supplier to the automobile industry. It is also expanding into other areas of the plastic industry, such as manufacturing storage reservoirs and water tanks.

Importance

ABC Plastic is prepared to meet fast-delivery requirements for any product from an in-stock inventory, and provide the delivery of parts to prevent prolonged and costly shutdowns of its customers' operations. However, Mr. Karel recognizes the fact that, in order to continue with his growth strategy, his company needs financial resources. He has difficult decisions to make regarding the investment needed for producing these pipes and fittings. Unfortunately, commercial banks and other lending institutions in the Czech Republic are not willing to provide the necessary funding for his growth plan.

Most of ABC Plastic's recent expansions were financed through internal funds. Therefore, maintaining a profitable operation is very critical to the survival and expansion of ABC Plastic in the future. The fact that ABC Plastic is operating in a highly competitive industry with numerous suppliers around the world makes the job even more difficult.

Impact of current economic conditions

The current global economic crisis is certainly expected to have a major impact on the demand for plastic pipes and fittings in the European countries. Although worldwide demand for plastic pipes is forecast to be 8.2 billion meters (or 18.2 million metric tons) in 2012, most of the gains will come from continued strong prospects in developing nations, particularly in China — countries in which ABC Plastic does not have any presence. In fact, China is expected to account for 30% of overall length demand gains for plastic pipes between 2009 and 2012.

According to Mr. Karel, "This crisis has slowed down our expansion strategy to some extent but it will not stop it." He sees no other alternative for his company but to grow. In recent months, however, the sales volume and the number of inquiries from potential customers, both domestic and international, have declined markedly. At the moment, ABC Plastic has stopped hiring additional employees but, as Mr. Karel puts it, "We will not terminate anyone. It is not easy to replace these trained and loyal workers. Most of them have been working with me for the last 12 years." To retain its highly skilled workers, ABC Plastic serves them with a free lunch in a small cafeteria at its headquarters.

Mr. Karel believes the current economic slowdown is temporary, as infrastructure development and economic growth in the European markets will resume and the demand for plastic pipes in network telecommunications and even residential home-building applications will increase soon. He also argues that ongoing efforts across Europe to upgrade water treatment systems will boost the demand for plastic piping used for water delivery and in drainage and sewage applications. In his opinion, PVC pipe, which accounts for two-thirds of ABC

Plastic's sales volume, will remain the leading plastic pipe in the market. PVC pipe is popular because of its low cost, durability, strength, and ease of extrusion, allowing it to compete against non-plastic pipes. However, ABC Plastic is also preparing itself to benefit from the increased demand for HDPE pipe, as it has introduced new HDPE pipes for uses such as small-diameter pipe for natural gas transmissions or as a conduit for electrical and telecommunications applications.

Future of the company

ABC Plastic plans to continue its growth in the future. Of course, this depends on the state of the economy. If the Czech Republic and other countries to which ABC Plastic exports its products make a quick recovery from the current economic crisis, Mr. Karel expects that the company could continue its current growth strategy. On the other hand, if the crisis lasts longer, the company, he asserts, will not be able to expand as fast as it has planned. He indicated that his company has done well in recent years. In fact, 2007 was its most successful year in terms of both sales and profit; the company reported annual sales of CZK 35 million, while employing 35 people. But he did not believe that the company would be able to match those sales numbers in 2008. Nevertheless, he is more optimistic about the next five years. In Mr. Karel's opinion, the greatest potential for his company's growth comes from overseas markets. He feels that his products are very price-competitive compared to other Western European companies, especially German and Austrian companies whose markets are the target for ABC Plastic's products.

Systematic decision-making process

ABC Plastic does not employ any systematic decision-making process. It is managed similarly to any other family-owned business around the world. Mr. Karel and his two sons, who are in charge of the production and marketing of the company, make all of the major decisions. Mr. Karel believes he has significant manufacturing experience, but agrees that neither he nor his sons have any broad experience in marketing their products, especially in other European markets. He argues that his limited financial resources do not allow him to hire a professional manager to direct his marketing department. Similarly, ABC Plastic does not have any systematic or regular planning for new products, new markets, or diversification into other businesses. Mr. Karel and his sons make all of these decisions, with little or no input from other employees into the introduction of new products or the diversification of operations. Generally, the production and marketing strategies are determined based on inquiries or requests from customers. The company does not employ any marketing research into potential new products or markets.

Initial markets

According to Mr. Karel, while domestic sales account for more than 80% of ABC Plastic's annual sales volume, international sales are growing fast. Its first international market was Germany in 2004, and that was started by coincidence during a trip to Germany to attend an international trade show. Today, ABC Plastic exports mostly to neighboring countries such as Germany, Austria, Poland, Slovakia, Bulgaria, and Croatia. Since its first successful export to Germany, the company has started exploring export opportunities not only in Germany but also in other countries. When asked whether he has considered employing an international agent or has advertised in international trade journals to promote his products, Mr. Karel answered no. He realizes that his company's inability to gather market information and maintain a continuous flow of communication with foreign customers as well as lack of experience in planning and targeting export sales in world markets are some of the shortcomings that ABC Plastic must overcome. But, again, the limited financial resources are obstacles to this expansion strategy.

Export obstacles

The most obvious reason companies do not seek to develop new markets is simply their failure to recognize that new markets exist. This lack of knowledge can be due to either the lack of effort to find out what opportunities exist or the lack of opportunities to explore new markets. New market development requires a firm to research the market, establish a local presence, sell, process and fulfill orders, and ship and deliver. Since ABC Plastic is a relative newcomer in international markets, finding prospective clients in foreign markets is one of its major obstacles. Similarly, poor knowledge of potential markets hinders ABC Plastic's export activities. Obtaining the information necessary to enter the export market is one of the biggest problems faced by would-be exporters. In addition, knowledge and skills about export procedures, documentation, and government regulations are another critical requirement for successful foreign market entry by smaller companies. Mr. Karel agrees that his firm must overcome obstacles such as the expense and time required to fill in the paperwork in order to comply with foreign regulations as well as cultural and language barriers. Although Mr. Karel speaks fluent Russian, his knowledge of other languages such as German, French, and English is very poor. He realizes that the ability to communicate with clients overseas and knowledge of different cultures are antecedents of an attitude toward successful exporting. Thus, Mr. Karel and his sons are well aware that they need to gain the additional knowledge and skills needed for exporting.

Problems caused by financial barriers such as credit collections, honoring letters of credit, dealing with banking institutions, and inadequate capital are also a major impediment to ABC Plastic's export activity. Mr. Karel indicated that, in order to keep his customers satisfied, he has expanded his payment terms from 60 to 90 days for his regular customers, but he emphasized that in the past he has had some problems with credit collections from newer customers. According to Mr. Karel, collecting money from a default customer is almost impossible in countries such as Germany, as going through the court system is very expensive. Since today's credit markets are tight and his financial resources are limited, he requires his new customers to prepay the full amount of the transactions.

The riskiest adventure occurs when a company is not totally committed to internationalization. Half-hearted efforts in acquiring the knowledge and skill make the process to successful exporting both slow and difficult. Successful exporting requires a well-thought-out strategy and commitment of human and financial resources. Although ABC Plastic has been very aware of the significant impact that international sales can have on its future, the lack of financial resources and its unfamiliarity with foreign markets have prevented it from taking advantage of the opportunities available in those markets.

Future markets

ABC Plastic's further expansion into European markets is doubtful, as all of these countries are going through their own economic slowdown. However, Mr. Karel emphasized that many of the multinational companies operating in the Czech Republic have become its regular customers, and he hopes to build on these relationships in order to become their supplier in other countries. For example, the company's new product that is used in the production of chassis for Škoda automobiles has provided an opportunity to sell other products to Volkswagen, Škoda's parent, in Germany. ABC Plastic is trying to build the same kind of relationship with Samsung and Kia Motors of South Korea as well as with Sony of Japan, which are ABC Plastic's customers in the Czech Republic.

Mr. Karel believes that international sales are more profitable than domestic sales. He believes that, in order for ABC Plastic to survive, it must expand its international sales. He indicated that he is willing to sacrifice short-term profitability if that would lead to an increase in his company's market share overseas. Also, in order to make his products more attractive to foreign buyers, Mr. Karel and his engineers have made sure that his products meet all European standards and he provides extensive after-sales support and even expert assembly of some of his products for his customers. He indicated that his willingness to go the extra mile for his customers' satisfaction has had some positive results.

Systematic exploration of international business opportunities

Mr. Karel claims that his firm systematically explores foreign opportunities; but when asked to give some examples of such foreign opportunity exploration, attending a trade show in Germany in 2004 was the only one he could recall. He has not attended any other trade shows overseas since 2004. When he was reminded that these trade shows are the best places to locate potential foreign customers, he mentioned the lack of financial resources as the reason for not attending any other trade shows.

Interestingly, increasing trade deficits and other economic problems have forced many nations to develop policies and strategies to encourage firms to enter the export field. Smaller businesses in particular can benefit from export assistance programs, but many firms are unaware of available assistance programs. It seems that current export assistance programs are not reaching their targeted audiences in an effective manner. Furthermore, there is a need for firms to increase their commitment to export-related activities, especially in the first few years when they begin to penetrate foreign markets.

Government promotion programs which provide technical assistance and information on export opportunities overseas can be particularly helpful to companies such as ABC Plastic to consummate an export sale. Creating good personal contacts with clients in foreign markets is important. Frequent visits to foreign markets and attendance at trade shows are absolutely critical in developing export markets. Mr. Karel indicated that the Czech government hardly provides any such assistance; but emphasized that any support such as help with participating in trade shows, assistance with trade leads, export counseling, export financing, or export tax credit could be very useful to his company.

Future prospects

According to Mr. Karel, the global demand for plastic pipes, pipe fittings, and plastic fans will continue to grow in the next 5–10 years. The development of more efficient and higher-performance materials as well as improvements in product engineering and technology, along with product innovations, are resulting in plastic pipe becoming increasingly economical and the opening up of new markets for the plastic industry. For example, further technical development is ensuring that the material polyethylene (PE) is becoming increasingly efficient. To this end, cost-effective pipe-laying techniques have been developed for PE pipes over the past few years. Therefore, Mr. Karel believes it is possible that public utility companies in the future will be able to lay their pipe systems in the drinking water and gas supply networks without the use of sand beds.

Positive future perspectives for the industry are also expected for other reasons. For example, ABC Plastic is expected to benefit from exports to other markets such as Russia and other developing nations. In Mr. Karel's opinion, the necessity to use natural resources sparingly also promises growth potential for ABC Plastic. Areas of applications such as geothermal energy and heat recovery, as well as further development in telecommunications along with the traffic and energy infrastructures, could be of great potential for ABC Plastic's expansion. In Mr. Karel's view, plastic pipes are almost predestined for the development of glass fiber networks because glass fiber strands require long-life, protective pipes.

Another positive outlook for the plastic pipe industry is promised by the need to restore and redevelop old, crumbling public sewer systems. According to Mr. Karel, local municipalities and private sewer system networks in Europe must invest billions of euros in order to guarantee well-functioning sewage disposal systems. Mr. Karel estimates that the majority of the Czech Republic's sewer connections are probably defective and thus in need of restoration.

An additional potential growth market for ABC Plastic is that of industrial plastic fans. Although this segment of ABC Plastic's operation is small compared with plastic pipes and fittings, the spectrum of applications for industrial plastic fans is constantly increasing. This applies, for example, to the chemical industry and to special applications such as biotechnology. The requirements placed on industrial plastic fans are usually diverse and, depending on the industrial sector and application area, the desired standards and material requirements can be high. The increase in metallic materials prices and the extended range of possible applications for industrial plastic fans provide a basis for growing demand for economically efficient plastic fans.

In view of the current uncertainty regarding further developments and trends in the financial markets and their effects on the real economy, a forecast for ABC Plastic is difficult (if not impossible) to make. Most current forecasts assume there will be a weaker economy in the next couple of years; this will also affect the plastic pipe industry. However, Mr. Karel hopes that this economic slowdown will only last for a relatively short period of time. On that basis, ABC Plastic could have a brighter prospect in the future.

Summary

ABC Plastic is a successful family-owned company with several years of experience in plastic processing. While the company continues to manufacture piping systems, it has branched out into other businesses such as water tanks and storage reservoirs as well as plastic fans.

In order to remain successful in global markets, ABC Plastic's strategy is to launch new high-quality products with competitive pricing. It hopes that the superiority of its design and the quality of its products will give it a competitive advantage which the company cannot afford to lose. The other element of ABC Plastic's strategy is to continue its diversification into other production lines.

ABC Plastic has done well in recent years. In fact, 2007 was its most successful year in terms of both sales and profit. However, the current economic crisis has impacted the company. The company has not yet let any employees go, but it will not be able to expand as fast as it has planned if the economic crisis lasts longer.

The company lacks any systematic decision-making process. Mr. Karel and his sons are in charge of all decision making in the company. Other employees in the company have very little input to any decision related to the company. Since neither Mr. Karel nor his sons have any broad sales and marketing experience, this could create a problem for the company as it expands its business not only in the Czech Republic but also in international markets where the company has the greatest growth potential. Its products are competitively priced compared to other Western European companies.

The company also faces numerous export obstacles, including financial, cultural, and language differences in dealing with foreign customers. But finding prospective clients in foreign markets is one of its major obstacles. The company is committed to its international efforts. It realizes that its half-hearted efforts to acquire knowledge and skills have made the process to successful exporting both slow and difficult. As more and more uses are found for plastic pipes and fittings, the future prospects for ABC Plastic seem bright. It is in a good position to take advantage of newer demands for its products.

The main characteristics of ABC Plastic are as follows: (1) a family business operated by the owner and his sons; (2) producing high-quality products with competitive prices; (3) operating successfully in both domestic and international markets; and (4) having a positive outlook for the future.

11.1.2 *KMF Limited*[2]

Company background

KMF Limited was established as JT Metal Fabricating Limited by Mr. Jon Tomas in the Moravia region of the Czech Republic in 1990 as a job shop with two employees, Mr. Tomas and his wife, Elena. Originally, the company was solely involved in fabricating metal garden furniture. Although Mr. Tomas has no formal training in metal fabrication, he stresses that since his childhood he has been fascinated with metalwork and that his hobby was to make garden furniture for his own home. After the collapse of the communist regime in the Czech Republic and the loss of his job with a state-owned company, together with encouragement from his wife, he started JT Metal Fabricating. Mrs. Tomas also quit her job with another company and joined JT Metal Fabricating as an accountant; she still handles the bookkeeping and other accounts of the company. JT Metal Fabricating became very successful and subsequently moved into larger production facilities, diversified its operations into metal guards for doors and windows, and increased its staff to 14 employees. Later, Mr. Tomas bought another company involved in manufacturing interior metal chairs and stools. Five years ago, the two companies were merged into one and renamed KMF Limited. Today, KMF employs more than 45 employees with annual sales of more than CZK 20 million in 2007.

Products

Currently, KMF operates several lines of business. The original, and still the biggest, part of its operation is manufacturing metal garden furniture. This includes picnic tables, lounge chairs, benches, and rocking chairs, as well as metal arbors for garden flowers. Metal garden furniture is usually made from powder-coated steel or aluminum.

---

[2] Professor Hamid Moini of the University of Wisconsin-Whitewater developed this case. The name of the company has been changed at the request of the owner-manager. This case cannot be copied or electronically reproduced in any form without written permission from the author.

Metal garden furniture has always been a popular way to decorate gardens in the Czech Republic. With proper maintenance, this furniture can easily last for many years. Metal garden furniture has both style and durability features, which make it the preferred choice of garden furniture. According to Mr. Tomas, the all-time favorite piece of metal garden furniture is the classic single ornate iron bench, which adds elegance to the garden in a way that no other furniture can. He stresses that this piece of furniture can also act as a focal point, and draw attention away from less interesting sections of the garden.

In recent years, KMF has introduced new garden furniture made of aluminum. These furniture pieces are often light and portable, and hence can be used in various areas of the garden. According to Mr. Tomas, aluminum sunloungers, tables, and chairs are all great pieces for times when one needs just a few more pieces of furniture on the patio to entertain friends and family. Aluminum outdoor furniture is an ideal combination of economy, durability, and beauty. Aluminum garden furniture needs very little maintenance, making it a popular option for outdoor settings.

KMF also manufactures school furniture. However, the vast majority of school chairs and tables that KMF manufactures are still of a classical design (a fixed slanted desk), which is widely used in Eastern and Central European countries but is now almost non-existent in most Western European countries. Petr Novak, a professional manager hired by Mr. Tomas, contributes the poor design and low quality of KMF's school furniture products to the limited educational budget of the Czech government for school furniture. In his opinion, this situation need not continue. He hopes that European Union (EU) membership will force the government to spend more money on replacing aging school furniture. He also indicates that, in order to make its school furniture more attractive to foreign buyers, KMF needs to redesign this line of products.

Interior metal furniture is the third line of products that KMF manufactures. KMF designs and manufactures high-quality modern aluminum and stainless steel chairs, bar stools, and other indoor furniture that is built to last. KMF products, which are often functional, have graced many homes, lofts, and offices in the Czech Republic and other European countries. As Mr. Tomas mentioned in his interview, "We have the ability to incorporate any type of material with our metal base, whether it is glass, wood, or whatever. We will make it work." KMF has come a long way from its humble beginnings making metal garden furniture to its current position where it is able to make products that can be showcased in beautiful homes.

KMF also manufactures products designed by its customers. Customers' ideas are easily transformed into products such as staircases, banisters, and gates for homes. All furniture designed by KMF is made from 11-gauge steel, which is generally more than twice as sturdy and durable than most steel furniture on the market today. Much of the steel furniture sold today is made from a grade of steel that is not as thick as 11-gauge steel and requires reinforcement, which is often disguised as a decorative feature. Pieces designed by KMF have a sense of permanency rarely seen in furniture. There is no assembly required. According to Mr. Novak, "Customers will never receive confusing directions on how to construct their tables. Our furniture arrives ready to be enjoyed. It's that simple. We could not have it any other way."

Focus

According to Mr. Tomas, his business has always been a job shop and he saw himself as a craftsman manager focusing on production capabilities. But as his business grew, he realized that he needed a professional manager to take the helm of the company. As a result, he hired Petr Novak, who has a background in marketing, to help manage the company. Mr. Novak, in Mr. Tomas's opinion, has brought the expertise that his company badly needed to compete in the current economic conditions. Since hiring Mr. Novak, Mr. Tomas has delegated most of his tasks to him, but all new product development projects and new market expansion decisions are made by the team of Mr. Tomas and Mr. Novak.

Competitive advantage

Pricing is by far and away the most sensitive profit lever that managers can influence. Very small changes in average price translate into huge changes in operating profit. KMF's success is mostly due to its competitive prices and the quality of its products. According to Mr. Tomas, KMF's prices are about half the prices of foreign-made products of comparable quality. In addition, through manufacturing high-quality products, KMF has been able to create value for its customers. The combination of superior quality and lower prices gives KMF a competitive advantage which is envied by its competitors. In addition, the recent drop in the value of the Czech koruna versus other currencies has put KMF in a more favorable position in dealing with its foreign clients. However, as Mr. Novak states, "We're actually losing customers in the Western European markets because they are unwilling to purchase our products even though they are cheaper in terms of the euro."

Importance

For KMF, keeping prices very competitive has not led to an increase in the sale of its products. Mr. Tomas argues that it is not enough for KMF to launch a low-price product; it must have a competitive quality product as well. Although he maintains that his products are high-quality products, his customers sometimes correlate the lower prices to lower quality for the products. He also stresses that his company could not survive very long without profit. Therefore, growth is not what is most important: profit is.

Certain other factors are also important for KMF to be able to compete and, furthermore, win customers in the Czech Republic and other countries. KMF must increase the efficiency of its production facilities, and vigorously pursue cost cutting through learning and cost control (especially for overhead costs). For KMF to achieve a superior return through this strategy, it needs to simplify its manufacturing and increase capacity to serve its customers in order to expand volume. The introduction of such a strategy demands high capital investment in up-to-date equipment, aggressive pricing, and the capacity to absorb some losses, in order to gain a larger market share. Unfortunately, this is easier said than done for a small company from the Czech Republic.

Mr. Tomas stresses that he and Mr. Novak do not always know how they are going to grow the business to the next level. One of the problems that KMF faces is the difficulty of securing financial support from banking organizations in the country. In the Czech Republic, smaller firms most often turn to banks for necessary sources of financing. Bank financing has long predominated in the Czech market and many credit products from various banking institutions exist here, from current-account overdrafts to special-purpose loans. Due to the current economic conditions, however, financial institutions in the Czech Republic are refusing to extend any credit, especially to smaller companies.

Impact of current economic conditions

The highly open Czech economy is set to slow down considerably, an effect of the deteriorating outlook for its main trading partners. Although gross domestic product (GDP) growth was still solid in the third quarter of 2008, both export and import growth slowed significantly. The global crisis was expected to adversely impact the real economy, particularly from the fourth quarter of 2008 through 2009. Czech external trade was down again in February 2009, with exports and imports falling year on year by 22.2% and 21.5%, respectively.

Obviously, the unprecedented volatility in the exchange rates and the economic slowdown have also affected KMF's sales in both domestic and international markets. The company has noticed a dramatic drop in its sales volume as well as its profit. Even the depreciation of the Czech koruna has not helped KMF's exports. Mr. Tomas is not expecting a repeat of 2007's record sales of CZK 20 million anytime soon. So far, the company has resisted laying off any workers; but he emphasized that, with its limited financial resources, the company may have to lay off some workers soon.

Future of the company

The current global economic crisis has lowered the potential future growth for companies such as KMF, but Mr. Tomas is hopeful that in the near future the recession in the Czech Republic and other European countries will be over. He believes his company will continue its growth, albeit at a lower rate than in the last 19 years. However, he realizes that, to achieve the desired growth for his company, he must rely mainly on internal financial resources, as the financial institutions and the government of the Czech Republic are not very helpful in providing financial support for entrepreneurs like himself. Mr. Tomas argues that his government is trying hard to move the country toward a service industry from its historical tradition as being one of the best manufacturing centers in Eastern and Central Europe. Thus, if there is any government support for smaller businesses, it mostly goes to service companies rather than manufacturing firms such as KMF.

Systematic decision-making process

Smaller firms in the Czech Republic, such as KMF, seldom pay any attention to the systematic decision-making process. They ignore the fact that systematic decision making can be an effective management tool. There are numerous reasons for the failure of smaller firms in the Czech Republic to have a formal process for coming up with product or market opportunities. While Mr. Tomas acknowledged that companies which engage in a systematic decision-making process are more successful than those which do not, he contributed the failure of KMF to have a formal systematic decision-making process to a lack of capability in determining and overcoming potential barriers. He also indicated that, since hiring Mr. Novak, he has implemented team-planning meetings between the two of them. However, there is little or no input from other employees in the company on critical decision-making issues such as introducing new products or entering new markets.

Initial markets

It was expected that the accession of the Czech Republic to the EU in 2004 would help smaller firms such as KMF gain easier access to

Western European markets. Although the proportion of Czech firms involved in foreign markets has increased over the last several years, domestic markets account for the lion's share of their annual sales. Currently, KMF sells more than 80% of its products in the domestic market. KMF's international markets are limited to Austria and the Netherlands, and account for less than 20% of its sales. Despite the relative ease of entering other EU-member markets, the poor quality of some of its products and the inability to meet the required standards of the Western European countries prevent KMF from having much more success in its export markets.

As was mentioned earlier, the school furniture that KMF manufactures today is outdated and no longer used in Western European countries. Thus, the potential markets for such products are most likely in the less developed countries of Africa and Asia, where KMF has no presence. On the other hand, KMF's other product lines such as garden and interior furniture are very suitable for EU markets. Mr. Novak contributes KMF's failure to sell more in EU markets not only to the poor quality of some of its products, but also to its lack of knowledge of foreign markets. KMF's limited capacity to acquire information about foreign markets and the use of resources are major factors explaining its low level of involvement and performance in export markets.

KMF's exports to Austria began by coincidence in 2000. Moravia is located next to the Austrian border, and KMF's original Austrian customer heard about the company by word of mouth and contacted KMF for a price quote on its metal garden furniture. After that successful transaction, both Mr. Tomas and Mr. Novak tried to expand exports to this market. Exports to the Dutch market started in nearly the same way. KMF's original Dutch customer was vacationing in Moravia and noticed its furniture. After inquiries about KMF and lengthy negotiations, exports to the Dutch market began. Today, more than half of KMF's exports are to this market.

Although these could be good examples of successful export marketing decisions being made on the basis of intuition and acumen, it is well known among academicians and practitioners that decisions based on marketing research information are an important factor in overall business success. It has been argued that the increased uncertainty posed by extending business to an unfamiliar market with unfamiliar environmental conditions intensifies the need for marketing information. This increases the urgency for KMF's executives to attend foreign trade shows and educate themselves about foreign markets targeted by the firm. Attendance at fairs and missions is a factor with the greatest influence on export expansion. Neither Mr. Tomas nor Mr. Novak has attended any foreign trade shows. They are both fluent in German, and attributed their knowledge of the German language as their main success factor in the Austrian market. When asked if they have tried to export to Germany, the biggest EU economy, they indicated their fear of entering such a big market.

Export obstacles

The most obvious reason companies do not seek to develop new markets is simply their failure to recognize that new markets exist. This lack of knowledge could be due to either a lack of effort to find out what opportunities exist or a lack of effort to explore opportunities in the new markets. The process of systematically exploring export possibilities is a very powerful discriminator between successful exporters and non-exporters. Generally, successful exporters put more effort into systematically searching for export opportunities than do non-exporters. Once Mr. Novak joined KMF, he created a process for evaluating foreign market potential. He acknowledged that, due to limited financial resources, the company is unable to explore all of those opportunities. In the past, KMF attempted several times to hire foreign agents to represent it in foreign markets. According to Mr. Novak, these attempts failed as many of the foreign agents declined to represent such a small client as KMF. When Mr. Novak was asked if KMF had considered advertising in any foreign journal to market its products, he indicated that, due to the high cost of advertising in foreign journals, it is unable to afford such a venture.

KMF's road to success in exporting to EU markets has not been an easy one. KMF has had to deal with numerous obstacles in dealing with its EU customers. Its main obstacle to exports today is the prosperity of the main "old" EU countries. The strengthening koruna could pose another barrier, but Mr. Tomas says that this cannot markedly hurt the conditions for KMF exports. Mr. Novak points out, "We try to diminish its negative influence by offering better-quality products with higher added value." He then continues, "Unfortunately, the share of know-how contributing to the value of our products is usually low, so when competing on global markets we have to stress low prices rather than the high quality and careful development of our products." Even though KMF offers goods that are comparable to those of Spain and Italy, for example, foreign customers still have the tendency to discount the prices of its products to about 60% of those of Western European competitors. According to Mr. Novak, "The hallmark of an Eastern European company is holding us back to a certain degree. If we succeed in improving our image, it would facilitate our position in those markets." However, KMF is learning how to move in the competitive environment of the EU, where it is better able to penetrate with goods mainly thanks to high quality, honesty, and good communication.

Future markets

In order to expand both its domestic and foreign markets, KMF has realized that it must restructure its production lines in order to capture new markets. As mentioned earlier, meeting new product standards in other countries is very critical for capturing new foreign markets. Since exports account for a small portion of KMF's sales volume, this suggests that these restructuring efforts have not been significant. For KMF to succeed in its efforts, it must understand customer needs in both domestic and foreign markets. It is agreed that understanding customer needs will contribute to the success of new products. Unfortunately, KMF has no formal planning process for evaluating the introduction of new products or market diversification. Although some of its outdated products are not suitable for Western European markets, KMF could find customers in less developed countries; however, KMF executives indicated no interest in offering its products in those markets.

International sales enhance profitability, improve capacity utilization, and reduce reliance on one market. Mr. Tomas agrees that, generally, KMF's exports are more profitable than its domestic sales. However, in his opinion, exchange rate fluctuations can have a major impact on export profitability. Until early 2008, while the value of the Czech koruna was relatively high compared to the euro and the U.S. dollar, KMF's profit from exports shrunk due to the fact that KMF had no choice but to invoice its foreign customers mostly in euros rather than koruna. But the value of the koruna has taken a major hit since mid-2008, which will make export sales more profitable for KMF. The substantial changes in exchange rates have not induced KMF to either enter new markets or exit the Austrian and Dutch markets in which it already operates. Mr. Tomas, however, hopes that the Czech Republic will join the eurozone countries in the near future as that would stabilize KMF's export profit.

Systematic exploration of international business opportunities

The establishment of JT Metal Fabricating, the predecessor of KMF, almost coincided with the transformation from a centrally planned economy to a market economy. According to Mr. Tomas, replacements were needed for virtually vanished markets in Eastern Europe and other countries of the Soviet Bloc. During the early years of transformation, many companies struggled. Slowly but surely, however, through constant improvement in their product quality, smaller companies such as KMF were successful in gaining a share of the demanding markets of the Western world. Mr. Tomas agrees that international trade plays an ever-greater role in today's ongoing globalization and in the continuing economic integration of the Czech Republic into the EU. The value of KMF's exports has increased every year, albeit more slowly than Mr. Tomas had hoped. Mr. Tomas, his company, and numerous other small- and medium-sized manufacturers have played a major role in revitalizing the Czech Republic's economy. This is evident by the observation that in the early 1990s, many exports from the Czech Republic were represented by raw materials and only some processed products; whereas today, the largest portion of exports includes manufacturing products with high added value. Highly developed foreign trade thus represents one of the core prerequisites of positive economic development in the Czech Republic.

The future prospects for KMF's products seem bright. Market demand for metal furniture in the Czech Republic is growing, as living standards continue to rise in what is one of Eastern Europe's richest economies. Although imports are also growing substantially, the bulk of the increase in consumption is currently being met by Czech manufacturers, including KMF which finds itself in a relatively strong competitive position. This is borne out by the rapid increase in manufacturing output and productivity, reflecting strongly growing exports and domestic sales in recent years. The opportunities, prospects, and problems facing KMF in the Czech Republic and other European markets are similar to those of other companies competing in those markets. Customers in European markets are demanding new product ideas and designs, and KMF must be prepared to meet these needs. The Czech market is also characterized by growth in demand for, output of, and trade in furniture.

After decades of communism, consumers in the Czech Republic are now making use of their right to choose, and KMF must be ready to respond to consumer wishes. This means moving to higher-quality products and catering to more discriminating customers. KMF has been quick to adopt design and manufacturing innovations and to integrate new materials into its products. Its high-quality and well-finished outdoor and indoor metal furniture with original designs has good opportunities not only in the domestic market, but also in Western European countries such as Germany. Mr. Tomas is mindful of the fact that the pressures of globalization are also creating better market opportunities for exporters from other countries such as China into the European countries. In response to this competition, KMF must emphasize its design input and import component parts from lower-cost sources, mainly in Asia.

KMF must develop a new marketing strategy specifically aimed at penetrating and building up sales in the European markets. Germany, as well as existing markets in Austria and the Netherlands, should be regarded as an integral part of KMF's overall market expansion. KMF is in a good position to enter Germany's market, given the proximity of Germany to the Czech Republic. Also, the fact that Mr. Tomas is fluent in German should help him communicate with potential customers. The use of metal materials by itself should give KMF an advantage, as there is a strong Green movement in Germany that discourages consumers from using wood furniture.

Working together with a local sales agent may offer the best and most cost-efficient method of establishing sales in the difficult business environment of the Western European markets, where communicating in the local language is often crucial. Finally, visiting and eventually taking part in relevant European and other regional fairs is a second step for action once an initial impression of the market has been obtained through market research.

Summary

KMF has been a successful family-owned business for almost two decades. It fabricates metal garden and interior furniture. Located in the southern part of the Czech Republic, the company is managed by the founder, Mr. Tomas, and a professional manager, Mr. Novak, who was hired to direct the company through tough economic times. As the company has evolved, the focus of the company's founder has changed from being a craftsman manager focusing on production capabilities to a rational manager who has acted in a logical and rational manner in spite of all the problems.

Over the years, the company has enjoyed an advantage by manufacturing high-quality products at competitive prices. KMF's prices are generally about half the prices of its competitors in Western European countries. Unfortunately, low prices have not met the expectations of increased sales growth for KMF. Mr. Tomas attributes this failure to an erroneous perception among his customers who correlate low prices for his products with low quality.

The current economic slowdown has affected KMF's sales and profit. So far, the company has not made any employees redundant; but the management of the company knows that, if the economic situation does not turn around soon, they may have no choice but to lay off workers. The current economic situation also jeopardizes the potential future growth of the company. In order to achieve its desired growth, the company must rely mainly on internal financing, as the financial institutions and government of the Czech Republic are not providing any financial support for small companies such as KMF.

Unfortunately, KMF has no formal planning process for evaluating the introduction of new products or market diversification. Although the management of the company acknowledges the benefits of such a process, they attribute their failure to have a formal systematic decision-making process to a lack of capability in determining and overcoming potential barriers.

More than 80% of KMF's sales are to customers in the Czech Republic. However, the company's international sales are growing. Through constant improvement in the quality of its products, KMF has been successful in gaining a share of the demanding markets of Western Europe such as Austria and the Netherlands. But the company realizes the need to further expand its markets. In order to achieve this goal, it needs to restructure its production lines in order to capture new markets. However, the efforts to expand exports have encountered numerous obstacles. The worsening economic conditions in Western European countries as well as customers' perceptions about the poor quality of products from Eastern and Central European countries are examples of these obstacles.

Nevertheless, the future prospects for KMF seem bright. Customers in European markets are demanding new product ideas and designs, and KMF is prepared to meet these needs. KMF must emphasize its design input and import component parts from lower-cost sources, mainly in Asia.

The main characteristics of KMF are as follows: (1) a family business operated by an owner and a professional manager; (2) producing high-quality products for general applications; (3) operating successfully in both domestic and growing international markets; and (4) possessing dynamic future growth due to the growing Green movement around the world.

11.2 Danish Cases

11.2.1 *Cembrit Holding*[3]

Company background and focus

The asbestos fiber-cement industry started in Austria during the beginning of the 20th century when an Austrian engineer, Ludwig Hatschek, invented a method for producing thin asbestos fiber-reinforced cement sheets. The method bore the name of the inventor and became known as the Hatschek process. The products of this process were considered to be superior to similar products on the market at that time — stronger, weather-resistant, thin, and light-weight. For these reasons, they were used in the production of various building materials including corrugated roofing sheets, wall coverings, and water pipes. Mr. Hatschek internationalized the production method by entering into license agreements with many cement companies in a number of European countries, including the Netherlands, Belgium, France, Norway, Sweden, Switzerland, and Denmark. He subsequently licensed the technology to companies outside Europe and, over time, asbestos cement became a common building material worldwide. Cembrit was established in 1927 under a Hatschek license agreement as a subsidiary of Aalborg Portland, a Danish cement company.[4] It started as Dansk Eternit Fabrik (DEF), and became Dansk Eternit Holding A/S (DEH) in 1994 and then Cembrit Holding[5] in 2008.

---

[3] Professor John Kuada of Aalborg University in Denmark developed this case with the permission of Cembrit Holding. This case cannot be copied or electronically reproduced in any form without written permission from the author.

[4] Aalborg Portland was, until 2003, a part of the FLSmidth & Co. Group, one of the world's major producers of cement processing equipment and factories with a turnover of approximately 20,000 million Danish kroner.

[5] The name "Cembrit" has its origins in the Cimbrians, nomadic tribesmen from Northern Jutland (around 100 B.C.) who fought their way through Europe in a "conquering" quest. By adopting this name, Cembrit's management would like to signalize the company's Cimbrian thrust for adventure and drive on the global scene.

Products

The company has two product lines, each serving a distinct market segment:

(1) Roofing materials — comprising corrugated sheets (used in the agricultural and industrial construction market segment) and roofing slates (used in residential buildings and other high-end construction projects); and

(2) Flat sheets — used for both exterior and interior wall cladding.

Competitive advantage

By the end of 2008, Cembrit had become the second major producer of fiber-cement products in Europe, holding about a 20% share of the market. The company's long-term growth can be attributed to a combination of strategies that has ensured technological improvements, product adaptations, new product development, and territorial expansion. It was one of only two companies in the world that embraced the challenge of converting asbestos-based production to asbestos-free products in the 1980s. This provided the company with a first-mover advantage in markets outside Denmark. But by the end of the 1990s, asbestos-free production technology became widely accessible within the industry and no longer provided Cembrit with a unique competitive advantage.

Importance

Today, the top management sees effective management, continued investments in R&D, keeping investments in sales, and its marketing platform as the most important determinants of corporate performance within the industry. According to Cembrit's business development manager, all fiber-cement producers can avail themselves of the technology required to produce fiber-cement products, but effective management can differentiate a company from its competitors. Cembrit therefore plans to continue to invest in R&D in order to continuously improve its products for the various market segments that it serves and to maintain a good brand image within the industry. Management has also begun to rely less on its production platform as a growth driver and more on marketing, customer relationship management, and value-added services to customers (e.g. finding new uses for its products by collaborating with key user groups).

Impact of economic and political decisions on the market

The 1970s witnessed an increased suspicion by the health authorities in Europe and North America that asbestos was hazardous to human health. This provoked a stream of legal restrictions to asbestos usage in these countries. The Scandinavian countries reacted promptly by banning asbestos in the construction industry and in products that come into direct contact with human beings and animals; the reactions were initially less dramatic in the Southern European countries. The negative publicity that the industry received in various European countries, combined with the legal restrictions, began to erode consumer confidence in asbestos-based products. This triggered a technological challenge within the industry to find substitutes for asbestos.

Prior to the 1980s, Cembrit's products were asbestos-based, just like other fiber-cement companies in Europe at that time. The company was therefore faced with the choice of leaving the business altogether or embracing the technological challenge of finding asbestos-free fiber substitutes. Shareholders' support was obtained to engage in R&D activities aimed at developing asbestos-free products. A series of experiments was conducted, and the results revealed that cellulose fibers were good substitutes for asbestos if the compound was subjected to "accelerated curing" under high temperature and high pressure. The R&D department also developed an alternative technology using various types of synthetic fiber. The two technologies were applied in the production of different products within Cembrit. By 1987, the company was able to convert all of its production lines to produce asbestos-free products. This meant substantial increases in the costs of raw materials and components as well as in investment costs for new technologies and equipment. With these developments, the company redefined its line of business, leaving the asbestos fiber-cement industry altogether and entering a new (non-asbestos) fiber-cement industry with higher-priced products, a new competitive arena (competing with different types of metals and aluminum products), and new growth opportunities.

Market trends and the future of the company

Cembrit considers growth trends in key markets as critical to its future performance. Industry analyses have revealed that Europe will continue to be a major market for fiber-cement products. The European market was estimated at some €1 billion in 2007 or approximately 1.5 million tons of fiber-cement products.[6] Western Europe now accounts for about 80% of the market, with corrugated sheets taking about 50% of this market; roofing slates, 25%; and flat sheets, 25%.

Central and Eastern European countries, which were major markets for asbestos fiber cement under communism, also changed to non-asbestos fiber products in the second half of the 1990s. The change provided Cembrit with an opportunity to enter the market in the mid-1990s, first by buying majority shares in EZA Sumperk a.s. (a Czech company) in 1993. Cembrit CZ was established in 1996. In 2000, Cembrit acquired Izopol (a Polish company); the company was restructured over a period of 3–5 years, during which a management team was established and it became fully integrated into the Cembrit group of companies.

In the U.S., asbestos fiber cement has historically been available but the market has been small compared to other parts of the world.[7]

---

[6] The volume of consumption of asbestos fiber cement in Europe in the pre-1980 era was by far bigger than the consumption of asbestos-free fiber cement today. But if we see asbestos-free fiber cement as a new industry which started in the 1980s, it makes sense to see consumption as growing steadily from zero in 1980 to a market worth €1 billion in 2007.

[7] Around the mid-1990s, fiber cement in the form of "siding" — imitation wood — started to gain popularity as a competitive product to real wood and vinyl plastic imitation wood siding.

After asbestos disappeared from the industry, the Australian company James Hardie developed a market-leader position in fiber-cement products in the U.S. by growing the market from scratch to about a 12% share of exterior siding claddings in the residential construction segment. This corresponded to annual sales of about US$500 million in 2007.

The Etex Group (of Belgium) has a dominant market position in Europe, with about 50% of the market share. With an approximately 20% share of the European market, Cembrit has the second-largest market share and is therefore a significant player on the market. Other major competitors in the industry include Swiss Eternit AG with about 10% of the market share, and Eternit-Werke Ludwig Hatschek (EWLH) with about 5% of the market share. The remaining 15% is distributed among other independent fiber-cement manufacturers.

Systematic decision-making process

Until 1980, Cembrit sold its products exclusively on the Danish market. Its internationalization process started in 1980, with a significant growth in exports, particularly in 1983 and 1984 due to orders received from England. This occurred at a time when the company was experiencing a significant decline in domestic demand for its products, partly due to a general economic downturn and the anti-asbestos debate in Denmark. The management established an export department in 1982, and engaged in deliberate export market search and entry strategies. As the business development manager explained, exports therefore helped the company to address the capacity utilization challenges that it faced in the 1980s, with the export share of total earnings rising steadily from zero in 1980 to 16% in 1989.

The growth in exports encouraged the management to pursue more aggressive export strategies, utilizing the fact that Cembrit was an early mover in terms of transforming its production systems to produce asbestos-free products. The export share of total turnover was targeted to reach 33% by 1992. In an effort to achieve this target, the company strengthened its position in a number of European markets in the early 1990s by establishing sales and/or production subsidiaries — first in the U.K. in 1986; followed by Finland, the Netherlands, and Germany in 1992; the Czech Republic in 1996; Poland and France in 2000; and then Sweden and Norway in 2003 (see Table 1 for details). The export target was exceeded in 1993 when the export share of Cembrit's total turnover climbed to 43%. By 2007, nearly 65% of the company's sales was generated outside Denmark and it had 13 subsidiaries in 12 European countries, with production units in Finland, the Czech Republic, and Poland (see Table 1).

Table 1   Overview of Cembrit's International Subsidiaries

Name of company	Country	Year of Cembrit involvement	Cembrit's shares (%)	Nature of business
Cembrit Blunn Ltd.	United Kingdom	1986	100	Sales and distribution
Oy Minerit AB	Finland	1992	100	Production, sales, distribution
Cembrit B.V.	The Netherlands	1992	100	Production, sales, distribution
Eurocem GmbH	Germany	1992	100	Sales and distribution
Cembrit CZ a.s.	Czech Republic	1996	96	Production, sales, distribution
Izopol S.A.	Poland	2000	100	Production, sales, distribution
Cembrit SAS	France	2000	100	Sales and distribution
Tepro Byggmaterial AB	Sweden	2003	100	Sales and distribution
Norsal as	Norway	2003	100	Sales and distribution
Eternit kft.	Hungary	2006	50	Production, sales, distribution
Cembrit SFS, s.r.o.	Slovakia	2006	100	Sales and distribution
Cembrit IBS, b.v.	The Netherlands	2006	100	Sales and distribution
Eternit s.r.l.	Romania	2006	50	Sales and distribution

In 2005, the company closed down its manufacturing plant in Aalborg, Denmark, which served as the only production factory until the 1990s. Now, with a staff of 40 people, the Danish subsidiary operates from Aalborg and serves the Danish market. The parent company — Cembrit Holding, which employs some 20–30 people in corporate functions — also has its head office in Aalborg. Thus, by 2009, Cembrit ceased to perceive itself as a Danish company with exports to other European countries; it now sees itself as a European company managing multiple domestic markets.

The function of the holding company is to exploit potential synergies of being a group, to implement coherent group strategies, and to avoid redundancy as the group expands with more and more subsidiaries. In response to this challenge, a new group management structure was adopted in 2003. This included the formation of a group management team with functional responsibilities for sales and marketing, production and administration, as well as finance, each headed by a functional executive group director. A Czech and a Finnish national were recruited internally for two of the group management positions. As of 2007, the group had about 900 employees worldwide creating a turnover of DKK 1,400 million (see Table 2).

Future markets

Cembrit has been considering two strategic market growth opportunities in recent years. One option is to continue its geographical market expansion, with a stronger focus on non-European markets where the demand for asbestos-free products has shown an increase. The other option is to increase its penetration of European markets. Top management considers the first option as requiring long-range planning and substantial resource commitment, but without commensurate economic gains. The second option has been assessed by management to be more achievable within a shorter time frame, since it is consistent with the company's past experience and competitive advantages. This assessment forms the basis of the company's current market growth strategies.

Table 2   Financial Performance of Cembrit for the Period 2003–2007 (in DKK million)

Turnover	2007	2006	2005	2004	2003
Denmark	433	394	418	308	303
Scandinavia	207	168	141	111	84
Europe	770	628	563	539	494
North America	9	10	6	7	6
South America	0	0	0	0	0
Africa	0	0	0	0	0
Australia	0	0	0	0	0
Asia	0	16	19	12	10
Net turnover	1,419	1,216	1,147	977	897
Production costs	945	804	771	925	683
Gross profit	474	412	376	52	214
EBIT	124	81	61	−397	−83
Profit/loss for the year	97	120	52	−400	−108

Obstacles to internationalization

Cembrit is now firmly established in European markets, with a local presence in all major markets and with a group structure coordinating its business activities. It has, however, been faced with several challenges in the internationalization process, each challenge providing management with new experiences and skills for further growth.

During the initial stages of its internationalization process, the company took over some of its importers' businesses in order to gain control over its operations and to increase its international business knowledge. The original owners remained with the company as local subsidiary managers. But in some cases, the original owners experienced difficulties in adjusting to their new roles as members of an international corporate management group, thus creating obstacles in integrating the companies into the corporate family. This led Cembrit's management to opt for a strategy of outright acquisition, i.e. without the continued participation of the previous owners.

Cembrit also faced challenges in product adaptation. Management noted that each country had its own traditions with respect to the size, shape, and color of preferred building materials. Internationalization therefore necessitated the modification of production technologies and processes in order to accommodate the differences in consumer preferences in the different foreign markets. This resulted in significant investment in new technologies and equipment.

Another major challenge that Cembrit faced was regarding its entry into the Central and Eastern European countries in the mid-1990s. The challenge was how to manage the local subsidiaries effectively without deploying Danish personnel there. For example, when the Czech joint venture was established, Cembrit hoped that it could retain the local managers at the top management level since they possessed the local business knowledge that was believed to be very important for successful operations. The Danish personnel who were sent to the country were to act as advisors to local management and, therefore, had no executive power. However, it quickly turned out that there were huge gaps between the Danish and local managers' understanding of how the business should be run. This was aggravated by the local managers' language difficulties. There were therefore several incidents of miscommunication and misunderstanding, resulting in difficulties in integrating the companies as rapidly as desired. In addition to this, many of the local top managers in the Eastern European companies that Cembrit acquired had been appointed to these positions due to their political affiliations. This meant that they did not necessarily have the right professional qualifications for the job. Cembrit's top management was thus compelled to replace them with Danish expatriates after the companies were acquired, although this resulted in higher costs.

In the case of the Czech companies, Cembrit addressed the staffing problem by recruiting and training younger local employees for the managerial positions in the companies. Some were trained in Denmark, and were guided to understand the vision and mission of the Cembrit group and to embrace its corporate culture. This approach proved successful. The Danes were withdrawn once the Czech managers were ready to take over. These subsidiaries are now managed by a qualified Czech management team, which adopts a leadership style that is consistent with Cembrit's corporate cultural values. The experience gained in the Czech Republic subsequently helped Cembrit to speed up the integration processes of companies acquired in Poland and Hungary in subsequent years.

Future outlook and strategies

Recent developments have encouraged the top management of Cembrit to look toward the future with optimism. In its estimation, the growth prospects in some of the European markets remain fairly good for the next five years. Management is therefore confident that it can move the company in a direction that ensures profitable and controlled growth and can strengthen Cembrit's position as the second major producer of asbestos-free products in Europe, after Etex (the market leader in Europe). Management has formulated the company's goals (and vision) for the next five years in the following words:

- "We will make Cembrit known as the leading promoter of fiber cement in Europe"; and
- "We will position fiber cement as the building material for innovative and aesthetical architecture."

These goals signal an ambition to pursue a strong proactive role in expanding the European fiber-cement market in competition with other types of building materials, rather than gaining market share at the expense of smaller fiber-cement producers. The management's main challenge is to formulate a coherent strategy that will help achieve this goal, taking changes in industry and market configurations into account but avoiding undue risks to the company. This requires taking actions in the following two areas:

- Strengthening Cembrit's low-delivery-cost capabilities; and
- Building a stronger corporate identity.

Reducing delivery costs partly entails improving the coordination of the company's logistics activities and streamlining its enterprise resource planning (ERP) systems. Substantial progress has already been made in both areas. All subsidiaries in Cembrit must now adopt the group's financial and management reporting system.

The adoption of the name "Cembrit" in 2008 is part of the corporate branding and identity development process. As shown in Table 1, all 13 companies comprising the Cembrit group had different names prior to 2008 and maintained unique national identities in their respective local operational environments. With the new name, all of the companies have been brought together into one corporate entity and with a common identity. Although some national differences may persist, Cembrit as a whole is now guided by a common vision and sense of direction.

Summary

Cembrit has developed from a local manufacturer of asbestos-based fiber-cement products for the construction industry to an international company producing asbestos-free products. It now has a significant market position in Europe, being a market leader in Scandinavia as well as in Central and Eastern European countries. Its growth has been driven by strategic investments in technology, improvements in operational efficiencies, and customer relationship management. The management still sees good growth opportunities in Europe and will pursue this, partly by increasing its competitive strengths relative to other fiber-cement companies and partly by adopting a proactive strategy in the growing fiber-cement market as a whole.

11.2.2 *Migatronic*[8]

Company background

Migatronic is a medium-sized manufacturing company located in a small town in the northern part of Denmark. The Migatronic story began in 1970 when the company was born in a chicken house (chicken hutch). Migatronic produces welding machines and, over the past 40 years, has developed from a village mechanic selling low-price CO_2 welding machines to an internationally recognized supplier of high-quality welding machines, including automatic, robotic, and electronic welding solutions for advanced industrial applications.

It all began when a salesman visited the mechanic in an attempt to sell him a welding machine to fix cars in his shop. The mechanic found the machine to be too expensive and not good enough, and decided to make one himself. He had some assistance from a friend who was an electrical engineer. Together, they developed a small welding machine that could be used for welding thin plates (0.5–2.0 mm) such as those on car bodies. At that time, it was unusual to be concerned with rust prevention on car bodies; it was cheaper to replace the parts. But car owners in Denmark practiced rust prevention, due to the high prices for cars and the high degree of corrosion caused by Danish weather.

Welding machines were well known, and were normally produced for general industry and for thicker metal plates (2.0 mm and above). For the first two to three years, Migatronic and a few others who became aware of the automobile market were the only producers of small welding machines. Later, in light of the oil crisis, most other European countries became interested in the upkeep of cars, which in turn required welding machines to be used when replacing the plates.

In the beginning, the mechanic and the electrical engineer produced and sold welding machines to local garages. The business grew

---

[8] Professor Olav Jull Sørensen of Aalborg University in Denmark developed this case with the permission of Migatronic. This case cannot be copied or electronically reproduced in any form without written permission from the author.

and, in 1971, they hired a mechanical engineer, whose main job was to document and systematize the production process. More people were hired in the following years. In 1972, the mechanic became fed up with all of the administrative work and sold his part of the company to the recently employed mechanical engineer.

From its small beginning, Migatronic expanded rather quickly during the 1970s and 1980s. In 1984, the company was quoted on the Copenhagen Stock Exchange. At that time, the electrical engineer wanted to sell his half of the company. The shares were bought by several people, including the mechanical engineer who became the majority shareholder and who has been the owner-manager of Migatronic ever since.

Today, Migatronic is among the 10 largest welding machine producers in Europe. It sold machines and accessories for around DKK 425 million in 2008. The largest European producer has a size two and a half times that of Migatronic. At the factory in Denmark, Migatronic employs around 300 people. Migatronic also has 200 employees abroad and produces more than 20,000 welding machines annually at its factories in Italy, India, and China, and maintains 10 sales subsidiaries in major European markets.

Focus

Migatronic has always emphasized good workmanship. In the late 1980s when quality control needed improvement, the company decided to aim for ISO 9001 certification, which was achieved in 1992. Migatronic engages primarily in order production. Parts of the production process are automated, the production equipment is flexible, and the company is able to deliver welding machines which are adapted to specific customer needs. The products are mainly different combinations of standard parts, but in some cases Migatronic even develops specific parts in order to serve the needs of just one customer. The company's added value is approximately 50% — a figure which emphasizes Migatronic's ability to produce in-house. This is partly a reflection of the company's somewhat isolated location with few nearby industrial support facilities. Over the past 40 years,

Migatronic has experienced waves of both insourcing and outsourcing; whether to insource or outsource has depended on the technology and the price. The welding machines currently produced have electronic smart boxes installed and these cannot be produced completely by Migatronic. In order to compete, in 2007 Migatronic established a joint venture in China to take advantage of lower labor costs. As the CEO explained in his interview, "It takes five to seven hours to put a welding machine together from its parts. The hourly rate is DKK 300 in Denmark while it is DKK 15 in China."

Good workmanship is still a hallmark of Migatronic. However, since no major technological breakthrough in welding technology has occurred since about 1980, competing products are relatively similar in terms of technology. The focus in Migatronic today is on intelligent welding machines, technical service back-up, and ease in use of the welding machines. Migatronic brands its products as "Switch on–Press–Weld," indicating that Migatronic machines are the most user-friendly machines on the market. In the words of the owner-manager, "Don't develop what is possible. Develop what the customers want."

Products

Since the first simple welding machine aimed at local garages for car repair, Migatronic has expanded its product program tremendously. This expansion has been guided both by specific market needs in various industries and by technological opportunities. Today, the inverter technology is the technology mostly used in its products.

Apart from its own Migatronic-brand welding machines, Migatronic also produces private-label machines for customers interested in having their own line of welding machines. Such orders, however, constitute only a small share of total sales.

In addition, Migatronic supplies various accessories. These are not produced by Migatronic, but by larger multinational companies which can capture economies of scale for these products. Migatronic procures standard products on the market or has the accessories produced according to Migatronic specifications. Some accessories are sold with the Migatronic brand; others are not. Sales of accessories are important, as the life span of a welding machine is seven years. As a rule of thumb, for each DKK 100 of equipment, the customers buy DKK 300 of accessories. Migatronic thus sees the sales of accessories both as a separate business and as part of its service package to customers.

The fact that a welding machine has an average market life of seven years creates a special problem for Migatronic, as it must continue producing and stocking spare parts. In addition, certain markets are rather conservative and favor the older generation of non-electronic welding machines, forcing Migatronic to run two production lines, making it more difficult to capture economies of scale.

In 1985, Migatronic established Migatronic Automation as a separate company in another small town closer to the regional capital. One reason for this location was that Migatronic Automation would require more engineers, and the expectation was that it would be easier to recruit engineers from the regional university if Migatronic Automation was located close to the city. Furthermore, although synergy between Migatronic and Migatronic Automation was expected, the business models were different in that Migatronic was based on serial production whereas Migatronic Automation was project-based. Migatronic Automation produces special equipment adapted to each customer, as well as more standardized products which can be sold to companies with robotics know-how. Migatronic Automation is also an agent for a Japanese company, FANUC Robotics, so Migatronic Automation is able to produce and sell complete robot solutions to its customers. Thus, Migatronic Automation differs from Migatronic because it operates in markets beyond the welding industry, especially in robotics. The robots may also be used by companies that do not have welding as part of their production but merely need the robots for something else. Today, Migatronic Automation employs around 60 engineers and technicians.

Whenever possible, Migatronic Automation buys the welding machines from Migatronic and integrates them in larger automatized set-ups, making the proper adjustments for the single customer. Migatronic Automation has, so far, carried out most of its export sales directly from Denmark, but now both Migatronic Automation and Migatronic are taking initiatives to coordinate sales and marketing through the foreign sales subsidiaries so that Migatronic Automation can take advantage of their market expertise. Automation is a growth area, especially in markets with high labor costs in which customers can save on labor costs by converting from manual welding to robot welding.

Competitive advantage through innovation

With the focus on quality, durability, and services, pricing has never been used as the key competitive instrument. Migatronic caters to the upper market of welding-based industries. Close contact to the market has guided the innovation activities of Migatronic, and this link to customers forms the basic competitive advantage of Migatronic. Up-to-date technology, easy access to accessories, and good technical service are the areas that make Migatronic remain competitive. Migatronic has an R&D department with 30 engineers who are responsible for both product and process development. Each year, Migatronic launches new products and features at major exhibitions; many of the new products focus on ease of use, including making the machines more intelligent, handheld, easy to move, safe to use, durable, and of high quality. The quality and stability are exemplified by the use of welding machines in the construction of the Øresund Bridge from Copenhagen to Sweden, where the machines were used seven days a week from January 1998 to October 1999 with no need for back-up machines and no welding failures.

Migatronic does take out patents on designs, technology, and software. However, it is not a big problem to copy the technology, the owner-manager claims, indicating that patents cannot replace a proactive innovation strategy. Combined with the sales and distribution strategy of Migatronic, it seems that Migatronic is market-driven but very technology-conscious.

Impact of economic conditions and local embeddedness

During its almost 40 years of existence, Migatronic has experienced ups and downs, both in sales and in profit, but in general has been able to expand and continuously consolidate the company. The present goals are for an organic growth of 10% per annum and a profit-over-sales ratio of 5–8%. In the auto industry, economic cycles may shift the market from producing new cars to having the garages repair old cars when people cannot afford to buy new ones. Obviously, Migatronic has benefited from the creation of the EU Internal Market and could thus also take advantage of the gradual expansion of the EU to include the Eastern European countries. Most of these countries have a legacy from the central planning era of metallurgical industries and therefore they have become an important outsourcing platform for Western European multinational companies; in other words, the latter acquired so-called "brown industries" (companies that have the land, buildings, and workforce, but have old technology).

The global trend to outsource to Asia has caused a shift in the world economic order. Migatronic has had to adapt to this by following its customers to these new markets. The present economic crisis is also harming Migatronic and sales are down. Migatronic is adjusting its organization, and this includes a reduction in the workforce both in Denmark and in the sales and production subsidiaries abroad. Migatronic is not in danger of collapse, as it has generally accumulated funds to overcome such fluctuations. However, Migatronic did expect a deficit in 2009.

Migatronic is — and has always been — very much embedded in local community affairs. Even though it is very much an international company, it has remained with the very small bank in town that trusted the then-young entrepreneurs and provided Migatronic with a loan. Migatronic has also participated in projects that respond to social problems in the local community, such as the inclusion of handicapped people in the workforce and the integration of foreigners, among others. The social orientation of Migatronic towards the local community is part of the company's value statement, which, according to the CEO, states that "Migatronic is conscious of its responsibility to the local community and takes community interests into account in its choice of suppliers, employment, etc."

Future of the company

In spite of the ups and downs, the owner-manager is confident of the future for Migatronic. In 1995, when Migatronic celebrated its 25th anniversary, he wrote in the Jubilee Brochure:

> Migatronic will always be needed. In 25 years' time Migatronic will still be in the welding industry. I dare not predict how our machines will look like by then, but the joining of metals will always be needed, and I can see no better, quicker and more efficient procedures than welding. Migatronic's challenge — and goal — will continue to be to stay in the forefront of welding machine development using the latest and most advanced technology, and introducing new components. Machines can satisfy the requirements for speed without compromising on quality and user-friendliness.

So far, 14 years later, he is right. The global market is estimated to be around DKK 10 billion and Migatronic's share is only 3%. Three events in 2007 and 2008 also testify to the fact that Migatronic is still a very active and cutting-edge player in the market. In 2007, Migatronic established a joint venture in China to stay price-competitive and also to establish a platform for entering the Chinese market; in the same year, Migatronic won a large contract from one of the leading European car manufacturers; and in 2008, Migatronic launched a new plasma welding machine. In 2006, Migatronic won the iF Product Design Award, showing that functionality is augmented with design.

The future will, however, bring changes to Migatronic. The owner-manager is in his mid-60s and he will soon face a succession problem. No official plans have been made, and the thoughts and reflections of the owner-manager are not yet apparent. The current economic crisis will also affect the company's future, depending on how deep and how long the crisis will be. For 2009, Migatronic adjusted both its sales and profit expectations downwards and also adjusted its workforce. This decline period is being used proactively to upgrade the workforce in various areas, for example, instituting the principles of lean production in order to increase productivity.

Systematic decision-making process

As in most start-ups, action was more important than planning in the early years. However, documentation of products and processes was essential, and this was the reason for hiring the present owner-manager in 1971. With his background as a mechanical engineer, he could assure documentation. He was also the person who ensured that Migatronic acquired the ISO 9001 certification in 1992.

Since then, Migatronic has introduced IT-based management systems in almost all areas, including production, sales, quality, finance, configuration of products, etc. "We control everything," the owner-manager says — and his statement is not meant to brag about the way the company is managed. He is very focused on avoiding too much bureaucracy. When bureaucracy increases, so do costs. "I get crazy, and then the bureaucracy curve goes down again," he says. The owner-manager is not against planning, but he also believes that there has to be room for making mistakes.

Good workmanship is a top priority for the owner-manager. He associates good workmanship with producing in-house as much as possible, including the processing equipment, the design of the factory, and the processing layout.

He is a man of "small steps" and he does not favor involving too many people in decision making. He seems to manage as he goes and monitors trends closely. Bigger decisions have been made over the company's 40 years of existence, including the bold steps related to opting for the Copenhagen Stock Exchange, establishing Migatronic Automation, and offshoring production to its Chinese joint venture.

Since 1984, Migatronic has been self-financing its development, including the factory which has been expanded three times. Migatronic is a well-consolidated company financially. The owner-manager does not want to be dependent on banks and other financial institutions. He wants to be able to move on his own when he sees a good opportunity in the market, including the possibility to acquire a competitor. Bankers would claim that he is overcautious with the result that the rate of return on his invested capital is modest.

As innovation is crucial to the competitiveness of Migatronic, it may serve as an example of how plans and decisions are made within the company. The innovation process at Migatronic is organized according to a number of stages, from the ideas to specification and design and further on to construction, testing, production trial, and then to the final stage, production. At each stage, a number of people are involved in an ad hoc working committee. The membership of the ad hoc committee is contingent upon which tasks have to be undertaken at the stage in question, and personnel from any white-collar department may be involved in the process. The R&D department is normally involved in each stage and also acts as the secretariat for a permanent product committee. The permanent product committee, which comprises the top managers and one of the product managers, initiates, supervises, and finalizes all projects.

Ideas for new projects may come from a number of sources. Sometimes it may be an outcome of formalized activities, while at other times it may appear as "spontaneous" ideas (however, even the "spontaneous" ideas are normally based on observations and contacts in the marketplace). Migatronic stays in close contact with its foreign sales subsidiaries in order to obtain knowledge about new needs and opportunities in the various export markets. Furthermore, ideas are sometimes conceived by an observation of competitor behavior or are suggested by some of the educational institutions within Migatronic's customer segments. Finally, ideas may appear through contact with Migatronic's industrial customers.

Even if Migatronic runs a very systematic innovation process, it is often the non-traditional solutions that count, such as when the owner-manager suddenly realized that all he needed for a specific innovation was the spring used in a ballpoint pen.

Initial export markets and market expansion

The first export order came from Sweden in 1972, two years after the company was established. The Swedish importer was in need of a broad range of welding machines to serve the various industries in the Swedish market. By 1985, Migatronic had developed and produced a wide range of welding machines based on different technologies. Around 1990, Migatronic was selling its welding equipment and accessories to eight different segments of the metal processing industry, ranging from heavy ship building to light industries such as bicycle manufacturing. In addition, Migatronic also sells to precious metal industries, chemical factories, the car industry, and various institutions including schools. The product lines are estimated at around 40 different machines, which are marketed to more than 30 countries, primarily in Europe.

Migatronic has a market share of 50–60% of the Danish market. Foreign sales are about 65–70% of total sales. This percentage of foreign sales has been rather stable over a number of years.

International expansion had a good start with the Swedish importer in 1972 and continued thereafter. Migatronic quickly established exports to all nearby markets, and subsequently to the more distant EU markets. This took place while the newer EU Internal Market was heavily debated in the 1980s and gradually implemented in the late 1980s and 1990s. Migatronic established sales subsidiaries in some markets. This was not a smooth process, as some of the sales offices were established due to the unsatisfactory performance of the importer or distributor. The first sales subsidiaries were established in 1979 in two of the largest markets in Europe, Germany and the U.K.; this was followed by one in France in 1980. After some revision of the sales and distribution strategy (see below), five new sales subsidiaries were established in 1991–1992 in Italy, Sweden, Norway, Hungary, and the Czech Republic. Today, Migatronic has 10 sales subsidiaries of various sizes in Europe.

Expansion continued to the more distant markets in Eastern Europe, the Middle East, the U.S., and South Africa. By 1980, the first export orders went to the U.S., China, and Egypt. Today, Migatronic sells its welding machines and accessories in about 40 countries.

During the strong international expansion in the 1970s and 1980s, profits, however, did not grow at the same speed as market

expansion. Migatronic therefore had to reconsider its strategy, perhaps even the role of internationalization in some way. Consequently,
Migatronic changed its strategy and started to concentrate on the distribution channel instead of just identifying and selling through
agents and importers. In 1994, the company launched the
"Distribution Campaign 1994", which had the basic aim of concen-
trating on and improving the distribution channels, especially in
Germany, the U.K., and France. The idea behind this campaign was
that the current range of export markets was too wide; hence, the distribution system was not efficient or intense enough mainly due to a
lack of service back-up. By increasing the number of distributors,
Migatronic wished to increase sales, establish closer contact with the
market, and assure improved knowledge of the needs of customers.
One of the main goals of the distribution campaign in other countries
was to increase the number of distributors in each country. As stated
by the marketing manager of Migatronic, "We want our welding
machines in the industry to be standing so close together that they
can have a conversation."

This new approach to distribution was, to a large extent, a replica
of the way Migatronic distributed its products in Denmark.
Migatronic implemented the new distributor system in Norway first,
and then in Germany and Sweden. This system builds on welding
centers, i.e. large distributors with a shop-in-shop and well-educated
personnel. The centers also contribute to advertising campaigns, participate in exhibitions, etc. The centers sell not only Migatronic
machines, but also Migatronic-brand filler materials and accessories.

Parallel to the distribution campaign, each sales subsidiary carried
out sales activities of its own. In markets where Migatronic did not
have a subsidiary but was represented by distributors, importers, or
agents, minor sales activities were launched. However, in general, the
activities and visits to these markets have been cut as part of the market rationalization process. This has resulted in a focus on eight
countries, including the three biggest outside of Denmark —
Germany, France, and the U.K. In these countries, the sales subsidiaries have been strengthened in order for them to work more
closely with the market and customers.

The goal for Migatronic is to be among the three largest companies (by market share/sales) in its most important markets. One of the means of reaching this goal, according to Migatronic, is by selling approximately 20% directly from the subsidiaries to the customers and the remaining 80% through distributors. The reason for this strategy is that it is less expensive and less troublesome to sell through distributors, as they do most of the field work. On the other hand, it is important to stay in touch with the market; therefore, Migatronic wants the subsidiaries themselves to have some direct sales to customers.

International expansion of production facilities

For 17 years, the business model of Migatronic was one of centralized production in one plant in Denmark and a flow of products from there to the many overseas markets. This required an expansion of the physical facility. The factory was not relocated, as Migatronic had acquired enough land at an early stage to manage even large expansions. Migatronic moved to the present site in 1976 and expanded the floor space in 1980, in 1985 by 2,000 m², and again in 1991 by 9,000 m².

In 1987, however, Migatronic acquired a producer in Italy. Migatronic was losing market share in the lucrative Italian market due to transport costs and the higher labor costs in Denmark as compared to Italy; Migatronic could not compete in the price-sensitive Italian market. Moreover, the Italian producer, in contrast to Migatronic in Denmark, relied to a large extent on subsuppliers for the parts. In recent years, the Italian affiliate has focused on development, especially of smaller and portable welding machines. This is done in conjunction with the company's innovation department in Denmark.

While the Italian venture aimed to hold on to a lucrative market, Migatronic has also considered the possibility of establishing production in other countries. In 1995, a study was made of the Hungarian market. The main conclusion was that the most appropriate method was to form a partnership with a Hungarian partner, due to legal, cultural, and other issues. The proposal for investment stressed the importance of quality and control, and examined how it would be possible to transfer the Danish model and technological level of production to Hungary. This plan, however, remained on the drawing board and was never realized as no suitable partner could be identified.

A study has also been made regarding outsourcing parts of production to Malaysia. It was proposed to establish a wholly owned manufacturing subsidiary and thereby benefit from Malaysian lower wages, good possibilities, experience in producing electronic products, and political stability. Again, the study never resulted in any real action, but the activities indicate Migatronic's continuous monitoring of and search for new opportunities.

In 2000, Migatronic entered a joint venture with an Indian company in the Madras area, the sole purpose of which was to enter and penetrate the Indian market. This factory was primarily for the assembly of components produced by Indian subsuppliers.

As a result of price pressure and the growth in certain Asian markets, Migatronic started investigating the possibility of outsourcing to China and in 2007 made the bold decision to enter a joint venture with a Chinese producer of welding machines in the Shanghai area based on in-house production as well as subsuppliers. This joint venture is using the newest technology, and aims at carving out a position in the fast-growing Chinese market. This market is growing both because China has become the manufacturing powerhouse for Western multinationals and because of economic growth in the domestic Chinese market, where almost all construction work is based on steel frames that need to be welded together.

Future markets and industry structure

A welding machine has a life span of 7–10 years. This means both a low rate of reselling and the need to keep spare parts for many years. However, it also creates opportunities for long-term servicing contracts and the associated selling of accessories.

The market in Europe is stagnating due to the outsourcing of much of the metal processing industry to Asia. The relative importance of the European market is declining due to the growth rates in Asia, although it is still a very important market for Migatronic. For these reasons, Migatronic is looking East both to outsource and to gain a share of the growth markets.

The industry is highly competitive in Europe. It has no dominant global players. Hardly any company has a market share beyond 15% in any market outside its home market. In most cases, each European market — the U.K. being one important exception — is dominated by one (as in Denmark) or a few local producers which may control half of the market, and a myriad of importers and small local producers. One of the reasons for this is the market for less sophisticated welding machines and associated services. Due to the big need for service back-up, a foreign producer also faces problems entering the market as it is difficult to acquire sufficient market share which would be large enough to cover the costs of an expensive service back-up system within a short span of years.

Although industry entry costs have increased over the years due to the development of welding machines equipped with electronics/smart boxes and other accessories, the industry is both old and new as there are still many newcomers that can carve a niche in the local market by producing a few models. Furthermore, although the big companies brand their products, they are also willing to produce private labels and even have their own second labels of possibly lesser quality.

The industry in Europe has seen relatively little consolidation and mergers and acquisitions. Migatronic is ready for a merger and acquisition in order to buy market share, and has the resources to do so. However, it is not very interested in buying production capacity as the industry already has excess capacity.

The industry consists of approximately 100 producers in Europe, 75 each in the U.S. and Japan, and 125 in other countries. Migatronic competes with around 12 producers in Germany (the largest market in Europe), 3 in France, 2 in the U.K., and 20 in Italy. Migatronic has 3 main competitors in the Czech Republic, and 2 in Hungary.

Very few of the competitors operate Europe-wide. Apart from Migatronic, there is 1 each in Finland, Sweden, and France, while there are 2 or 3 in Germany and also some in Japan and the U.S. A few operate worldwide: 1 each from France and Sweden, 1 or 2 from Japan, and 2 or 3 from the U.S.

Export versus domestic profit

It is a general characteristic of the welding equipment industry that the home market is important for manufacturers with international operations. They all have a relatively large home market share, and their intensive distribution and service system prevents foreign manufacturers from becoming dominant players in those markets. Apart from a better margin on the home market, this home-market position provides the advantage of working closely with advanced customers for development purposes.

Export obstacles

Within the EU market, the obstacles for exports are minimal, although some technical standards may vary from one country to another. Instead, the main barriers to exports are the differences in traditions and conventions in the various industries that Migatronic is targeting. Migatronic and its competitors will have to adapt to such differences in order to enter and penetrate foreign markets.

Outside the EU, there are more barriers and the industry traditions are different. For example, Migatronic has never been able to penetrate the U.S. market, as customers in the U.S. prefer larger and sturdier welding equipment and car bodies have always used thicker metal plates than in Europe.

The cost structure of Migatronic has been an internal obstacle for exports and has forced the company to look for cheaper places to produce, as was the case with Italy, India, and most recently China.

Systematic exploration of export opportunities

The owner-manager of Migatronic thinks and investigates before he acts. He does not necessarily conduct elaborate analyses, but pays frequent visits to markets. To some extent, this cautiousness has been an obstacle to international expansion, but at the same time it has prevented the company from any large-scale international failures. This way of operating also seems to fit in an industry with a relatively fragmented structure and incremental innovations.

Future prospects

Looking through Migatronic's lenses, the potential for survival and company growth is there as Migatronic has only 3% of a DKK 10 billion global market and the joining of metal (and composites of metals) will always be needed, as the owner-manager expressed when Migatronic celebrated its 25th anniversary.

Both innovation and a customer orientation are needed to stay competitive and gain a share of the global market. Migatronic has had an international orientation almost since its establishment. For many years, it focused on exports and Europe; but, especially in the new millennium, Migatronic has been forced to adopt a more global orientation and also focus on establishing production abroad. Innovation is also being internationalized partly due to the problem of hiring engineers in Denmark and partly due to the need to adapt products to local market needs.

Thus, the market is there, but to reach it and establish a solid market position is a challenge for a company the size of Migatronic. Financially, Migatronic is well prepared, but it is crucial for Migatronic to establish an organization that can coordinate widely scattered sales, production, and innovation activities. The owner-manager is a key figure in this development, and his experience and insights are valuable. However, to assure optimal coordination and knowledge sharing among the many units, Migatronic will have to develop its organization further.

The structure of the industry is, as mentioned, relatively fragmented, with a small and relatively stable set of companies operating in Europe and worldwide as well as a number of small newcomers which come and go in the industry. This pattern seems to be repeating itself in the Chinese market. Migatronic is ready to acquire competitors or enter joint ventures, but one challenge for Migatronic is that it is not so interested in buying production capacity as the industry has more than enough capacity. What it wants to buy is market access and access to distribution channels that can implement its service package.

Summary

Migatronic has been a successful business for almost 40 years, and has been controlled and managed by the dominant owner-manager since around 1984. The company is located in a semi-rural area in the northern part of Denmark. It produces a wide assortment of welding machines for a number of different industries. Migatronic has its own brand, but it also produces and sells private labels.

Migatronic produces high-quality products for the higher-end market, which focuses on good back-up service, durability, and user-friendliness. Migatronic has a tradition for producing in-house and for developing the production technology and factory layout by itself. Migatronic has an innovation department with 30 engineers for both product and process innovation. Migatronic also supplies accessories as part of its service package. Accessories may have the Migatronic brand, but Migatronic does not produce accessories; rather, it buys them from specialized suppliers.

Ever since Migatronic adopted the ISO 9001 standard in 1992, standards, documentation, planning, and the introduction of various administrative and management systems have been part and parcel of Migatronic. At times, however, the owner-manager has put his foot down and installed a temporary stop to what he sees as a risk of too much bureaucracy or the killing of innovative spirit. Migatronic monitors the market primarily by visiting and participating in the market, for example, by frequently taking part in international exhibitions. In terms of decision making, Migatronic prefers to take small steps and learn from them before moving on. It is incremental decision making that laid the foundation for the development of the company.

Soon after its establishment, Migatronic began exporting — first to Sweden, followed gradually by more and more European countries. When the Eastern European markets opened up in the 1990s, Migatronic continued its expansion. With a firm export basis in Europe, Migatronic also started to establish production abroad in

Italy, India, and, since 2007, China. Recently, the original joint venture in China was turned into a 100%-owned subsidiary by taking over the 49% share owned by the Chinese partner. In this way, Migatronic hopes to improve the synergy between its European operations and Chinese operations.

The Danish home market is still important. Migatronic has a market share of 50–60% in this market, and the Danish market is used to experiment with new concepts and practices before rolling out the successes to the European markets. Recently, for example, the service teams from Migatronic and Migatronic Automation were integrated into one service team in Denmark, and this team introduced a new service concept which enables customers to receive service within 24 hours.

Migatronic's internationalization process has been a gradual one aimed at securing a good position in the European region. Other markets have been served through importers and distributors. Development in Asia, however, has forced Migatronic to move beyond an export strategy and follow its customers, who are increasingly outsourcing their production to Asia. At the same time, the Asian markets themselves have also grown, making it attractive to establish production and sales units there to serve domestic demand in Asia.

Migatronic is sensitive to economic fluctuations, and the present crisis is hard on the company. Adjustments in expectations for 2009 were made in terms of sales, profit, and the workforce. Nevertheless, the financial position of Migatronic is strong enough to survive (provided that the crisis is not too deep or too long). On the other side of the crisis, Migatronic is confident that it will be able to continue its global expansion.

11.2.3   *Scan Tracking Systems*[9]

Company background

Scan Tracking Systems (STS) was established in 1952 to provide automation solutions to businesses in the areas of telecommunications, marine, energy, environmental preservation, and computer electronics. During the first 45 years of its existence, it served as a subcontractor to Crisplant (now FKI Logistex),[10] providing it with information technology (IT) solutions in relation to specific projects. The partnership with Crisplant enabled STS to grow steadily, moving from rented premises where it started to its own building with a staff of 45 employees in 1997. In 1998, management decided to extend its range of business lines in order to reduce its dependence on Crisplant. STS therefore began to develop competencies in track-and-trace applications, with a focus on software-driven solutions for airports and the logistics service sector. These new business lines developed rapidly, with airport baggage and cargo handling becoming the company's high-growth market segment from 2000 onwards. By 2008, STS had 190 employees (70% of whom were software engineers) and operated in 60 countries with its customers listed among the Fortune 500 companies.

The new growth strategy necessitated some changes in the ownership and structure of the company. In 1994, STS had eight owner-managers, all of whom were involved in strategic decision making as well as in running the various divisions of the company. By 2006, only two owner-managers remained in the company and most decisions were made by professionals who had no direct ownership interests that could cloud their considerations. This has led to more speedy decisions with regard to investments and new market entries.

---

[9] Professor John Kuada of Aalborg University in Denmark developed this case with the permission of Scan Tracking Systems. This case cannot be copied or electronically reproduced in any form without written permission from the author.

[10] Crisplant engages in the development, design, manufacture, sale, marketing, and on-site services of system solutions to the liquid gas industry.

Focus

The successful implementation of the business strategy initiated in 1998 redefined the company's business focus. Management broadly defines STS's present mission as helping other service companies to serve their customers effectively through optimal monitoring of item flows. In specific terms, the company is engaged in designing, installing, maintaining, and controlling track-and-trace systems using radio-frequency identification (RFID) technology. The integrated RFID software systems provide an effective means of identifying and tracking moving items from their points of delivery to their destinations.

Products

STS's solutions and services are targeted at four business segments:

(1) Airports and airlines;
(2) Postal services;
(3) Supply chain and logistics services; and
(4) Control services.

Airport solutions support overall logistics at airports and help optimize baggage operations by increasing flow capacity and reducing the amount of mishandled bags, trolleys, and other items, as well as improve passengers' travel experiences. Solutions provided for the postal service sector include the Automatic Mail Quality Measurement (AMQM) system, "quality of service" diagnostic measurement system, transport management, and track-and-trace systems used in monitoring, analyzing, optimizing, and managing postal processes. Management estimates that STS's software and automation systems now serve 55 postal service companies and approximately 85% of the world's mail flow. The supply chain management solutions include warehouse management, food and product traceability, and container goods handling. Solutions offered to the control services segment include automation of control systems for conveyors, sorters, and data management systems.

Competitive advantage

Two factors have shaped STS's competitiveness within the industry: technology and customer service. During the past 10 years, the company's engineers have developed special competencies in integrating company-specific RFID solutions into larger RFID networks, thereby strengthening the reliability of the systems that customers use at a global level. These competencies have positioned STS as a strong and reliable partner within the rapidly growing global logistics sector. The acquired knowledge has also been extended to new market segments, thereby accelerating STS's growth and competence development. As a result, STS became the first company to implement an RFID-enabled system for the postal service sector due to its innovative capabilities.

Customer relationship strategies at STS are guided by two main principles:

(1) Provision of superior customer value — according to an airport division manager, "STS must offer more than its competitors, but at the same price."
(2) Overall customer satisfaction — "STS must not bring a project to a close until the customer is fully satisfied."

These principles reflect management's awareness that the success of STS depends on the success of its customers. It has been a lot easier for the company to win new customers through references and endorsements from existing satisfied customers than through its own marketing efforts. Management expressed this customer-oriented philosophy in the following words: "Our customers are our kings and queens; they are our employers; it is because of them that our business exists. If they leave us, they leave with a chain of others; if they remain, they bring in a chain of others." This awareness has motivated STS's management to emphasize the provision of 24/7 service to its customers.

Importance

Four factors have been critical to STS's growth within the industry:

(1) Partnership;
(2) Integration;
(3) Product development; and
(4) Added-value creation.

Since STS's strength lies in customized software development, management considers it prudent to encourage the cooperation of its staff with a number of leading software and computer companies whose technologies play an important role in the design of the solutions it offers. These partner companies include HP, IBM, OMRON, Oracle, Intermec, and Philips. The collaborating partners deliver standardized and/or adapted platforms on which STS's engineers design their solutions.

The uniqueness of STS's customized solutions depends partly on their integration into existing system configurations. This differentiates STS's solutions from standardized solutions on the market, and thereby renders it difficult for customers to compare its solutions with solutions from competitors. In this way, STS is able to reduce the bargaining power of customers.

Integration is also important at other levels. For example, the needs of three distinct interest groups must be taken into account in all airport projects: the airport itself, the airlines, and the handling agents.[11] The challenge for companies such as STS lies in coordinating the needs of the various interest groups and taking due cognizance of them in designing their solutions. It is also important for the company to be able to communicate effectively with all three stakeholders in the project implementation processes in order for

---

[11] A handling agent is a local company which supplies services to airlines in airports. Instead of each airline having its staff located in every airport to handle services such as baggage handling and check-in, local agents are engaged to deliver such services for a fee.

them to feel that their needs have been carefully considered. Building RFID-enabled software is therefore not merely an engineering task; the engineers involved must also have good management skills to be able to deliver good products and services.

Staying ahead of competitors requires that STS maintains consistency in its efforts to develop new products. This has been made possible by building an organizational culture of learning using the potentials inherent in industry-based operating systems and procedures to the fullest. One of these industry-based sources of knowledge is ISO certification. STS is therefore ISO 9001:2000 certified. In practical terms, this means that STS employees are guided by standard procedures and documentation when executing projects. They are thus able to learn cumulatively and to share their knowledge with each other by working on projects in teams.

Added-value creation is seen as a differentiation strategy. As noted earlier, this is at the core of the company's customer orientation. STS's engineers are therefore required to have good insight into the nature of the businesses that its customers undertake and the challenges that they face in tracing, tracking, and monitoring the flow of items connected with their service delivery. This knowledge then forms the foundation of the software that engineers design for any particular customer.

Impact of current economic conditions

Economic conditions have a mixed impact on STS's operations. On the one hand, STS's services usually form an integral part of long-term investment decisions of nations, institutions, and companies. As a result, demand for its services is not directly subject to short-term fluctuations in macroeconomic conditions. For example, budgetary decisions related to building new airports and/or airport terminals, or to modifying/extending existing terminals, are usually made several years prior to the actual project implementation. Economic changes may delay the project for a while, but they rarely lead to its cancellation. Thus, STS can forecast the demand for its services with a fairly good degree of certainty, based on planned investments in various target countries and institutions.

On the other hand, economic trends tend to influence the level and volume of the activities of STS's customers. Taking the airport market segment as an example, management has observed that global economic conditions determine the number of passengers who use airports as well as the volume of cargo transport. This has recently been demonstrated by the negative impact of increased fuel prices and the global economic recession on the airline business.

A number of non-economic factors also impact the company's business opportunities. As the airport division manager explained, recent events such as the 9/11 terrorist attack in the U.S. as well as the SARS and bird flu epidemics in Asia have affected air transportation. Airports have been compelled to change their security, control, baggage handling, and passenger identification systems. In effect, new service needs emerged while others became redundant because of the changes. STS must be able to adapt its solutions to the consequences of such events.

Future of the company

STS's goal is to be known within the industry as a world-class supplier of logistic solutions through innovative, user-friendly, and reliable solutions, and to capture 20% of the global market. Although the company has experienced some shortfalls in customer orders, management remains optimistic about the future and sees the current global economic crisis as temporary. The airport division manager maintains that, when the world economy picks up again, several emerging market economies will demand RFID solutions in areas of logistics, postal services, and baggage handling at airports. This will result in an increase in demand for STS's services. The challenge is to meet the increasing competition in the industry with innovative products at good prices, i.e. to be prepared for better times ahead.

Systematic decision-making process

The dominant engineering culture at STS has encouraged the adoption of a systematic decision-making process in the company. Information about the construction of new airports and airport terminals or new postal services is systematically collected, using a variety of sources including members of business networks to which STS belongs. The information is then analyzed for new market opportunities, and potential customers are identified for targeted marketing efforts. Since each single customer can constitute a key account, deliberate efforts are made to examine the needs of each prospective customer. When a company shows an interest in STS's offer, management quickly assigns it to a team of skilled software engineers related to the specific type of solution that is required and a project manager is selected to head the team to prepare a tender document. The team works out a set of alternative solutions that would fulfill the needs of the potential customer, given different price assumptions. This increases STS's chances of winning the contract.

Systematic approaches are also adopted in staff recruitment, development, and deployment. The company is rather conservative in recruiting new staff and laying off existing ones. The policy is to retain employees for as long as possible in order to reduce knowledge loss and to ensure cumulative growth in organizational competencies and capabilities.

Initial markets

The internationalization process of STS started in 1998 when the company participated in an international tender and won a contract with the International Post Corporation (IPC) in Brussels, Belgium. The project required STS to design an AMQM solution for IPC. The execution of this project triggered the development of other new solutions and enhanced the overall knowledge base of STS engineers regarding the application of RFID technology.

Top management decided to use the new knowledge as a springboard to explore new business opportunities in new geographical regions of the world, but with a particular focus on North America (where top management believed STS had a good chance of doing well). Investigations led it to open a sales and service office in Frederick, Maryland, in the U.S., from where the company currently serves its 60 U.S. customers. STS also acquired two RFID technology companies in Toronto, Canada, in 2001 and 2003, respectively, and gained a foothold in the Canadian market. Activities at the Toronto subsidiary have subsequently been broadened to include manufacturing and R&D, turning it into one of the leading RFID innovation centers in the world today.

In 2005, management turned its attention to the Central and Eastern European region, establishing a sales office in Bucharest, Romania. This office now provides project management, software development, and technical services for a small but increasing number of customers in the region.

Export obstacles

STS's management has identified four obstacles to the internationalization process of companies within the industry. The first is the amount of investment required in facilities, product development, knowledge acquisition, and networks of relationships in order to operate in foreign markets. As noted earlier, the needs of each given customer are unique in some respect, since the services designed must fit the contextual requirements of the customer. Although some aspects of the technology used are standardized, adaptations are required, and this can run into several man-hours. Investments in facilities and the effort to find qualified staff for top-quality service delivery may therefore act as a barrier for new entrants into the industry or for the growth of existing companies. This explains STS's current personnel policies regarding the retention of existing staff.

Second, local presence is a market entry requirement. The local presence may take the form of either setting up local offices or finding appropriate partners which can provide services on demand. Such local presence provides customers with the assurance that the service provider is close by and ready to handle any difficulties that might arise in the implementation of the software. This explains why STS had to open offices in the U.S. and Romania as well as acquire companies in Canada. Subsequent international expansion will require making additional investments in offices in other parts of the world or finding appropriate local companies with which to partner.

Continuous knowledge acquisition and sharing is another obstacle. Since the adaptation of RFID technology to new business lines requires new knowledge, companies within the industry must develop dynamic learning capabilities. This again explains STS's human resource management policy of not firing its engineering staff and software developers unless absolutely necessary. The current global economic crisis has, however, compelled the company to lay off some of its staff. This, in the words of the airport division manager, "has led to significant loss of valuable knowledge that would be hard to replace when STS begins to expand its operations again." Furthermore, since most engineers take pride in their individual achievements and want to be acknowledged for them, it is difficult to place them in teams and encourage them to share their knowledge with each other. STS's management believes that it has been able to handle this conflict with a reasonable degree of success, and has now created an organizational culture that balances the gains of individuality and team spirit.

The fourth challenge is keeping project costs under control. This strikes at the heart of the engineering culture which dominates companies within the industry. As the airport division manager explained:

> There are two parallel cultures within STS — a technical culture and a business economics culture. We have engineers who love to develop and deliver the world's best solutions, irrespective of the cost; projects constantly exceed cost calculations and the engineers don't really seem to care. The management, with its business economics mindset, tries to control costs. But it is difficult to deliver good-quality projects on time and within the stipulated budget.

This remains a challenge for STS's management.

Future markets

Assuming a quick global economic upturn, STS's management expects to increase its market share within the four market segments that the company currently serves: airports, postal services, logistics and supply chains, and control systems. Opportunities are believed to be available in both the North American and European markets as well as in the emerging market economies. However, competition is also expected to be tougher in the coming years.

Taking the airport market segment as an example, the airport division manager states that globalization has resulted in increased standardization and modernization of airport facilities, since identical requirements have to be adhered to at all major airports in order to meet international standards. At present, there are only four airports in the world that have installed RFID technology-based solutions. STS supplied three of the four solutions installed between 2004 and 2008, and continuous efforts are being made to win new customers.

In addition, many industries have yet to become aware of the potentials inherent in RFID technology and to exploit them in their specific service delivery processes. For example, in the agricultural sector, food traceability can be greatly enhanced through the use of the technology. The military industry also offers good potential for RFID applications in such areas as battlefield surveillance (wearable electronics), gravitational and inclinational applications (helicopter altitude detection, measurement of inclination for parachute drops), remote sensing (passive, miniature, unattended ground sensors), and biological/chemical attack detection. The potential for the adaptation of RFID technology to these specific areas of application remains to be explored.

Future prospects

As indicated earlier, STS's management is aware of the huge unexplored potentials for applying RFID technology beyond the four segments in which the company's activities are currently concentrated. For example, there are enormous possibilities for application in military operations as well as in the aeronautical, pharmaceutical, and automotive industries (e.g. the design of tire pressure monitoring sensor systems).

There is some evidence within the industry that some larger companies are exploring possibilities of partnering with RFID solution providers to perform significant research and development work in order to develop the related middleware for these industries. This trend is expected to continue to accelerate not only in North America, but also on a global basis. STS's management is therefore currently investigating possibilities for participation in such RFID middleware development programs. Its immediate focus, however, remains in the more familiar areas and involves the exploitation of STS's current competencies through simple extensions of its activities into related areas. Projects that are receiving management attention include linking RFID data into enterprise resource planning (ERP) systems, and building and/or managing RFID-enabled warehouses.

Summary

STS is a small RFID technology-driven company that has experienced dramatic growth during the past 12 years as a result of deliberate top management strategies to reduce dependence on a single key customer. This has led to a restructuring of the organization (including a new ownership structure), a greater focus on learning and new competence development, as well as aggressive internationalization efforts. Global economic, political, and social events in recent years (such as the 9/11 terrorist attack) have produced a mixed impact on demand for the company's services and provide new market opportunities in the future. Top management is optimistic that, by granting the required resource investments and partnering with other companies in the industry, it can intensify its internationalization efforts by entering new markets and business lines.

11.3 Swedish Cases

11.3.1 *Martinsons Trä AB* [12]

Martinsons Trä AB is the marketing and sales division of Martinsons Group AB, and specializes in sales of sawn and planed wood. It is an independent entity. Martinsons Group AB is known for its positive approach to markets, its innovative technology, and its long tradition in the sawmill business. Martinsons Group AB has evolved through aggressive growth, a series of acquisitions, and highly focused innovations. Martinsons Group AB sells about 75% of its lumber unplaned and about 25% planed through Martinsons Trä AB. Martinsons Trä AB arranges custom fabrication of wooden products. It markets in the Swedish and foreign markets. About 50% of its annual turnover is generated from Scandinavian markets, and the rest from international markets.

Although Martinsons Group AB is well established in several foreign markets, it is experiencing increasing competition especially from Russia, the Baltic countries, and Central Europe. At the same time, markets for sawn and planed products are also changing. Even branded sawn and planed products with extensive quality performance records are becoming mere commodities, particularly in the construction and building markets. Buyers of these products are less loyal to their suppliers; they expect shorter delivery times and lower prices. Sawmills which focused on efficient sawing and planing and which specialized in calculating the exact amount of lumber that could be obtained from a single tree are now forced to focus on the needs of the market. Martinsons Group AB is no exception.

The market focus at Martinsons Group AB is apparent in the necessary shift away from emphasizing its sawing and planing efficiency and productivity of high-quality branded products to understanding the needs of its customers. In some way, the new

---

[12] Professors George Tesar of Umeå University and Anders Söderholm of Mid Sweden University developed this case with the permission of Martinsons Trä AB (http://www.martinsonstra.se). This case cannot be copied or electronically reproduced in any form without written permission from the authors.

focus is the result of the introduction of new product dimensions and standards in the construction and building industries. These developments require major changes in the strategic and operational philosophies of the entire Martinsons Group AB. One part of Martinsons Group AB directly impacted by the organizational changes is the marketing and sales organization managed by Kenneth Wallin. He is directly responsible for the sales of sawn and planed products. One of his current tasks is to design a new sales organization. However, designing a new sales organization in an industry sector that is faced with major turmoil is not a simple task, especially for a line of products that is moving towards becoming a commodity — sawn and planed wood.

The new Martinsons Group AB is not only a well-established sawmill with a long family tradition in Bygdsiljum, a vibrant village in northern Sweden, but also a highly innovative wood-processing operation. Martinsons Group AB was introduced as the new parent company in January 2005, along with Martinsons Såg AB which is responsible for softwood production at the sawmill in Bygdsiljum. Martinsons Såg AB is also responsible for the production, marketing, and sales of all products in the field of Glulam and Solid Wood components and systems (Glulam and Solid Wood are proprietary names). Martinsons Trä AB, also introduced in January 2005, is responsible for the marketing and sales of softwood produced by all sawmills in the group, with the exception of Glulam and Solid Wood components and systems.

Martinsons Group AB employs approximately 276 employees in several locations. Its website (http://www.martinsonstra.se) provides substantial information about the entire company, including Martinsons Trä AB which is responsible for all softwood marketing and sales activities. Some financial data for Martinsons Group AB is also available on the corporate website.

Family history and close family ties are important to Martinsons Group AB. The company's early beginnings can be traced back to the late 1920s, when Sigurd Martinson operated a transportable sawmill in the populated areas around Bygdsiljum in northern Sweden. In 1939, the concept of a stationary sawmill was developed, and the

Martinsons' sawmill has stayed in the same location ever since. Martinsons Group AB has always been known by its competitors as being highly competitive, forward-looking, and dynamic in both the Swedish and international markets. Many of its competitors are located in neighboring Finland.

Since its early beginnings, Martinsons Group AB has embarked on an aggressive acquisition program. In 1996, it acquired Hällnäs Såg AB from the Baltic Group. This is a sawmill with a long tradition dating back to the turn of the last century and is located on the Vindelälven (Vindel River), not far from Umeå. In 1998, Martinsons Group AB purchased a half interest in Svenska Träbroar AB — a company that specializes in building timber bridges — which at the time was owned by Wallmarks Såg. In the summer of 2003, Martinsons Group AB acquired Wallmarks Såg in Kroksjön from Sorb Industri AB along with the other half of Svenska Träbroar AB. This was an interesting turn of events because Sorb Industri AB originally wanted to acquire Martinsons at that time. Wallmarks Såg, established in 1925, offers a full line of products. In addition to acquisitions, Martinsons Group AB has also developed new lines of products including a range of glued and laminated products and structures. In January 2005, Martinsons Trä AB was named as the official marketing and sales organization for all softwood products manufactured under Martinsons Group AB management.

Martinsons Group AB's location in northern Sweden does not limit its international outlook. Its export markets for sawn and planed products include a number of countries in Europe, North Africa, Southeast Asia, North America, Japan, and other global destinations. In most of these markets, Martinsons Trä AB sells directly through sales agents and sales representatives, but it manages its own sales force in the U.K. The U.K. is one of Martinsons Trä AB's largest markets for sawn and planed products; approximately 20–25% of all exports, or between 25,000 m^3 and 30,000 m^3 of timber, are delivered there each year. According to corporate sources, the advantages of the market in the U.K. include strong current demand and a favorable price structure. Corporate expectations are that markets in Germany, the Netherlands, France, and Japan will also grow in the future.

Martinsons Group AB also has a long history of technological innovations. Early on, a unique lifting truck was developed in order to move materials more easily around its sawmill operations. This invention was followed by the development of highly specialized timber-cutting techniques used to calculate how much lumber a given tree would yield. During the early sawmill operations, a quality control process was introduced for sorting cut lumber into different grades of lumber. In an ongoing process of innovation, Martinsons Group AB opened the most modern computer-operated, electronically controlled sawmill in Northern Europe in 1976. Technological progress continues today.

Developing sales organizations for corporations operating in major industry sectors is always a challenge. It is an even greater challenge when a new sales organization must be developed after a series of mergers and acquisitions (M&As) of companies that are well established in the market and that have operated under respected brand names. Integrating several sales forces into a single new sales force after a merger or acquisition is virtually impossible. Different corporate cultures, different sales approaches, and even differences in the perception of buying habits in the market create enormous inconsistencies and conflicts in any new sales organization. Ownership of brand names and trademarks also presents sales conflicts and obstacles. The perceptions from the market may be conflicting; customers may have preferences for one brand over another; and sales personnel might be forced to promote one trademark over another, which might create additional conflict within the sales force. Establishing a new identity and a new brand name is costly and time-intensive.

Many companies develop comprehensive sales plans and strategies before mergers or acquisitions are completed. The assumption is that pre- and post-M&A plans and strategies are needed to determine what the resulting expectations and outcomes might be. Sales games and simulations are designed to answer questions about future performance and the competitive positioning of the sales force with respect to the expected performance of the new sales force.

When markets change dramatically, sales organizations must respond to the changes. Frequently, outside specialists need to be hired to deal with the changes. Such specialists understand the changes and can respond to them objectively and systematically. Sales managers sometimes argue that they do not include such specialists earlier because the market changes are gradual and initially difficult to detect, and making small incremental changes in the sales organization is not economically feasible. When changes in market orientation also require a change in corporate orientation, for example from domestic to international, a new sales force may also have to be hired.

Markets today are more international (or global), and require increasing knowledge of sales management and sales techniques. An increasing number of major corporations are redesigning their sales organization and staffing their sales force to accommodate broad market changes. Typically, the sales organization and the selection of the sales force are a function of the types of products that will be sold. The more differentiated the products are, the more specialized the sales force will be. Conversely, if the sales force is responsible for selling commodities, the less specialized it will be.

Efficient sales organizations are managed by a sales manager who reports to the chief marketing director. A sales organization needs to include an individual trained in sales planning, forecasting, and budgeting. This individual provides the direction for the entire sales effort. Another important individual in sales organizations is the person who deals with major customers, distributors, and supply chain coordinators. This individual is sometimes perceived as someone who deals with special, more valued contacts. The other side of a sales organization focuses on the actual management and performance of the sales force. There is a need for an individual who is responsible for day-to-day management and coordination of the sales personnel and their sales efforts. Finally, there must be someone who can objectively evaluate the performance of individual sales persons and the overall sales force.

Sales force management has, over the past few years, experienced some changes. The traditional ways of assigning territories, product lines, accounts, and markets have been replaced with more flexible approaches of assigning responsibilities to individual members of a sales force. In some cases, individuals are free to select customers and markets based on their own expertise or training. A few companies have decided to let their sales personnel alternate between domestic and foreign customers and major accounts.

Since the issues of internationalization, market changes, and product changes impact the design and development of a sales force, new approaches must be developed to accommodate these issues and changes. Marketing and sales researchers suggest that a product- or market-structured sales force can be flexible enough to respond to internationalization issues, market changes, and product changes. However, these types of sales organizations require better-educated and trained sales specialists.

The forest industry sector in northern Sweden faces many challenges and opportunities. With the use of satellite technology in the forest industry, managing forests today requires a great deal of technical expertise, high levels of investment, a better-educated labor force, and extensive value chains. Developments in plant sciences and sophisticated knowledge about growing trees are also adding efficiency to forest harvesting and transport of raw material out of the forest. Owners and managers of large tracts of forests in northern Sweden have, over the past few years, considered new forms of forest management, such as leasing out tracts of forests to subcontractors, contracting out harvesting operations, or jointly managing forests with their downstream customers.

Some of the development centers for high-technology forest equipment are located in Northern Scandinavia. In particular, the forest industry boasts a strong presence in Västerbotten, where specialized machinery, cranes, communication technology, and simulation and training facilities for the world market are developed. The forest industry cooperates with the nearby universities in plant science research and off-road vehicle development. This cooperation further strengthens the industrial cluster in Västerbotten.

Globally, the increasing consumption of sawn and planed wood products, along with the downward pressure on prices combined with changing construction and building specifications, in a number of international markets immensely complicates relationships in the forest industry sector. The entire value chain is highly sensitive to these changes. Market demand for less expensive wood is driving down investments in new tree growing, sawing, and planing technology. The returns on investment in the forest industry sector are becoming progressively smaller. Sawmill operations are also directly affected. The market changes are further complicated by technological changes.

Another important issue is the level of vertical integration in the forest industry. Sawmills have a choice of integrating their operations either downstream or upstream because they are typically in the middle of the supply chain — between forest owners and providers of final goods. Most commonly in Scandinavia, large forest owners have invested in sawmills. Independent sawmills purchase timber on an open market. During periods of market instability, this market works like a futures market where buyers and sellers constantly compete to obtain favorable contracts for future delivery of timber. The tendency today is that future contracts are shorter and prices change more frequently.

The use of highly capital-intensive, satellite-based forest harvesting technology is not necessarily a global phenomenon. Forest management companies in the Northwestern United States harvest large tracts of forest using highly advanced techniques of tree harvesting, and their investment in new technology is increasing. In comparison, Russian Siberia employs relatively labor-intensive methods to harvest large forested areas for both domestic use and export markets. The rainforests in South America and tropical forests in Southeast Asia produce enormous amounts of timber that are shipped unprocessed to countries with more advanced wood-processing technology. Even marginal forest management companies in Australia are now harvesting rural areas that were previously considered to contain inferior timber-producing trees, primarily because of the globally expanding demand for wood. Consequently, economists and researchers specializing in the forest and wood industry sectors forecast that the increasing demand for wood will force the forest industry to harvest inferior-quality trees in the near future using obsolete tree harvesting and sawing techniques.

Internationally, forest harvesting is under increasing scrutiny. Pressure from interest groups opposed to uncontrolled forest harvesting is shaping the opinions of local, regional, and national governments to limit forest harvesting in protected areas such as the Northwestern United States or the Amazon rainforest. Concerns over the rainforests of South America also have international implications. According to environmentalists, there are social, political, environmental, and cultural justifications for these concerns. Many environmentalists suggest that major lifestyle changes and market adjustments are needed to protect the existing forests. Some discussions focus on issues related to changing consumption habits among consumers in the more developed countries, while others point out that industry sectors using wood-based products need to find alternative materials to produce their products.

Traditional wood-based products — ranging from private homes and commercial buildings to building components, furniture, tools, and utensils — have become accepted products in most cultures. Some wood-based products in many cultures have a tendency to be invisible, or even transparent, to the average individual. Wood-based products used in the construction of public and private buildings, private homes, or even public infrastructures are seldom noticed. The use of wood in paper making, in the production of packaging material, and in personal hygiene products is also significant. Market demand for these types of products is growing and therefore driving the costs of production higher and the market prices for finished consumer goods lower. The lobbying groups concerned with forest management and forest protection argue that something has to change.

Some social values in the consumer markets are gradually evolving. Consumers are changing their lifestyles and are more open to recycling paper products. In some countries, especially in Northern Europe and North America, municipal recycling of paper is becoming a routine part of waste collection activities. Other parts of the world are only beginning to think about recycling. Consumers are also changing their habits and the way they shop and bring home their groceries; most major stores offer a choice of either a paper or plastic bag. However, these are relatively minor changes in the overall scheme of things.

The construction and home-building industry sector is faced with major developments. The demand for construction and building materials is growing, and thus the demand for lumber is increasing; however, the supply of lumber is decreasing. Some countries and municipalities responsible for building codes and safe construction of homes and commercial structures are changing the building codes and the specifications for the type of lumber that can be safely used. In some cases, the standard dimensions of conventional lumber are being changed to accommodate the shortages of construction-quality lumber.

Steady increases in the cost of lumber are driving up construction costs and therefore the prices of new private homes. Younger families find it difficult to purchase their first home; home maintenance and remodeling are also becoming a major challenge for many homeowners. This rise in the price of lumber used in industrial construction is forcing building companies to look for innovative alternatives. Architects and builders are integrating materials such as glass, plastics, stone, and steel to replace wood as the preferred traditional construction commodity. Even the laminated plastics industry is investing in research and development to introduce viable products for the home-building industry. In response, municipalities are changing building codes to accommodate new materials and building technology.

These developments are particularly relevant to the sawmill industry sector. Sawmills are a key link between the forest management companies and the rest of the value chain for lumber and similar wood-based products. They receive raw material right out of the forest and attempt to maximize usable output from every tree as best as they can. Their expertise was traditionally based on their ability to efficiently cut each log into usable lumber. However, increasing market prices for lumber in the construction and building industry sector, changing building codes, and innovative building techniques are compelling sawmill operators to rethink their production, sales, and marketing strategies and focus on the changing needs of their customers throughout the entire value chain.

The above changes in the market for sawn and planed wood products clearly suggest that they are becoming tradable commodities sold in large quantities without any brand identity or loyalty. Tradable commodities without any significant differentiable advantage are difficult to market and sell. With respect to this case study, Kenneth Wallin is in charge of the challenging task of forming a new sales organization for Martinsons Group AB's line of sawn and planed wood products — a line of products that is rapidly moving from privately branded products to commodities. Marketing and selling branded products is substantially different to selling commodities, and this is one of the key challenges in forming a new sales organization. At the same time, the markets are looking for products sold in bulk.

About 75% of the wood sold by Mr. Wallin's organization is saw-cut but not planed, whereas 25% is finished. The main reason why only 25% of the wood is finished is because of the limited capacity to plane wood. The assumption here is that if the capacity to plane wood was increased, more planed wood could be sold.

Martinsons Trä AB is faced with four distinct segments for its products: (1) retailers (large retailers or wholesalers) who sell to builders and related customers; (2) industries which make products from wood, such as window manufacturers; (3) companies which finish wood; and (4) bulk buyers (large customers). Approximately half of the annual turnover comes from Scandinavia, while the other half comes from international markets. Some of the foreign markets are serviced directly by a sales force, while in the U.K. and Ireland the products are sold by sales agents. Current expectations are that the markets for sawn and planed wood will increase in Asia and Australia. The future sales force will be responsible for both domestic and foreign markets.

In designing the new sales organization, Mr. Wallin is confronted with several problems. The January 2005 reorganization brought together well-established brand names owned by Martinsons Group AB — Martinsons Såg AB, Wallmarks Såg, and Hällnäs Såg AB — each with its own brand name and individual identity; all three now have to be integrated into the Martinsons Trä AB marketing and sales organization. The new sales organization will function as one unit representing the three sawmills and will sell the products under one common brand name: Martinsons. However, through an end mark (brand name identification), customers will be able to distinguish in which sawmill the final sawn or planed products were produced.

Another problem faced by the new sales organization is the market for sawn and planed products. The market as well as the buying habits and loyalty of customers are all changing. These changes provide a major challenge for the sales organization as a whole and for individual sales persons in the market. Targeting key accounts, selling to major construction and building industries, and identifying individual clients in international markets have become more complicated and cumbersome tasks.

Identifying appropriate supply channels and establishing a meaningful sales presence in these channels are also difficult and time-consuming. Moreover, foreign competition is growing. Suppliers from Finland represent strong competition; the Baltic countries, Russia, and Central Europe are also actively competing within these channels with lower-priced products. The new sales organization needs to clearly understand the implications of these challenges.

In reality, the new sales organization of Martinsons Trä AB will have to confront the market changes regarding the supply of and demand for sawn and planed wood products, develop a strong understanding of its international competitors, clearly identify its sales opportunities, and participate in major supply chains. The overall task of the new sales organization will be to build on its previous brand identity and international connections to maximize its sales effectiveness.

11.3.2 *Norrmejerier*[13]

One dairy that is responding to changes in the market for dairy products is Norrmejerier in northern Sweden. Norrmejerier is an international company; in addition to Sweden, its products are sold in Finland, the U.K., Ireland, Denmark, Norway, Austria, Russia, and the U.S. It is a cooperative, owned by dairy farmers in Norrbotten, Västerbotten, and the northern part of Ångermanland. Its mission is to collect, process, and market the owners' milk production with the greatest possible respect for the environment.

Norrmejerier is an important employer in the region. It has approximately 470 employees, and in total generates about 5,000 jobs in the rural areas of the region. It perceives its operations as a driving force in the development and preservation of life in the countryside.

Norrmejerier operates five dairy plants in Burträsk, Luleå, and Umeå. Norrmejerier also operates several specialty ventures, an ultra-high-temperature (UHT) plant in Luleå, storage facilities for its famous Västerbotten cheese (Västerbottensost®) in Ånäset, and a berry-pressing plant in Hedenäset. As part of its diversified services, it also offers additional animal farm services including artificial insemination of livestock, animal breeding, and animal health and feed services, among others. Moreover, Norrmejerier's strategic investments suggest developments and improvements in cheese processing, storage, and retailing.

Norrmejerier stresses close management of environmental factors as its operating objective. It strives to balance its approach to the economy, the ecology, and the environment. Specific environmental performance goals are clearly stated and implemented both out on the farms as well as in its laboratories. Environmental management issues, such as soil cultivation, recycling, waste collection, and other related

---

[13] Professors George Tesar of Umeå University and Anders Söderholm of Mid Sweden University developed this case with the permission of Norrmejerier. This case cannot be copied or electronically reproduced in any form without written permission from the authors.

issues, are systematically considered as a part of day-to-day operations. Independent, certified environmental specialists perform regular environmental audits.

According to the corporate philosophy, Norrmejerier views its customers and individual consumers as principals in its business, and frequently conducts proprietary marketing research studies to communicate with its consumers and improve its products and services. The results from marketing research studies are also used to develop new product concepts and, eventually, new products. Marketing research studies are an important part of the overall managerial philosophy. Norrmejerier's marketing research studies focus on consumers and their needs, and also on the environmental and lifestyle changes of consumers. The results of marketing research studies are carefully examined and converted into new market opportunities.

Västerbottensost® is one of Norrmejerier's most famous products. It is well known in Sweden and internationally. It has a very long history and is associated with pioneering work in trademark development, marketing, and quality. The cheese was produced for the first time in 1872.

The dairy industry in Sweden has been significantly impacted by changes in the marketplace. The demand for milk with lower fat content is increasing globally, while the consumption of butter and other high-fat products is decreasing. But, at the same time, the production of milk is increasing. The U.S., China, Australia, and New Zealand are major global milk producers where the supply of milk is growing. The European Union (EU) is also a major milk producer with a surplus. Although countries such as Sweden, Norway, and Finland produce significantly lower quantities of milk, even the milk processors in these countries are faced with an increasing oversupply of fresh milk. Since many milk dairies in these countries are cooperatives and the farmers own shares in them, it becomes rather difficult for the milk dairies to refuse their supply of milk.

Internationally, the dairy industry is a heavily regulated industry. Governments are continuously negotiating export and import quotas for milk and milk products. Even in the EU, there are major concerns over milk production. The concerns over milk production and marketing of milk products have increased even more with membership in the EU by countries such as Poland and Hungary, both of which are heavily agricultural countries. Since most governments are reluctant to restructure milk production at the farm level, they are more interested in protecting their current farm interests and the food-processing sector at the same time.

Individual milk-processing plants operate within a framework of set rules and regulations on the one hand and a growing and inflexible supply of milk on the other hand. These constraints produce a rather difficult situation for managers who face consumer demand for milk and milk-based dairy products. In recent years, dairy marketing has become a major managerial tool to deal with some of these issues. Today, dairy marketing focuses on stimulating increased consumption of milk and milk-based products.

As a result of market studies, dairies have introduced a variety of milk-based products as substitutes for soft drinks, as dietary supplements, and as post-operation recovery food products. These products have their specific functions and target markets. However, additional attempts are being made to introduce milk-based products in new target markets that are based on the changing lifestyles of consumers. This is a major challenge for dairy marketers because, in most instances, they need to think about new approaches to product development and new marketing strategies in order to create additional value for consumers interested in consuming lifestyle-related milk-based products.

Dairy marketers work closely with several sectors of the food industry. They cooperate with fast food franchisers, motivating them to serve more milk and offer milk-based products in their franchised outlets. Dairy marketers suggest that the menu in upscale restaurants includes using existing products such as yogurt as a natural salad dressing or replacing a high-fat cheese with a low-fat cheese in after-dinner offerings. In-store demonstrations are used to educate consumers about new milk-based products and their health benefits. Many of the general marketing concepts relevant to the marketing of other consumer products are now finding their way into dairy marketing.

Dairy marketing managers have two fundamental choices: they can strive to increase demand for dairy products, or they can concentrate on developing new products from the raw material (milk). It appears that the option of increasing potential demand for existing dairy products is costly, time-consuming, and difficult to implement. Many milk-based products today are perceived as inconsistent with today's dietary needs because they contain fat, as pointed out in marketing research studies of many consumers. The other option is to introduce new milk-based products into new emerging markets. Although this effort may also be relatively capital-intensive, it focuses on more innovative market segments such as the health, exercise, or aging markets, which may be more open to the introduction of milk products.

It appears that milk processors need to re-examine milk as a raw material suitable for developing a new variety of lifestyle-related products that meet the taste requirements and expectations of the new types of consumers. This is a challenge that may take some time to implement. The new generation of dairy marketing managers will have to carefully study the changing market landscape for milk and milk-based products, and creatively communicate with their existing and potential consumers to develop new and suitable product offerings based on a single natural resource: milk.

Research suggests that the Swedish dairy sector contains about 417,000 dairy cows cared for by approximately 11,000 dairy farmers. This means that the average farmer milks about 38 cows. The entire herd produces a total of 3,290,000 metric tons of milk per year, or about 300 metric tons per average farm per year. Many Swedish farmers are increasing the size of their herd in order to increase their income. At the same time, an increasing number of farmers are shutting down their dairy operations and leaving their farms.

In Sweden, seven dairy companies process almost 99% of the milk. Typically, dairies in Sweden are cooperatives owned by dairy farmers in their respective regions. Because of regional distribution patterns, most milk-processing plants in Sweden operate in geographically defined monopolistic markets. Within the EU, Sweden is a major player in milk production and in the processing and retailing of milk-based products.

The Swedish dairy sector was heavily regulated until 1990, when the Swedish Parliament deregulated it. In the following years, price controls and government subsidies for dairies were abandoned. Due to deregulation, cooperative arrangements and alliances were transformed to meet new competition. The former regional monopolies could not compete with the more aggressive dairies that began to penetrate the Swedish market.

When Sweden joined the EU in 1995, it became even more critical to foster domestic competition among dairies. Sweden's EU membership also introduced new regulations such as production quotas. Several mergers materialized among Swedish dairies during the 1990s. For example, Arla, a major Swedish dairy, made several acquisitions, only to be later advised by the authorities that it was in danger of violating the EU competition law. A number of smaller Swedish dairies went through a similar process of mergers and acquisitions, which resulted in large and more comprehensive dairies.

The dairy industry in Sweden also internationalized during the 1990s. Dairies from the other Nordic countries entered the Swedish market, and Swedish dairies in turn entered the other Nordic markets. Arla, the major Swedish dairy, sought a Nordic partner and eventually merged with a Danish company, MD Foods. Internationalization had additional benefits. For example, it promoted the product development needed to introduce products with a longer shelf life to accommodate greater geographic distribution.

Norrmejerier offers a broad line of dairy products in several consumer markets, including milk, yogurt, fermented products, cream, edible fats such as butter and butter-based spreads, and cheese. It also offers a line of fruit drinks. All of the products are marketed under well-established brand names. Some of the products, such as milk, tend to have a geographically narrow distribution; while other products, including the fruit drinks and butter-based spreads, have broad national distribution.

The markets for Norrmejerier's products tend to be relatively stable. Consumers tend to perceive most of these products as necessary convenience goods. Other markets may be changing slightly, but are subject to unstable consumer preferences. Changes in consumer habits or the introduction of new lifestyles may significantly impact these markets.

Markets for consumer products are changing rapidly all over the world. Consumers are examining their consumption values and changing their lifestyles accordingly. They are concerned about their health, eating habits, physical condition, and other aspects of their everyday lives. Young and old consumers alike are confronting the producers of consumer products, challenging them to review their product lines and marketing strategies and pay more attention to consumers' new needs. Some consumers go so far as to leave the traditional marketing system altogether, and instead seek other options where food products are grown organically or where farmers and other food producers sell directly to customers. Even a cursory look at today's evolving consumer needs suggests that the entire market for food products is changing and will change even more dramatically in the future.

Other major changes are taking place on an international level. The entire food industry is responding to new consumer demands. Examples include introducing international food products that focus on various ethnic groups, changing product ingredients to respond to local tastes, removing chemical preservatives from prepared foods, and adding value in general by offering healthier and more nutritious products. Food producers — sometimes by choice and at other times at the urging of their governments — have also recently introduced smaller packages or smaller product servings, and have included daily dietary recommendations on product labels.

Although some of these changes have a significant impact on business operations, sometimes lowering profit expectations, food producers continue to seek new product opportunities to increase their profitability. For example, in the food processing industry in the U.S., where manufacturers are urged to introduce smaller packages by both federal agencies and consumer lobbies, often entire production lines need to be modified or completely rebuilt in order to respond to these challenges. In some countries where food processors used chemicals to conserve or extend a product's shelf life, they are now obligated to demonstrate that their processes are safe for human consumption and for the natural environment. In addition, consumer advocates are calling for uniform international standards for the production of consumer food products. This is a broad international movement among consumers; even in Japan, housewives are beginning to question the eating and sleeping habits of their husbands and children.

With advances in food technology, government regulations, and consumer demands, food producers are developing and marketing new, healthier products such as products made from natural ingredients including soybeans, grain, or natural oils. A variety of milk-based drinks are also offered in the international market. All of these food innovations require significant management decisions by the food producers, and frequently require re-examination of their entire marketing strategy along with their marketing research practices and approaches to new product development.

The fast food industry is also feeling the pressure of changing consumer lifestyles. Several major international fast food franchising operations have announced reductions in food size servings and have become more concerned about the nutritional aspects of their offerings. Other segments of the fast food industry have publicized other concessions that will widen their current product offerings and give customers greater choices by including more naturally and organically grown foods obtained directly from their own exclusive suppliers. Some fast food restaurants are offering milk and milk-based products as alternatives to carbonated and non-carbonated soft drinks.

Not only are consumers' lifestyle changes being accepted by food producers internationally; but some governments are also directly concerned with changing lifestyles, to the point that government agencies are actively involved in educational programs for their population. These programs focus on eating, exercise habits, and health maintenance issues. Walking programs in Finland or community exercise meetings in North America are examples of such programs. Individuals have become more concerned about their own health status in response to the increase in obesity and the consequences of a non-healthy lifestyle, such as heart and blood circulation problems, which are often communicated by the media.

Other changes are taking place along with the major changes in the market for processed and fast food. An increasing number of individuals are signing up for exercise classes, attending exercise facilities, and participating in outdoor sports. Most of these individuals seek products that will help them exercise more and feel better after they exercise. Some segments of the food processing industry are examining product opportunities in these markets and are rapidly introducing a variety of products. These products range from pure bottled water to a range of energy products, post-exercise recovery products, and low-carbohydrate products. Occasionally, these products find their way into everyday use.

The aging market is also becoming a significant market for the types of products introduced by the food processing industry. In countries where an aging population dominates, food producers have introduced products especially for them. These products are frequently highly nutritious, conveniently packaged, and easy to use. Many of the large global food producers clearly indicate that this is a rapidly growing market.

Gainomax Recovery is a milk-based recovery drink that does not need refrigeration. Its production started in 1990, and Norrmejerier purchased the rights for the product in 1997. The product was repositioned in 2000 when the package was redesigned to be more compatible with an active and healthier lifestyle. The "recovery" concept was added to indicate that the drink was intended for active individuals to regain their energy level after active exercise. The repositioning process also meant changing focus from communicating with a "strong male" to a gender-neutral approach. Today, Gainomax Recovery is seeking its own market position and is becoming recognized by all types of sport-minded individuals as a satisfying drink for those who want to recover their energy level quickly after vigorous exercise.

Although Gainomax Recovery was previously distributed in retail stores in Västerbotten and Norrbotten, and in the rest of Sweden via training facilities, in 2004 the product became available in retail and convenience stores all over Sweden. It is anticipated that retail sales will reach the SEK 30 million level. The product is supported in the market by a strong promotional effort including newspaper advertising, athlete and sports team sponsorship programs, television commercials, and magazine advertising. In addition to its Swedish distribution, Gainomax Recovery has successfully entered several export markets including Finland, Ireland, Denmark, the U.K., and Norway. It was estimated that the product would generate retail sales revenue of SEK 20 million in export markets by the end of 2004.

Gainomax Recovery is an interesting product when it comes to its actual market positioning. The product belongs to the broad category of "sports drinks"; however, it is in its own category of "recovery drinks" which is generally a subcategory of sports drinks, along with another subcategory of sports drinks called "energy drinks". Since Gainomax Recovery seeks an ideal display position in stores, it is typically displayed somewhere on the side of other sports drinks and sometimes in the dairy section of the store.

There are several reasons for this anomaly. The ideal target market for this product is not sufficiently educated to fully understand the benefits of recovery drinks. Under ideal conditions, Gainomax Recovery should be in its own separate display in the drinks section along with sports drinks, rather than among dairy products or soft drinks, so that consumers could make a simple purchase. A considerable public relations effort might be needed to inform consumers about this drink.

A similar dilemma also exists in export markets. In Finland, Gainomax Recovery is distributed in sports facilities as well as retail and convenience stores, the same as in Sweden; but in the rest of the export markets, it is distributed only through sports facilities. At the same time, the target market in export markets is rapidly shifting from body-building markets to fitness and leisure markets. In reality, in both the Swedish and all of the export markets, Gainomax Recovery is searching for its identity in the market and even within its presumed target market. This is one of the challenges faced by marketing managers at Norrmejerier. Market competition is gradually emerging and the marketing managers at Norrmejerier must respond.

Gainomax Recovery is an important product for the entire international marketing effort at Norrmejerier. It is a milk-based product that does not require refrigeration. It is a UHT product, which translates to a long-shelf-life product for the end consumer. It can be distributed along with other products throughout the distribution channels leading to conventional retailers. Since it is a milk-based product, any increase in its demand can be met due to the surplus of milk availability.

At the same time, the future of Gainomax Recovery is confronted by many challenges. On the retail level, it suffers from an identity crisis — being an unknown brand name serving a need for recovery that is not very well known by consumers. What is it? Is it a sports drink or a specialty recovery drink? Although competition is slowly moving into the market, especially in export markets, Gainomax Recovery is a milk-based product and not too many competing products are milk-based.

Another challenge faced by the marketing managers at Norrmejerier is how to define the recovery drink market. The idea of "recovery" is important, but it presents a major concern in relation to its relatively narrow target market. One of the fundamental questions is whether the recovery target market is slowly evolving based on the perceptions of consumers in that market, or whether the target market needs to be clearly defined and developed through an integrated marketing communication process. How big is the recovery market in the first place, and can it be assessed both qualitatively and quantitatively?

The export markets present interesting challenges. The market for sports drinks is expanding worldwide. Which markets should be entered, and how should Gainomax Recovery be positioned in those markets? Should one uniform marketing strategy be developed and implemented in all export markets, or should each export market be evaluated separately and Gainomax Recovery positioned accordingly? Alternative questions that might be posed relate to the domestic market, which is relatively large in comparison to the export market. Should the domestic market be expanded further at the expense of the export markets?

These are important questions that the marketing managers at Norrmejerier are asking about the implications of international business operations. Domestic competition is emerging in the company's home market. Based on the relatively short-term experience in export markets, it appears that the potential is relatively significant. According to Norrmejerier's management, the key issues regarding Gainomax Recovery can be summarized in two simple questions: how should Gainomax Recovery be marketed in its domestic market in Sweden, and how should it be marketed abroad?

11.3.3 *Seaflex AB* [14]

Seaflex AB produces and markets flexible mooring systems for pontoons, floating docks, and marinas worldwide. It is located near the city of Umeå, close to the Bay of Bothnia, in northern Sweden. Its initial business operations started back in the 1960s when Bertil Brandt, a Swedish innovator and inventor active in the mining industry, invented a very durable rubber compound for lining ore mills. In 1968, he visited a fishing harbor in Cannes and witnessed the chaos that occurred when fishing boats were berthed. He constructed a simple and secure rubber mooring arrangement. During his work in Cannes, he realized that mooring single pontoons was an even bigger problem. Back home in Sweden, he continued to develop a secure mooring system.

The firm was established when Bertil Brandt thought about ways of securing pontoons, floating docks, and floating wave attenuators in marinas after having observed their vulnerability to storms and powerful waves. The first Seaflex[15] product was installed in 1975. The initial business started as a hobby with his children in their spare time.

In 1991, Lars Brandt, the current president and CEO, took over operations and created an export business that secures everything from pontoons to floating docks in large marinas in Sweden and around the world. His management team consists of 11 highly skilled professionals with many years of experience. The team includes the president and CEO as the key decision maker, a market director, a market manager, an export manager, two sales managers, an IT and web development manager, a financial manager, a design engineering and project manager, an installation supervisor, and a secretary responsible for logistics and economy support. One of the major recent accomplishments of his marketing team was winning an order

---

[14] Professors George Tesar and Dan Frost of Umeå University developed this case with the permission of Seaflex® AB (http://www.seaflex.net). This case cannot be copied or electronically reproduced in any form without written permission from the authors or Seaflex® AB.

[15] The present name of the firm is "Seaflex AB", and the product is referred to as "Seaflex".

to secure pontoons in the Qingdao Marina during the 2008 Olympic Games in China.

Seaflex products are unique. They are flexible mooring systems that accommodate water variations in seas, lakes, and rivers. The products resist natural forces, and stabilize moorings for pontoons and marinas. The products are simple to install, easy to ship, and weigh much less than competing alternatives such as metal link chains. Because of their flexibility (the products have the ability to stretch and flex within limits depending on specifications), the products prevent jetties, marinas, and pontoons from being destroyed in storms and adverse weather conditions. Seaflex products can handle variations in water levels from 0.2 to 25 meters.

The products are based on rubber technology and are reinforced by a comprehensive computer-based software program called JFlex, which helps customers design a mooring system to their specifications. The products are fabricated with special elastic rubber cables combined with high-quality acid-resistant stainless steel and plastic components. The ropes used in these products are GeoSquare Polyester and DynaOne component parts supplied by the Gleistein und Sohn GmbH manufacturing company, which is located in Germany. The production and quality control of all Seaflex products are carried out in its own plant, which is located a few kilometers south of Umeå in northern Sweden. Seaflex AB's plant and its management center are located in a pleasant rural setting.

Both Seaflex products and the JFlex design software provide an interesting platform for sales, marketing, and engineering operations. Seaflex AB exports approximately 97% percent of its production to the global mooring market through its dealers. For a smaller manufacturing firm such as Seaflex AB, its distribution network is extensive. It spans over 29 countries in Europe represented by 79 distributors, 2 countries in Africa with 4 distributors, 3 countries in North America represented by 5 distributors, and 3 countries in South America with 5 distributors. Asia is represented by 3 countries and 6 distributors, while 12 distributors from 10 countries represent the Middle East; Australia and New Zealand each have a single distributor.

The production of Seaflex products from various component parts is a relatively technology-intensive process. All of the components, parts, and materials are custom-manufactured to Seaflex AB's specification. Experienced craftsmen on customized machines complete the final assembly. During the manufacturing process, quality control is implemented along with final inspection of each finished product. The suppliers of all component parts are mainly Swedish, with the exception of one (the German supplier), and are subject to rigid quality requirements and standards set by Seaflex AB. The proximity of suppliers to the final production point assures close coordination with suppliers, and speeds up the production and delivery process for customers.

Seaflex AB is an aggressive exporter of its products. Although the market is strong in Sweden, foreign markets are steadily growing. According to the company website, Seaflex products can be found from Skellefteå in northern Sweden to Guam in the Pacific Ocean with principal markets in Europe and the U.S. Internationally, Seaflex products are used in small and large marinas, and in boat clubs for jetties and buoys; more recently, a potential use has been identified in the fish farming industry.

Seaflex AB's management is constantly trying to improve communication with its current dealer network and, at the same time, expand the network by identifying additional new dealers who have a good grasp of the mooring market. New product inquiries or potential orders are automatically referred to the appropriate dealer who can respond to the inquiry or order in their own sales territory. Seaflex AB's management subscribes to the philosophy that it is the dealer and the end customer who determine the value of its products. If its philosophy is viable, Seaflex AB will grow and expand.

The technology embedded in Seaflex products is very much in the mainstream of environmental concerns. Concern over the environment is a priority issue for many national, regional, and local governments. Governmental agencies in the U.S., Canada, Australia, and many other countries around the world are increasingly concerned about the deterioration of sea, river, and stream bottoms. The devices used in mooring floating bodies can seriously damage the water bottom around the mooring anchors. Chains or other similar devices have a tendency to move the anchors around during storms or other water disturbances, and can severely damage the water bottom. In the U.S., corkscrew-like anchors are often installed to secure mooring devices. In Europe, concrete blocks are frequently placed on the water bottom and the mooring devices are attached to these concrete blocks. Seaflex products, however, are designed not to make contact with the actual water bottom.

It is increasingly common for government agencies, such as the state departments of natural resources in the U.S., to specify what kind of mooring devices can be used. Any suppliers of mooring devices, or contractors installing them, must closely follow these specifications. Seaflex AB finds these specifications favorable because of the inherent differential advantage based on its unique technology.

There are other environmental issues connected with the old chain mooring technology. Chains have a tendency to rust over a relatively short time span and so have to be inspected periodically, especially if used in older installations. Because Seaflex products are made from parts and rubber components that do not rust, they need to be inspected less frequently, and consequently generate significant savings for the owners of marinas, pontoons, and other floating devices.

Although Seaflex AB confronts competition from suppliers of similar devices, often inferior in quality, it does not maintain a monopolistic position in the market. Because Seaflex products are environmentally friendly and specified by government agencies, they tend to be copied and retro-engineered. Seaflex AB works very closely with many environmental agencies worldwide, especially with state environmental agencies in the U.S., to further demonstrate the environmental safety of its products.

In addition, because Seaflex products do not disturb animal life or damage plants, environmental groups in various international markets occasionally favor them. In Sweden, Seaflex products are used exclusively in Bohus County. Seaflex AB has also received an environmental award in England for its mooring installation in the May Yacht Harbor.

Because of their environment-friendly characteristics, Seaflex products have the potential to expand in other markets such as fish farming, water-based housing, and wave-generated electric power, among others. With population increases and major lifestyle changes, many of these markets are evolving along with a broad range of environmental concerns. The critical concern faced by Seaflex AB may be reflected in the cost of tracking major developments in these markets and the necessary investment that needs to be made in information gathering and technology assessment. From an environmental perspective, it appears that Seaflex AB may have a strong potential to develop with environmentally driven markets in the future.

From the perspective of governmental regulatory agencies around the world, there is another side to environmental concerns regarding the mooring of pontoons, floating docks, and marinas. The growth in leisure sports such as boating creates situations that may be environmentally untenable. As the leisure boating industry grows, the need for additional marinas increases. Thus, the boating industry (particularly the leisure boating segment of the population) is putting more pressure on environmental standards. Several countries in Europe, as well as some states and provinces in the U.S. and Canada, already limit the number of leisure boats that can be moored at individual marinas. They also regulate where marinas can be developed and how large the marinas can be. In the future, these regulations may severely limit market growth for mooring products.

However, there might be another dimension impacting the environmental issues for firms such as Seaflex AB. Ownership of private shore properties is growing internationally. Individual boat enthusiasts are buying shore properties at an accelerated rate. Many of the owners are installing piers, pontoons, and floating docks for their boats. In order to stabilize the growth of this phenomenon, many state departments of natural resources in the U.S., for example, are declaring many lakes and waterways motorboat-free. Nevertheless, many property owners resist regulations and opt for the installation of piers and pontoons to access their lakes and waterways anyway.

In a recent exercise designed to identify the strengths, weaknesses, opportunities, and threats of Seaflex AB (a SWOT analysis, in managerial terminology), the entire staff was involved and the analysis produced some interesting observations. It indicated that the present size of the firm can be an advantage but, at the same time, also a liability. Seaflex AB is growing steadily and has strong potential for future growth. Increased growth may bring necessary and sometimes unpredictable changes. The entire organization needs to respond to such changes. Additional resources will be needed when the market begins to pressure a relatively small firm such as Seaflex AB to offer additional services, expand its distribution system, and respond more quickly to customers' needs.

Among other things, the SWOT analysis indicated that technical expertise is one of Seaflex AB's strengths. However, the key question is how long it can maintain that strength. Sustainability of technical expertise may be a challenge for Seaflex AB. Although Seaflex AB has cutting-edge technology in mooring floating devices, a new competitor could enter the market with more advanced technology.

The regulatory environment in which Seaflex AB operates is changing rapidly. New specifications for mooring pontoons, floating docks, or marinas are constantly issued by regulatory agencies worldwide. Concerns over ecology and the preservation of waterways, lakes, rivers, and seas lead to new regulations almost daily. Seaflex AB's products are environmentally friendly, and that is another important advantage.

Smaller manufacturing firms with unique products are frequently challenged by large market opportunities. Seaflex AB is no exception. New mooring applications are constantly developing. Seaflex AB's products represent cutting-edge technology in a niche market, but what if a much larger market opens up? For example, fish farming will most likely expand and new demands for ecologically compatible mooring of fish farming beds will be legislated by governmental regulatory agencies. What if these agencies specify a mooring technology similar or identical to the technology owned by Seaflex AB? Would this be a strength or weakness from a managerial perspective?

Another concern that the SWOT analysis identified is the unpredictability of Seaflex AB's financial position and, more specifically, its cash flow. Seaflex AB is similar to many smaller manufacturing firms in this respect. Orders may not come in a steady and easily predictable fashion. There may be a backlog of orders at one point and a shortage of orders at another time; or, there may be one large order followed by a series of small orders, followed by a period without any orders. A smaller manufacturing firm needs to plan for financial contingencies. It has to manage its capital needs very closely. If strong demand for its products suddenly materializes, a smaller manufacturing firm needs access to sufficient financial resources. This may become a challenge for a smaller firm as bankers may not be willing to provide bridge loans, venture capital may not be available, and customers may not be willing to prepay their orders.

These concerns are some of the day-to-day realities of Seaflex AB, and top management is actively seeking solutions to these challenges. Seaflex AB is doing relatively well from the perspective of top management. But, is it prepared for the world of the future?

There is also the question of globalization. Smaller manufacturing firms with unique products such as Seaflex AB become global operators almost instantaneously. With the use of email over the Internet and the major improvements in air travel, marketing and sales personnel of smaller manufacturing firms have the same communication opportunities and flexibility as their large counterparts.

Can a smaller manufacturing firm become a global player? Can a smaller firm located far away from centers of international commerce gain a global reputation? Even though a firm may have a strong technological advantage and may produce unique products for a narrow niche market, it may have difficulty being recognized as a global player if it is physically located away from distribution hubs. These are questions that many managers of smaller manufacturing firms ask today.

In theory, however, the age of the Internet has changed the rules of the game for smaller manufacturing firms. The Internet allows firms to communicate instantaneously with their distribution channels. The Internet can also provide information for potential and existing customers wherever they are in the global marketplace, and it can supply marketing and technical information for anyone who is interested anywhere in the world. Theories concerning the internationalization of smaller manufacturing firms using the Internet are common topics in international and global marketing courses at most universities today. The fundamental question that needs to be explored by the top management of Seaflex AB is whether these theories work in everyday management.

Globalization of marketing operations among smaller manufacturing firms has one major flaw: physical transportation from the point of manufacture to the point of consumption or installation. In business-to-business marketing, this means from the point where the product is produced to the point where it will be used further in a production process as a part, component, accessory, or other semi-manufactured product. This flaw is being addressed systematically in the global marketplace by the growth and expansion of international shipping and transportation companies such as DHL in Europe, Federal Express, UPS, and many other private trucking companies which use freight forwarders to arrange for local and global shipping options. For many smaller firms located far away from centers of commerce, international shipping and transportation companies become an extension of their internal operations.

Another challenge faced by the management of many smaller manufacturing firms entering the global marketplace is how to identify, attract, and maintain market opportunities from far away. Internet exposure is not a solution to all of their marketing problems. Marketing personnel of such firms need to attend trade shows, participate in selling missions, and use other opportunities where potential and existing customers may communicate directly with both the marketing and engineering sides of the firm. Typically, marketing and engineering professionals working in a small manufacturing firm environment are reluctant to travel and participate in such activities as trade shows, missions, or conferences. Yet, the future of many of these firms from rural and remote areas is dependent not only on the Internet and its potential, but also on the firms' willingness and ability to communicate directly with their distributors and customers in the global marketplace. Firms that are willing to be proactive in the global marketplace at the physical level may have a stable and secure future ahead.

On the other hand, top managers of smaller manufacturing firms are typically interested in other aspects concerning the future of their firms. Steady and uniform growth of their firms over a long time period allows them to set priorities for other goals. Top managers become protective of their products and markets, and frequently neglect to look for new opportunities. They tend to perceive that their unique products will maintain their competitive advantage forever. They may become complacent about their patent protection, or less aggressive towards imitators and potential competitors. Systematic development and management of new potential markets that can provide new growth opportunities are frequently neglected.

One more important concern that faces top management in smaller manufacturing firms is managerial succession. When a smaller manufacturing firm, especially a firm located in a rural area, begins to grow and expand and needs additional professional managers, where will it find these managers? Or, what if present management recognizes its limitations and decides to turn over the management of the firm to more experienced professional managers? Will the future-hired professional managers be able to manage the firm in a way that meets the expectations of the present owners or managers? Seaflex AB is addressing these questions and concerns.

According to its own marketing literature, Seaflex AB is a cutting-edge firm in the business of mooring floating devices all over the world. Its business concept is to develop, manufacture, and market mooring systems to the global market. Its vision is reflected in a simple but powerful statement: "Seaflex AB shall be the world-leading supplier of mooring systems for marina environments." To this end, "Functionality and quality shall provide the customer with the most value-creating solution and be their natural primary choice." Although both the business concept and vision create somewhat demanding expectations, the current management team is fully committed to carrying them out.

Currently, Seaflex AB is a successfully functioning smaller manufacturer operating in a niche market with a unique technology. It markets a line of mooring products that are relatively complex and require a great deal of engineering support. In order to facilitate some of the support, the firm developed its JFlex software for use by its customers. In addition, an extensive international dealer network supports Seaflex products. Its marketing approach to present and future markets is good. In general, top management is relatively satisfied with the overall performance of the firm.

Additional research of the mooring market suggests that mooring products will have to be increasingly supported by product-related services. Although the JFlex software program provides an important platform for the engineering design of mooring devices, regulatory issues will likely be just as important as engineering design issues. The JFlex program may have to be broadened to include additional design parameters that may be beyond normal engineering practices.

Another concern in the day-to-day management of Seaflex AB is the ever-changing financial situation. In order for Seaflex AB to maintain its successful market position, it will have to build more flexibility into its financial management side.

The final concern relates directly to Seaflex AB's technology and its research and development strategy. Technology in general is changing rapidly and products are experiencing shorter market life cycles. This means that smaller manufacturing firms need to invest additional funds into their research and development efforts. Seaflex AB needs to do the same.

When all of these concerns are examined together, it becomes rather obvious that smaller manufacturing firms face a set of common problems. These are typically management, marketing, and financial problems. Technologically advanced firms such as Seaflex AB also need to consider their research and development capabilities, including the design of future products and supporting services. They must also consistently expand their engineering services to keep up with the expectations of their customers and other stakeholders. This may be a difficult challenge given the level of resources available within these firms.

The key question asked by Seaflex AB's top management is whether or not it can maintain its present position and become a true long-term global player. More specifically, Seaflex AB might ask whether or not a small manufacturing firm located in the woods of northern Sweden can become a major long-term player in the global market niche for mooring floating devices. The outcome of the recent SWOT exercise seems to be very positive. Perhaps it can!

Chapter 12

Comparison of the Wisconsin and European Perspectives

When comparing the Wisconsin and European perspectives on internationalization, researchers found both similarities and differences. One similarity is that all enterprises were started by individuals who decided to internationalize. They started smaller manufacturing enterprises because they had an innovative idea, technology, or product that had the potential to make a major impact on the industry, the manufacturing process, or consumers' lifestyles. The original owner-managers eventually passed on the management of the enterprise to more experienced managers. Both Wisconsin and European smaller manufacturing enterprises believe in their strengths or competitive advantages, a belief that has helped them to grow. Almost all managers believe that their products have unique attributes and are competitively priced.

Wisconsin managers of smaller manufacturing enterprises were most likely to make the decision to internationalize after receiving an unsolicited order from abroad, or were motivated to internationalize because they perceived technological or product advantages. On the other hand, their European counterparts decided to internationalize because of the smaller size of their markets and their close proximity to neighboring countries. For the Wisconsin managers, internationalizing operations seemed to be a difficult decision that has had a major impact on the entire enterprise and its resources, while European managers found the internationalization process to be a normal extension of their domestic operations. Wisconsin enterprises served their closest market and also had the option of serving the entire U.S. market,

279

whereas European smaller manufacturing enterprises could not expand domestically and had to look for markets in neighboring countries.

Once they decided to internationalize, both the Wisconsin and European smaller manufacturing enterprises could opt to formalize and internalize the decision. However, managers of Wisconsin enterprises frequently have not chosen to do so. When Wisconsin managers receive orders from abroad, they examine them one at a time, assess the potential risk in filling the order, and then decide if they will fill the order. A relatively small percentage of Wisconsin smaller manufacturing enterprises introduce fixed policies and formal procedures to routinely manage international operations. In contrast, the European managers of smaller manufacturing enterprises tend to introduce policies and procedures concerning international orders earlier, and generally rely on decisions made by a team rather than decisions made just by managers. Danish and Swedish enterprises use the team approach in internationalizing their enterprises.

Wisconsin smaller manufacturing enterprises made their entry into foreign markets exclusively by first exporting products. As they gained more international experience, they used other methods to enter foreign markets such as licensing, joint ventures, or direct investment. Some Wisconsin enterprises were taken over by foreign competitors and now function as a U.S. subsidiary of the former competitor. The European enterprises tended to internationalize operations by setting up sales offices, distribution, and even manufacturing abroad much earlier in the internationalization process than their Wisconsin equivalents. In some cases, European managers were willing to purchase licenses to manufacture or distribute foreign products in their domestic markets.

European managers of smaller manufacturing enterprises also evaluate the potential of foreign markets more systematically and objectively than do the Wisconsin managers. The European managers not only feel closer to potential customers in the other (mostly European) markets, but they also note similar applications for their products, particularly in evolving industries or economic sectors. They learn from these experiences and improve their products to meet the needs of foreign customers. Wisconsin managers are more likely to fill orders without identifying foreign customers and without understanding the applications for which their products are used. That is, Wisconsin managers are likely to be more reactive than proactive regarding foreign sales and customer focus.

Although both Wisconsin and European managers look for geographic market expansion, they tend to view future markets differently. Wisconsin managers look for growing markets for their products and occasionally for major consumption changes. Wisconsin managers emphasize marketing existing products with as little modification as possible. On the other hand, European managers tend to look for future markets based on how their products could be adapted to foreign customers' applications; local industry standards or use requirements become important in entering foreign markets.

Wisconsin and European smaller manufacturing enterprises also differ in how they view obstacles to international transactions. Perceived obstacles for Wisconsin managers are closely related to shipment and associated transactions such as shipping documents, financial transactions, or understanding of business practices in foreign countries. As Wisconsin managers gain experience, they look for information about customers and markets. In contrast, European managers look for information that describes the actual needs of potential customers, market requirements, and industry standards.

Furthermore, researchers found differences between Wisconsin and European smaller manufacturing enterprises in how the enterprises have evolved. Internationalization as a process has evolved among European enterprises over a much longer time period than for Wisconsin enterprises. Danish and Swedish enterprises have a long tradition of operating internationally and of using several modes of operations. In fact, many internationalization approaches were developed by Danish and Swedish enterprises. Wisconsin smaller manufacturing enterprises began their international operations relatively recently. The Czech smaller manufacturing enterprises are the newcomers; they have a very short history of internationalization.

Finally, Wisconsin and European smaller manufacturing enterprises display different approaches to managing growth. Wisconsin enterprises tend to be innovative in introducing new products, technologies, and manufacturing processes, which provide bases for start-ups in other industries; consequently, many Wisconsin enterprises are purchased or taken over by domestic or foreign competitors. Many of them change ownership and managerial structures early in the growth stage and are subsequently internationalized by new owners. European enterprises tend to be more stable. The original owner-managers grow the enterprise and internationalize it in a manner that is appropriate with its growth. At this point, it is not clear what the owner-managers of the Czech enterprises will choose to do. Will they grow their enterprises or change ownership? The fundamental difference between the Wisconsin and European enterprises is in terms of their longer-term management orientation. Wisconsin smaller manufacturing enterprises are most likely to change ownership, while European owner-managers retain ownership and grow their enterprises.

Part V

Conclusions and Suggestions for Future Research

Preliminary interviews, three surveys with each successive one completed 10 years apart, and a series of final interviews covering a 35-year period provide the basis for conclusions concerning the internationalization process of smaller manufacturing enterprises. Some conclusions relate to a need for additional research. This part outlines concepts and generalizations that need additional exploration.

Chapter 13

Conclusions

The researchers' objective was to focus exclusively on smaller manufacturing enterprises, a subset of small- and medium-sized enterprises, and to provide a longitudinal perspective on the internationalization experience of such enterprises over a period of 35 years. The research concerned operations, growth, and internationalization in the U.S. state of Wisconsin. The study on which this work is based focused on individual managers — frequently, owner-managers — of these enterprises. Researchers also compared the internationalization experiences of Wisconsin smaller manufacturing enterprises to those of the Czech Republic, Denmark, and Sweden. They believe that such comparisons are useful in attempting to understand internationalization as a managerial phenomenon in different countries.

The internationalization of smaller manufacturing enterprises is extremely important in light of the growing global marketplace and international competition. In order to survive, even locally focused smaller manufacturing enterprises need to examine their competitive posture, assess their market position, and evaluate their technological competence in the international context. Global markets and competitive environments have changed for smaller manufacturing enterprises. Today, they are expected to participate in international supply chains and complex value chains, and to rely on foreign sources of supply. Managers of smaller manufacturing enterprises need to consider these unavoidable international developments and respond to them appropriately.

The internationalization process — more specifically, the decision to internationalize among smaller manufacturing enterprises — consists of several distinct stages. Before managers of smaller manufacturing enterprises decide to internationalize, they need to understand who they are, define their goals, know their strengths and weaknesses, and formulate plans for their enterprises. Once they understand their management style, managers of smaller manufacturing enterprises may decide to internationalize. This is not an easy decision for smaller manufacturing enterprises. Managers need to understand both the internal and external implications of internationalization for their enterprises and consider the decision to internationalize. After considering whether or not to internationalize, some managers may make a formal, well-documented decision; while others may make an informal, undocumented decision that may conveniently change from one situation to the next. Managers of smaller manufacturing enterprises may anticipate obstacles to internationalization that will influence the final decision to internationalize. The number and types of obstacles are substantially reduced as they gain more experience.

Once they decide to internationalize, managers of smaller manufacturing enterprises tend to manage international operations inconsistently. For example, in the U.S. domestic operations frequently take precedence over international operations, primarily due to the large size of the domestic market. Managers have to be motivated to respond to foreign offers and inquiries. They need to understand what motivates them internally to make the decision to internationalize and start international operations, and what motivates them externally. Some managers believe that their strengths and weaknesses have an impact on the decision to internationalize; however, they can also be motivated by external forces such as foreign competitors or encouragement from various private or public entities.

The comparison between Wisconsin and European smaller manufacturing enterprises shows that those enterprises which have successfully internationalized their operations and are aggressively managing in the global marketplace are growing and expanding their market share. However, there are fundamental differences between Wisconsin and European smaller manufacturing enterprises in the way they have evolved, how they decided to internationalize, and how they manage their growth.

The Wisconsin smaller manufacturing enterprises were established and have evolved in a relatively large domestic market with sales potential for their products. Initially, they focused on markets geographically close to their operations; eventually, they expanded into the larger national market. Internationalizing their operations was not important. In the context of expanding global markets and intensified international competition, the internationalization of smaller manufacturing enterprises may be important for their community, state, or even the whole country, but it is not necessarily important for how managers manage their growth. Local, regional, and national governments, on the other hand, are concerned about employment, taxes, and economic stability, and so they want to help smaller manufacturing enterprises succeed and survive in the international environment.

The internationalization experience is different for European smaller manufacturing enterprises. Typically, they were established and have evolved in much smaller markets. Thus, they had to operate beyond their national borders early in order to reach the efficiency of production necessary to stimulate growth. For the European enterprises, internationalization of operations was a natural step in their growth and market expansion strategies; they had to consider the domestic along with the European markets and, more recently, the global marketplace. European smaller manufacturing enterprises are internally driven to internationalize, and are encouraged to do so by public entities much less than their Wisconsin counterparts.

Another fundamental difference between Wisconsin and European smaller manufacturing enterprises is in their approach to how they manage growth. Wisconsin managers tend to be innovative in introducing new products, technologies, and manufacturing processes, which provide bases for start-ups in other industries. These same new products, technologies, and processes frequently explain why many start-ups are quickly purchased or taken over by domestic and foreign competitors. Shortly after they become profitable and operational, many smaller manufacturing enterprises change ownership or management; internationalization follows shortly thereafter.

European managers manage their smaller manufacturing enterprises more evenly and over a longer time period. The original owners grow their enterprises slowly and deliberately, and they take a more systematic approach to evaluating their market options. When the internationalization decision needs to be made, it is made appropriately and consistently with expectations of growth. The exceptions to this approach in Europe are the recently established Czech smaller manufacturing enterprises. It is relatively early to speculate as to how Czech managers, with rather limited experience in managing enterprises in the global marketplace, will approach the decision to internationalize their operations.

Although smaller manufacturing enterprises are faced with many challenges in the global marketplace and are confronted with increasing and more dynamic international competition both at home and abroad, they have no option but to internationalize their operations. With the increasing adoption of new Internet-based business models, it is even more imperative to undertake the internationalization of operations early in the growth cycle. Today, it is not necessarily the new products, technologies, or manufacturing processes of an enterprise, but rather its international Internet visibility that provides the basis for market acceptance, growth, and a successful future.

Chapter 14

Recommendations for Future Research

This study examined smaller manufacturing enterprises in the U.S. state of Wisconsin over the past 35 years, and has produced a great deal of information about a small number of enterprises compared to the variety of enterprises that exist worldwide. Wisconsin is unique economically, socially, legally, and technologically — each state in the U.S. is unique. In Wisconsin, the existing infrastructure encourages the establishment and growth of new enterprises; it tends to produce a large number of technological innovators who start new enterprises. Close examination of some of the high-technology start-ups suggests that researchers know relatively little about what leads managers to prosper or to be technologically innovative. We know little about their management styles and how they see their opportunities and options in an international arena. We need to learn more.

In this study, we explored the managerial styles of smaller manufacturing enterprises. However, these management styles evolved more than 35 years ago, when the conditions for starting and managing enterprises were completely different. The Internet had not been introduced and international communication options were limited. Today, younger managers and innovators have been exposed to new concepts and theories of management, information technology, and internationalization. To promote internationalization and competitiveness among smaller manufacturing enterprises, researchers need to examine management styles today and relate them to efficient and effective international expansion strategies and business models in today's world.

Researchers, and even managers, of smaller manufacturing enterprises are aware of many different internationalization strategies and business models. In this book, we have compared Wisconsin and European smaller manufacturing enterprises. Additional comparisons are needed of similar entities in Africa, South America, and Southeast Asia. Studies in these parts of the world could provide a better understanding of how managers manage, grow, and internationalize their smaller manufacturing enterprises. Each country provides a unique environment for smaller manufacturing enterprises. Researchers need to explore how differing local environments stimulate the founding, growth, and internationalization of such enterprises in both positive and negative ways.

Researchers frequently think of small- and medium-sized enterprises as all types of enterprises offering a variety of services, products, and processes. But, this definition is too broad in the context of the contemporary global marketplace. As researchers, we need to focus on homogeneous sets of enterprises that can be identified and studied by using the latest qualitative and quantitative research methods and knowledge. Researchers need to systematically explore the smaller high-technology service enterprises that tend to be internationalized very soon after their inception.

The decision to internationalize carries different implications in differing economic and political systems. Economic and political changes stimulate the establishment of smaller manufacturing enterprises, but managers of these enterprises may not have the knowledge to grow, compete, and internationalize. The Czech experience certainly illustrates how quickly managers of smaller manufacturing enterprises need to learn about internationalization after their founding in order to compete.

The introduction of the Internet has presented many challenges for both old and new smaller manufacturing enterprises. Does the Internet play an important role in how smaller manufacturing enterprises secure their presence in domestic and foreign markets? This is an issue that researchers need to explore.

Finally, in order to generate statistically significant results, it is important to conduct future studies that include a substantial number of enterprises which are contained in an environment that can be well defined. Researchers need to learn more about the smaller manufacturing enterprises of today to provide a strong knowledge base on which future enterprises can begin and thrive.

Selected Bibliography on Internationalization

1960s

Farmer, Richard N. (1968). *International Management.* Belmont, CA: Dickenson Publishing Company, Inc.

Filley, Alan C. and Robert J. House (1969). *Managerial Process and Organizational Behavior.* Glenview, IL: Scott, Foresman and Company.

Kindleberger, C.P. (1969). *American Business Abroad.* New Haven, CT: Yale University Press.

1970s

Bilkey, Warren J. (1970). *Industrial Stimulation.* Lexington, MA: Heath Lexington Books.

Bilkey, Warren J. (1978). "An Attempted Integration of the Literature on the Export Behavior of Firms." *Journal of International Business Studies,* 9(Spring/Summer): 34–49.

Bilkey, Warren J. and George Tesar (1977). "The Export Behavior of Smaller-Sized Wisconsin Manufacturing Firms." *Journal of International Business Studies,* 8(1): 93–98.

Chandler, Alfred D. Jr. (1977). *The Visible Hand: Managerial Revolution in American Business.* Cambridge, MA: Harvard University Press.

Cunningham, M.T. and R.I. Spigel (1971). "A Study in Successful Exporting." *British Journal of Marketing,* 5(Spring): 2–12.

Johanson, J. and Jan-Erik Vahlne (1977). "The Internationalization Process of the Firm — A Model of Knowledge Development and Increasing Foreign Market Commitments." *Journal of International Business Studies,* 8(1): 23–32.

Johanson, J. and F. Wiederscheim-Paul (1975). "The Internationalization of the Firm — Four Swedish Cases." *Journal of Management Studies,* 12(3): 305–322.

Levitt, Theodore (1974). *Marketing for Business Growth.* New York: McGraw-Hill, Inc.

Maccoby, Michael (1976). *The Gamesman: The New Corporate Leaders*. New York: Simon & Schuster.

Mason, R. Hal, Robert R. Miller, and Dale R. Weigel (1975). *The Economics of International Business*. New York: John Wiley & Sons, Inc.

Pavord, William C. and Raymond G. Bogart (1975). "The Dynamics of the Decision to Export." *Akron Business and Economics*, 6(Spring): 6–11.

Preston, Lee E. (1970). *Markets and Marketing: An Orientation*. Glenview, IL: Scott, Foresman and Company.

Shull, Fremont A., André L. Delbecq, and L.L. Cummings (1970). *Organizational Decision Making*. New York: McGraw-Hill Book Company.

Simpson, Claude L. and Duane Kujawa (1974). "The Export Decision Process: An Empirical Inquiry." *Journal of International Business Studies*, 5(1): 107–117.

Vernon, Raymond and Louis T. Wells, Jr. (1976). *Manager in the International Economy*, 3rd ed. Englewood Cliffs, NJ: Prentice-Hall, Inc.

Wilkins, Mira (1970). *The Emergence of Multinational Enterprise*. Cambridge, MA: Harvard University Press.

Wilkins, Mira (1974). *The Maturing of Multinational Enterprise*. Cambridge, MA: Harvard University Press.

Zenoff, David B. (1971). *International Business Management: Text and Cases*. New York: The Macmillan Company.

1980s

Aaby, Nils-Erik and Stanley F. Slater (1989). "Management Influences on Export Performance: A Review of the Empirical Literature 1978–88." *International Marketing Review*, 6(Winter): 7–26.

Bartlett, Christopher A. and Sumantra Ghoshal (1989). *Managing Across Borders: The Transnational Solution*. Boston: Harvard Business School Press.

Cooper, Robert G. and Elko J. Kleinschmidt (1985). "The Impact of Export Strategy on Export Sales Performance." *Journal of International Business Studies*, 16(Spring): 37–55.

Corey, E. Raymond, Frank V. Cespedes, and V. Kasturi Rangan (1989). *Going to Market: Distribution Systems for Industrial Products*. Boston: Harvard Business School Press.

Czinkota, Michael R. (1982). "An Evaluation of the Effectiveness of U.S. Export Promotion Efforts." In: *Export Policy: A Global Assessment*, eds. Michael R. Czinkota and George Tesar, New York: Praeger Publishers, 63–71.

Czinkota, Michael R. (ed.) (1983). *Export Promotion: The Public and Private Sector Interaction*. New York: Praeger Publishers.

Czinkota, Michael R. and George Tesar (eds.) (1982). *Export Management: An International Context*. New York: Praeger Publishers.

Czinkota, Michael R. and George Tesar (eds.) (1982). *Export Policy: A Global Assessment*. New York: Praeger Publishers.

Drucker, Peter F. (1989). *The New Realities: In Government and Politics/In Economics and Business/In Society and World View*. New York: Harper & Row.

Dunning, John H. (1988). "The Eclectic Paradigm of International Production: A Restatement and Some Possible Extensions." *Journal of International Business Studies*, 19(1): 1–31.

Ettlie, John E. (1988). *Taking Charge of Manufacturing: How Companies Are Combining Technological and Organizational Innovations to Compete Successfully*. San Francisco: Jossey-Bass Publishers.

Glickman, Norman J. and Douglas P. Woodward (1989). *The New Competitors: How Foreign Investors Are Changing the U.S. Economy*. New York: Basic Books.

Johanson, Jan and Lars-Gunnar Mattson (1987). "Internationalization in Industrial Systems: A Network Approach." In: *Strategies in Global Competition*, eds. N. Hood and Jan-Erik Vahlne, Dover, NH: Croom Helm, 287–314.

Johnston, Wesley J. and Michael Czinkota (1982). "Managerial Motivations as Determinants of Industrial Export Behavior." In: *Export Management: An International Context*, eds. Michael R. Czinkota and George Tesar, New York: Praeger Publishers, 3–17.

Kotler, Philip, Liam Fahey, and S. Jatusripitak (1985). *The New Competition: What Theory Z Didn't Tell You About Marketing*. Englewood Cliffs, NJ: Prentice-Hall, Inc.

Levitt, Theodore (1983). *The Marketing Imagination*. New York: The Free Press.

Luostarinen, Reijo (1980). *Internationalization of the Firm*. Helsinki, Finland: The Helsinki School of Economics.

Piercy, Nigel (1982). *Export Strategy: Markets and Competition*. London: George Allen & Unwin.

Porter, Michael E. (1980). *Competitive Strategy: Techniques for Analyzing Industries and Competitors*. New York: The Free Press.

Porter, Michael E. (1986). *Competition in Global Industries*. Boston: Harvard Business School Press.

Reid, Stan D. (1981). "The Decision-Maker and Export Entry and Expansion." *Journal of International Business Studies*, 12(Fall): 101–112.

Reid, Stan D. (1982). "The Impact of Size on Export Behavior in Small Firms." In: *Export Management: An International Context*, eds. Michael R. Czinkota and George Tesar, New York: Praeger Publishers, 18–38.

Reid, Stan D. (1986). "Is Technology Linked with Export Performance in Small Firms?" In: *The Art and Science of Innovation Management*, ed. Heinz Hubner, Amsterdam: Elsevier Science Publishers, 273–283.

Robinson, Richard D. (1988). *The International Transfer of Technology: Theory, Issues, and Practice*. Cambridge, MA: Ballinger Publishing Company.

Root, Franklin R. (1982). *Foreign Market Entry Strategies*. New York: AMACOM.

Stobaugh, Robert and Louis T. Wells, Jr. (eds.) (1984). *Technology Crossing Borders: The Choice, Transfer, and Management of International Technology Flows.* Boston: Harvard Business School Press.

Telesio, Piero (1984). "Foreign Licensing in Multinational Enterprises." In: *Technology Crossing Borders: The Choice, Transfer, and Management of International Technology Flows,* eds. Robert Stobaugh and Louis T. Wells, Jr., Boston: Harvard Business School Press, 177–201.

Tesar, George and Jesse S. Tarleton (1982). "Comparison of Wisconsin and Virginia Small- and Medium-Sized Exporters: Aggressive and Passive Exporters." In: *Export Management: An International Context,* eds. Michael R. Czinkota and George Tesar, New York: Praeger Publishers, 85–112.

Tesar, George and Jesse S. Tarleton (1983). "Stimulation of Manufacturing Firms to Export as Part of National Export Policy." In: *Export Promotion: The Public and Private Sector Interaction,* ed. Michael R. Czinkota, New York: Praeger Publishers, 24–36.

1990s

Ackoff, Russell L. (1999). *Re-creating the Corporation: A Design of Organizations for the 21st Century.* New York: Oxford University Press.

Acs, Zoltán J. and Bernard Yeung (1999). *Small- and Medium-Sized Enterprises in the Global Economy.* Ann Arbor: The University of Michigan Press.

Chandler, Alfred D. Jr. (1990). *Scale and Scope: The Dynamics of Industrial Capitalism.* Cambridge, MA: The Belknap Press of Harvard University Press.

Dunning, John H. (1993). *The Globalization of Business: The Challenge of the 1990s.* London: Routledge.

Hills, Gerald E. (ed.) (1994). *Marketing and Entrepreneurship: Research Ideas and Opportunities.* Westport, CT: Quorum Books.

Moini, A.H. (1995). "An Inquiry into Successful Exporting: An Empirical Investigation Using a Three-Stage Model." *Journal of Small Business Management,* 33(3): 9–25.

Moini, A.H. (1997). "Barriers Inhibiting Export Performance of Small and Medium-Sized Manufacturing Firms." *Journal of Global Marketing,* 10(4): 67–93.

Moini, A.H. (1998). "Small Firms Exporting: How Effective Are Government Export Assistance Programs?" *Journal of Small Business Management,* 36(1): 1–15.

Ohmae, Kenichi (1990). *The Borderless World: Power and Strategy in the Interlinked Economy.* New York: Harper Business.

Root, Franklin R. (1994). *Entry Strategies for International Markets.* New York: Lexington Books.

Schonberger, Richard J. (1990). *Building a Chain of Customers: Linking Business Functions to Create the World Class Company.* New York: The Free Press.

Tesar, George and Hamid Moini (1998). "Longitudinal Study of Exporters and Nonexporters: A Focus on Smaller Manufacturing Enterprises." *International Business Review*, 7(3): 291–313.

Tesar, George and Hamid Moini (1998). "Planning for Product Development Among Smaller Manufacturing Enterprises: A Longitudinal Study." *Journal of Global Marketing*, 11(4): 95–106.

Tesar, George and Hamid Moini (1999). "Long-Term Analysis of Technologically Focused Small Manufacturing Enterprises." *Scandinavian Journal of Management*, 15(3): 239–248.

Thorelli, Hans B. and George Tesar (1994). "Entrepreneurship in International Marketing: A Continuing Research Challenge." In: *Marketing and Entrepreneurship: Research Ideas and Opportunities*, ed. Gerald E. Hills, Westport, CT: Quorum Books, 255–268.

2000s

Acs, Zoltán J., Randall K. Morck, and Bernard Yeung (2001). "Entrepreneurship, Globalization, and Public Policy." *Journal of International Management*, 7(3): 235–251.

Czinkota, Michael R. and I.A. Ronkainen (2006). *International Marketing*, 8th ed. Florence, KY: South-Western College Publishing.

DePalma, Donald A. (2002). *Business Without Borders: A Strategic Guide to Global Marketing*. New York: John Wiley & Sons.

Keegan, Warren and Mark C. Green (2007). *Global Marketing*, 5th ed. Upper Saddle River, NJ: Prentice Hall.

Larimo, Jorma (ed.) (2006). *Contemporary Euromarketing: Entry and Operational Decision Making*. Binghamton, NY: International Business Press.

Morgan, Glenn, Richard Whitley, and Eli Moen (2006). *Changing Capitalisms? Internationalism, Institutional Change, and Systems of Economic Organization*. Oxford: Oxford University Press.

Pope, Ralph A. (2002). "Why Small Firms Export: Another Look." *Journal of Small Business Management*, 40(1): 17–26.

Prashantham, Shameen (2007). *The Internationalization of Small Firms: A Strategic Entrepreneurship Perspective*. Florence, KY: Routledge.

Sorge, Arndt (2006). *The Global and the Local: Understanding the Dialectics of Business Systems*. Oxford: Oxford University Press.

Tesar, George, Steven W. Anderson, Sibdas Ghosh, and Tom Bramorski (eds.) (2008). *Strategic Technology Management: Building Bridges Between Sciences, Engineering and Business Management*, 2nd ed. London: Imperial College Press.

Index

ABC Plastic Limited   180
added-value creation   240
adequate assets   36
advertising   39, 159
aggressive exporters   74, 75, 83, 101, 102, 106
Alpha Technology Corporation (ATC)   118

bankruptcy   123, 148
Bio-technology and Horticulture Unlimited (BHU)   126
born global   96
brand   220, 234, 250, 255, 256, 262
budgets   169
business-to-business company   167
business-to-business markets   2

cash flow   120, 274
Cembrit Holding   207
competition   28, 57, 117, 129, 159, 285
competitive advantage   5, 16, 24, 33–35, 115, 120, 127, 139, 147, 154, 166, 177, 184, 196, 208, 222, 238, 277
competitive position   162
competitive price   37
consultants   47, 58, 64

contribution to the development of the U.S. economy   26, 73
craftsman managers   19, 22, 28, 29, 47, 49–51, 63, 68, 81, 93, 101, 102, 114
cultural barriers   188
cultural differences   159
culture   58, 116, 141, 170, 215, 244, 250
Czech Republic   176

decision-making process   23
Denmark   176
development and/or security of markets   27, 73
distribution   39, 105, 128, 228, 270
distributor   19, 58
diversification   7, 51, 129, 161, 184, 202
documentation   83, 159, 188, 225
dynamic sales force   38

economic growth   14
efficient distribution   39
efficient marketing   39
efficient production   40
email   3, 275
environmental concerns   271
environmentalists   150, 254

European smaller manufacturing
    enterprises 287
export 7, 26, 57, 60, 64, 68,
    131, 211
export agent 19
export assistance programs 190
export decision 90, 95
export obstacles 132, 150, 158, 170,
    187, 201, 232, 243
export operations 44
exporting 2, 32, 89, 122, 131, 160,
    178, 280
external environment 23, 25, 32
external growth 48
external motivators 105

family business 127
family operations 113
family-owned business 205
financial barriers 188
financial support 198
financing problems 160
first export orders 92
fixed policies 73
foreign competition 30, 46, 59, 65,
    85, 96, 97, 108, 144
foreign languages 160
foreign market entry 97
foreign markets 52, 58, 74, 85, 97,
    158, 200, 280
    representation in 82
foreign opportunities 82
formal structures 73

Gainomax Recovery 265–268
global economy 3, 117, 128
global environment 62
global marketplace 3, 23, 59, 74,
    160, 275, 276, 285, 286
global markets 46
global warming 133
globalization 204, 275

government agencies 57, 61, 64, 69,
    92, 108, 264, 271
growth 7, 17, 73, 148, 155, 167,
    177, 178, 184, 186, 197, 287
growth rate 28

human resources 29, 46

information technology 3, 4, 96,
    108, 289
initial markets 142
innovation 222, 226, 250
inquiries from abroad 102, 106
internal growth 48
internal motivators 104
international trade 203
internationalization 2–4, 8, 32, 44,
    52, 64, 285, 289
    challenges of 58
Internet 3, 4, 93, 95, 96, 100, 108,
    275, 288, 289

joint venture 32, 60, 122, 220, 230,
    280

KMF Limited 194
know-how 29, 60, 122

language barriers 188
language difficulties 215
leadership 20
letter of credit 3, 72
licensing 32, 60, 280
longitudinal study 6

manufacturing 6, 157
manufacturing process 16, 19
market position 285
market positioning 266
market research 131
market share 51, 97, 129, 167, 189,
    231, 286

marketing   7
marketing expertise   19
marketing philosophy   38
marketing research   34, 130, 187,
   200, 259, 264
marketing strategy   34, 204, 264
Martinsons Trä AB   247
merger   20, 62, 231, 250, 262
Migatronic   218

national distribution   51
new market development   50, 188
new market opportunities   168
new product and market development
   162
new product development   49, 168,
   264
new products   202
Norrmejerier   258

obstacles to exporting   89
obstacles to international operations
   116, 178
obstacles to international transactions
   281
obstacles to internationalization   79,
   214, 286
original equipment manufacturers
   (OEMs)   163
Outdoor Advertising Company (OAC)
   137
outsourcing   3, 30, 41, 46, 59, 61,
   148, 220, 223, 230
owner-managers   15
ownership   8, 282

Packaging Container Services (PCS)
   145
passive exporters   74, 75, 82, 83,
   101, 102, 106
perceived advantages   33–35
PJ Manufacturing Inc.   153

planning   47, 162, 169, 187, 202,
   225
pricing   40, 97, 159, 196
Process Controls International (PCI)
   165
profit   197
profit rate   28
profitability   25, 73, 143, 148,
   155, 167, 170, 178, 189, 203,
   263
promoter manager   20, 22, 26, 28,
   29, 47, 49–51, 63, 69, 81, 93,
   101, 102, 114
promotion   40, 159
proximity to the market   41
public policy   4, 61

rational manager   21, 22, 26–29,
   48–51, 63, 70, 93, 102, 114
regulations   79, 123, 124, 131, 138,
   188, 260, 262, 264, 273, 274
resource allocation   62
restructuring   202, 246
risk   19, 32, 92, 102

sales agent   19
Scan Tracking Systems (STS)   236
Seaflex AB   269
security of investments   29, 73
service providers   58
shipping   62, 97, 276
small- and medium-sized enterprises
   5
smaller manufacturing enterprises   5,
   13
   strengths of   33
social values   254
socio-cultural differences   14
stage model   95
start-ups   4, 13, 14, 16
strategic planning   141
strong management   42

supply chains   3, 30, 57, 59, 100,
    150, 285
sustainability   133, 134
Sweden   176

team   42, 178, 213, 215, 242, 244,
    269, 280
technical expertise   274
technical knowledge   19, 43
technology   43, 121, 177, 238
top management succession   8
trade fairs   57, 92, 122
trade shows   190, 201, 276

uncertainty   19, 191, 201
unique product   37, 43, 115

unsolicited export orders   91, 102
unsolicited first orders   94
unsolicited orders   3, 93, 100

value chain   3, 30, 57, 59, 100, 147,
    150, 252, 255, 285
value creation   41

Wisconsin managers of smaller
    manufacturing enterprises
    279
Wisconsin Manufacturers Association
    7
Wisconsin smaller manufacturing
    enterprises   7, 113, 280,
    287